Praise for
Inheriting the Holy Land

"Jen Miller's personal story about young Palestinians' and Israelis' efforts to renounce violence and war will certainly contribute to the new atmosphere of détente in the Middle East. Their quest for mutual understanding and peace communicates a moving appeal for faith in hope."   —ELIE WIESEL

"*Inheriting the Holy Land* underscores the importance of cross-cultural understanding and dialogue as a basis for peace and reconciliation and the power of hope and imagination to transform the future, even in the most difficult conflict environments."   —HER MAJESTY QUEEN NOOR

"A hopeful book about a conflict that often seems hopeless."
—*Booklist* (starred review)

"A collection [of interviews] that would make even a seasoned *New York Times* reporter's mouth water . . . It is Miller's attempt to steer clear of politics and delve into the personal that makes *Inheriting the Holy Land* unique."   —*Forward*

"With her honest prose, her inquisitiveness, and her willingness to allow Israeli and Palestinian youth to speak for themselves, Miller builds a story that is less about the details of land and more about the people caught in a violent conflict."
—*Pages*

"A thoughtful book that encourages dialogue between young people on both sides of the issue."   —*Kirkus*

"Stands on its own merit . . . If *Inheriting the Holy Land* teaches anything, it's the importance of dispassionate decision making and strategic long-term planning."   —*Jerusalem Post*

Inheriting the
Holy Land

Inheriting the Holy Land

AN AMERICAN'S SEARCH
FOR HOPE
IN THE MIDDLE EAST

Jennifer Miller

BALLANTINE BOOKS / NEW YORK

2006 Ballantine Books Trade Paperback Edition

Copyright © 2005 by Jennifer Miller
Map copyright © 2005 by David Lindroth, Inc.

Published in the United States by Ballantine Books,
an imprint of The Random House Publishing Group, a division
of Random House, Inc., New York.

BALLANTINE and colophon are registered trademarks of
Random House, Inc.

Originally published in hardcover in the United States by
Ballantine Books, an imprint of The Random House Publishing Group,
a division of Random House, Inc., in 2005.

Library of Congress Cataloging-in-Publication Data
Miller, Jennifer.
Inheriting the Holy Land: an American's search for hope
in the Middle East / Jennifer Miller.
p.   cm.
Includes bibliographical references and index.
ISBN 0-345-46925-9
1. Arab-Israeli conflict—1993–   2. Miller, Jennifer.   I. Title
DS119.76.M52 2005
956.9405—dc22   2004066349

Printed in the United States of America

www.ballantinebooks.com

2 4 6 8 9 7 5 3 1

Book design by Victoria Wong

For my parents
In memory of Ruth Ratner Miller

Preface

Three days before I left the Middle East and returned home to the United States, I took an extraordinary journey. I didn't realize it at first. I was driving toward Tel Aviv—nothing so exciting about that. I had traveled this stretch a number of times in the last six months, scrambling to make my interviews on time. But this trip was different. Somewhere along the highway of lush farmland and advertisements for Israeli-brand hamburgers, I began to consider where I was coming *from*. Not fifteen minutes before, I'd been in Gaza. And this journey from Gaza to Tel Aviv, one that took a mere hour and held little more peril for me than a possible traffic jam, was unimaginable for most Israelis and Palestinians.

I should have felt special for being able to cross such a boundary. Instead, I felt sad. I thought how absurd this situation would be if I was in the United States. There, an hour's drive is rarely extraordinary or unimaginable. On the other hand, crossing the physical, cultural, and emotional distances of the Middle East is intensely difficult. To embark on such a journey you need important provisions, including rock-hard determination and an endless supply of hope. After spending the past six months among Israelis and Palestinians, I knew most of them had run short of both.

For the next three days, as I wrapped up my interviews and cleaned out my apartment, I was stuck on the idea of the journey I had made, both in the car and in the last year. For months, I'd been making trips like the one from Gaza to Tel Aviv, but I still didn't know what I was looking for. Israelis and Palestinians had spent years searching for a solution, and look how far they had come. The thought was sobering. Why had I spent months traveling from city to city, following the lives of young Israelis and Palestinians and questioning their national leaders? Why did I care about these people? It seemed neither nation gave a damn about the other, so why was I wasting my time investigating and trying to enlighten others about their plight?

I felt as if I were stuck in a Monty Python movie. Only a few weeks before, I had watched *Monty Python and the Holy Grail*. It was the fifth or sixth time I'd seen the movie, but I needed a dose of lighthearted humor. My research had recently taken me to some of the most devastated, depressed places I had ever seen, and I had spent the morning writing about a friend of mine who'd been killed in the second intifada.

In the film, God instructs King Arthur to find the miraculous Holy Grail, and with it build Camelot into a kingdom of unrivaled prosperity and peace. Arthur sets upon his quest with great purpose, following the vision of the Grail the Lord has shown him: a brilliant, ethereal beacon accompanied by ridiculous bursts of inspirational music. And despite the fact that nearly all of Arthur's endeavors go awry, we have never seen a more determined knight. Hideous creatures cannot cow him. Bloody battles do not bow him. With the vision of the Grail always illuminated, Arthur presses through any peril. At long last, he comes within reach of his God-given claim. Then, in true Monty Python style, the British police pull up, handcuff Arthur, and throw his knights in the back of a truck. The movie cuts off. That's it. Or, as the Palestinians say, *"Khallas."* Finished.

The first time I saw this movie I thought the ending was a joke. It's not really over, I told myself. They're playing a trick. In another thirty seconds the movie will come back on and Arthur will win the day. He *can't* fail now! Ten minutes later the videotape ran out and I was left staring at television static. I'd had my first experience with Monty Python, and the joke was on me.

Watching Monty Python eleven years later in Jerusalem didn't cheer me up at all. I was living in an environment where the carnage on the news was, in some cases, outside my front door. I had been resensitized. One of the funniest scenes in the movie—where Arthur battles the Black Knight—left me wanting to vomit, not laugh. Suddenly, it wasn't so humorous to watch our hero slice through the knight's arms, sever his legs, and chop off his head. Most notably, I found nothing laughable about the Black Knight's refusal to give up the fight even when Arthur observes in his highbrow British accent, "But I've cut your head off!"

At the time, I thought it was only the blood and gore making my stomach turn. After that trip from Gaza to Tel Aviv, I realized the connection between this silly movie and what I'd witnessed for months in the Middle East. As in *Holy Grail,* there is a great deal of absurdity about the Israeli-Palestinian conflict. It seems simply illogical for two peoples to continue fighting after they have already torn each other to shreds. Just like the movie, blood continues to soak the ground. Only here the blood is real, and the absurdity isn't comic; it's tragic.

Like King Arthur, many Israelis and Palestinians are also on a quest. They, too, are after a vision: a place where they can live freely and securely, where their rights and needs are respected. This vision of the Holy Land has proved to be as elusive as the Holy Grail. If you ask Israelis and Palestinians what they think now about the Oslo process that began in 1993 and ended with the failure of Camp David in the summer of 2000, they'll look at you with a cynical eye and say: "It was all a trick. We were taken as fools. The joke was on us." This is the most pervasive attitude I encountered among adults in both societies: the feeling that the future is as black as a dead movie reel.

Living among Israelis and Palestinians had made me cynical and frustrated, but not, I discovered, hopeless. In my heart, I knew it was worthwhile to study the conflict and write about the people caught up in it. Not every epic quest ends in failure. Growing up, I loved *Star Wars, The Lord of the Rings, The Odyssey.* No matter how difficult their circumstances, the heroes and heroines of these tales pressed on. Failure wasn't an option for them, and it isn't for Israelis and Palestinians.

You may believe you know the ending to the Israeli-Palestinian epic—where one side, the Good, will triumph over the other side, the Bad. After all, don't all epics highlight the battle of good versus evil? I don't agree. Look closely at any adventure story, and you will see they are not so black and white. The heroes of Shakespeare, Greek mythology, Tolkien, or even Lucas wage moral battles within themselves.

It's the same with Israelis and Palestinians. My father spent twenty-five years as a negotiator working at the Department of State on Arab-Israeli issues and attended all the Oslo interim agreement negotiations, including Camp David. During that time, he watched Palestinian and Israeli security and intelligence officials—hard men with blood on their hands—laugh, joke, and feel for one another. I myself have listened to Israelis talk admirably about the same Palestinians they once deported. These societies are not primordially wired to hate each other. Hatred, mistrust, and bias are learned. They can be unlearned, but it's a risky endeavor. Sit on your sofa with a prepackaged TV dinner, and you know exactly what you're getting. Go out to a restaurant and sample an array of foreign foods, and you risk upsetting more than your stomach; you may find your long-held beliefs less easy to swallow, your preconceived notions more difficult to digest. Getting a taste of this diversity is the only way to understand the moral complexity of the Israeli-Palestinian conflict—and the only basis for solving it.

My last trip from Gaza to Tel Aviv—in fact, my entire six months in the region—acquainted me with the diversity outside my own small life. It was a challenging, often lonely trip, but I never could have experienced the complexity of the Israeli-Palestinian conflict without taking it. I am not the only one traversing such boundaries. I have watched Israeli and Palestinian adults travel this same road, but most of all, I've had my eye on the young people.

Like most epics, the Israeli-Palestinian saga is generational. These societies have long-term memories, especially when it comes to the pains and traumas of the past. It is going to take generations to heal such wounds if the Israelis and Palestinians are truly to reconcile, but this process must start soon. The leaders, Ariel Sharon and the late Yasir Arafat, may seem like the big shots, but I believe the fate of the Israeli-Palestinian conflict lies in the hands of the fifteen- to twenty-four-year-olds. The majority of Israeli and Palestinian youth are growing up with the same prejudices as their parents, and with good reason; they see violence and death on a daily basis. The small group of young leaders you will meet in the following chapters also experience this turmoil. They, too, are fiercely opinionated and full of national pride. Yet unlike so many of their peers, they have seen a world outside their own national identities and historical grievances. They have embarked on a journey of open-mindedness, tolerance, and dispassionate decision making. They understand that there is no predictable ending to their epic.

It seems to me that Israeli and Palestinian leaders are failing to reconcile their conflict—and failing their young people—largely because they believe the opposite. Cynical and preoccupied with revenge, they have lost their imaginations, their passion for the possible. They have allowed their youth to slip into the hands of extremists, and into the hands of apathy. It's telling that out of all the young people I interviewed, only a few could name a national leader he or she respected and admired. Of course, politics isn't the only way to affect societal change. But what are the consequences for those countries whose brightest, most capable future leaders shun the political arena?

It is easy to blame the current leaders and to write off the existing political structure, but that would be naive. Growing up in a political household, I have seen how people outside the government take it for granted. For this reason, I spent a great deal of time interviewing Israeli, Palestinian, and American national leaders. What the older generation may lack in imagination, they make up for in experience. Understanding the decisions they've made, their successes and, as important, their mistakes, is vital to untangling the current Israeli-Palestinian knot. There *is* hope to be found among this older generation. Many of them once hated each other, but told me that when the historic opportunity for reconciliation arose, they forced themselves to excise that hatred. This is perhaps the greatest lesson the leaders have to teach the younger generation.

Acknowledgments

The great hospitality and openness of all the young adults in *Inheriting the Holy Land* made this book possible. I want to thank Sari, Reem, Omri, Mohammad, Yara, and their families for making an American stranger welcome. Ruba, Uri, Yoyo, Hamdan, Badawi, Koby, Dalal, and Nardin were superb guides and unfailing friends. Thank you to the Seeds of Peace Jerusalem Center staff for their support. I would also like to thank Sa'eb Erekat and Nahum Barnea for going far beyond the call of duty, and Irit Gazit for being my mother away from home.

I was also given tremendous encouragement from back home. My *argileh bar* conversations with Gamal Helal provided indispensable insights. Ken Stein helped me get my history straight, and Tom Friedman rid me of my apprehension. I want to thank Thalia Field for giving me a chance and Celia Strauss for getting the book process started. Brian McLendon, Sarina Evan, and Lindsay Prevette were stellar publicists, and I thank them for their commitment. I can't say how lucky I am to have Allison Dickens and Julie Barer as my editors and advocates. They invested more energy, spirit, and skill into this book than I ever could have hoped. Finally, I want to thank my parents who provided unquestioned love and support throughout a trying half-year away from home; I could not have completed this project without them.

Contents

꧁꧂

ARMIES AND INTIFADAS

WHO INHERITS THE HOLY LAND?

A Word About Palestine

Historic Palestine refers to the land between the Mediterranean Sea, southern Syria, the Jordan River, and the Negev Desert. The name "Palestine" originated from the Philistines, the biblical people of Greek ancestry who once conquered the land that is today the State of Israel and the occupied territories. The actual term "Palestine" did not enter into common usage until A.D. 135, when it was adopted by the Roman emperor Hadrian. It was employed through the Muslim conquests in the seventh century and fell out of usage with the fall of the Christian crusader kingdom in 1099. The territory was informally called Palestine under the Ottoman Empire, which controlled the area from 1517 through the end of the first world war. With the collapse of the Ottoman Empire, the British officially revived the name under their mandate.

Today, there is no internationally recognized State of Palestine. Instead, the United Nations refers to the Palestinian people as living in a Palestinian National Authority (PNA) with undefined borders. I have made a conscious decision, however, to refer to the Palestinian country, though physically undefined, as "Palestine." I do this because the term is widely used by Palestinians, Israelis, and Americans. I mean neither for the word to connote specific borders nor to negate Israel's existence.

Time Line

1947   United Nations General Assembly votes to partition Palestine

1948   Israel established; first Arab-Israeli war begins

1949   Israel signs armistice agreements with its Arab neighbors

1957   Yasir Arafat founds Fatah organization

1964   Palestine Liberation Organization (PLO) founded

1967   Military confrontation between Israel, Egypt, Jordan, and Syria;
Israel captures East Jerusalem, West Bank, Gaza Strip, Sinai Peninsula, Golan Heights;
UN Security Council passes Resolution 242

1969   Yasir Arafat becomes head of PLO

1973   Military confrontation between Israel, Egypt, and Syria

1977   Menachem Begin elected Israel's first Likud prime minister

1977   Anwar Sadat visits Jerusalem and addresses Israeli Knesset

1978   Menachem Begin and Anwar Sadat sign Framework Agreement at
Camp David brokered by President Jimmy Carter

1979   Israeli-Egyptian peace agreement

1987   First Palestinian intifada begins

1988   Arafat accepts UN Resolution 242; U.S.-PLO dialogue begins

1991   Madrid peace conference

1993   Yasir Arafat and Yitzhak Rabin sign Oslo Declaration of Principles under auspices of President Bill Clinton

1994   Jordanian-Israeli peace agreement

1995   Rabin assassinated

1996   Palestinian presidential and legislative elections; Yasir Arafat elected Palestinian president

2000   Yasir Arafat and Ehud Barak meet at Camp David; Second intifada begins; confrontations between Israeli police and Israel's Arab minority

2001   Ariel Sharon elected prime minister of Israel

2002   Israeli Operation Defensive Shield

2004   Yasir Arafat dies

2005   Mahmoud Abbas elected Palestinian president; Israel dismantles Gaza settlements

2006   Ariel Sharon experiences massive stroke; Deputy Prime Minister Ehud Olmert becomes Prime Minister; Hamas wins a majority vote in the Palestinian Legislative Council

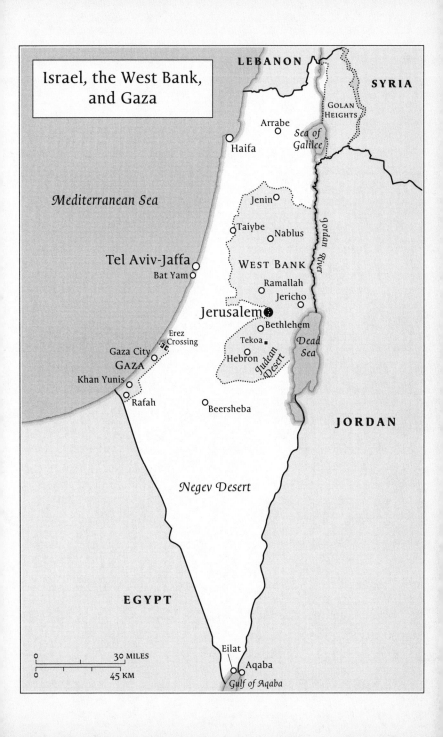

Israel, the West Bank, and Gaza

LEBANON

SYRIA

GOLAN
HEIGHTS

Arrabe

Sea of
Galilee

Haifa

Mediterranean Sea

Jenin

Taiybe

Nablus

WEST BANK

Jordan River

Tel Aviv-Jaffa

Bat Yam

Ramallah

Jericho

Jerusalem

Bethlehem

Erez
Crossing

Tekoa

Dead
Sea

Gaza City

GAZA

Hebron

Judean
Desert

Khan Yunis

Rafah

Beersheba

JORDAN

Negev Desert

EGYPT

30 MILES

45 KM

Eilat

Aqaba

Gulf of Aqaba

Introduction

B efore I move forward and tell you more about the journey I took in the Middle East, it's important to go back and explain how a twenty-three-year-old from Chevy Chase, Maryland, ended up living with Israelis and Palestinians in the first place. I also have to tell you who I am, because everything you read in the following pages will be filtered through me—through my experiences, my perspective, my biases. The heroes of adventure stories are always advised at the outset: "Don't trust anyone." In fact, every person I met on my travels tried to sell me his or her version of the truth. This bias wasn't always intentional. One person's suicide bomber is inevitably another's martyr, freedom fighter, or terrorist. I might agree with only one of these definitions, but refusing to consider the others is a dangerous trap. It would mean blocking out numerous other stories—other voices—that are equally important. So I won't tell you that I'm completely objective or that my story is the "right" one. To do this would leave you feeling as tricked or as duped as so many Israelis and Palestinians. I will only assure you that my story is not a polemic. My goal is to give voice to some stories that have not yet been heard: stories that I hope will show you where the humanity in the Middle East lies, and why those of us outside this conflict have to take the Israeli-Palestinian plight much more seriously.

Handshakes are rarely historic. But the morning of September 13, 1993, was a turning point in history. I was thirteen, too small to see above the crowd in front of me, and sweltering in the fancy sweater my mother had put me in for the occasion. And what an occasion it was; the leader of the

Palestine Liberation Organization (PLO) and the prime minister of Israel had just shaken hands on the White House South Lawn. They stood two feet apart, but the actual distance between them was interminable.

The handshake was a product of secret negotiations between Israeli and Palestinian officials that had begun the previous year in Oslo, Norway. Until this point, Israel had refused to accept the Palestinians as a legitimate national group, and the majority of Palestinians had refused to legitimate the Israeli state. The Palestinians had been living in the West Bank and Gaza under the occupation of Israel's military, and their national leadership, including Yasir Arafat, was in exile. Historically, the Palestinian leadership's attitude toward Israel was one of violent opposition, and this violence continued even after Arafat recognized Israel's legitimacy in 1988.

The handshake between Yasir Arafat and Yitzhak Rabin was a symbol of mutual recognition between Israelis and Palestinians, and it initiated the Oslo peace process. Oslo was designed as a series of steps—interim agreements—through which Israel would return land to the Palestinians and grant them political autonomy in exchange for Palestinian security cooperation and control over terror. It allowed for the exiled Palestinian leaders to return to the West Bank and Gaza and for the creation of a Palestinian government, called the Palestinian Authority. Only after the interim agreements had been completed, and sufficient trust established between both sides, were Israeli and Palestinian negotiators to discuss a final settlement on issues of security, territory, Jerusalem, and refugees. The Oslo documents make no specific mention of Palestinian statehood, but it was the Palestinian expectation that a final summit would indeed grant them a state. The Palestinian Authority desired this state to be based upon June 4, 1967, borders—territory the United Nations Security Council asked Israel to return to the Palestinians after the 1967 war.

Everyone at the Oslo ceremony as well as Israelis and Palestinians in the Middle East understood that it would be a long road from the White House South Lawn to permanent status talks at Camp David. We knew that some Israelis and Palestinians, including extremists on both sides, opposed a negotiated settlement and were willing to take any action to stop the talks. We did not foresee, however, that two years later one of these extremists would assassinate Prime Minister Yitzhak Rabin, and that the start of the new millennium would see both the collapse of the Oslo process and an intense renewal of Palestinian violence, the second intifada.

That bright September day, the crowd around me was filled with optimism and hope. Former president Bill Clinton wrote in his memoir that it was one of the proudest moments of his life. But it was neither the presence of Clinton, the late Yasir Arafat, nor that of Yitzhak Rabin that held my attention. I was much more interested in a particular group of teenagers wearing green T-shirts sitting in the front row. They were obviously important; President Clinton made special mention of them in his speech. This was my first interaction with the Seeds of Peace: forty-five Israeli, Palestinian, and Egyptian youths who had spent their summer at the Seeds of Peace Camp for Conflict Resolution in Maine. I envied their adoration. These kids were hardly older than myself, but everyone was calling them heroes.

That these forty-five young people had met as enemies and were now standing together as friends was a testament to the vision of John Wallach, Seeds of Peace founder and president. After the first World Trade Center bombing, Wallach left his job as chief diplomatic correspondent for Hearst newspapers to plan what most people considered impossible: a summer camp where Israelis and Arabs would learn to coexist. Since 1993, Seeds of Peace has expanded to include eight Middle Eastern countries as well as youth from India, Pakistan, the Balkans, Cyprus, Greece, Turkey, the United States, and Afghanistan. In thirteen years, they have graduated over three thousand young people.

The joke among my friends is that Middle East peace is the Miller family business. I attended the Oslo signing because my father was closely involved in Arab-Israeli negotiations at the State Department. A historian by training, with a Ph.D. in Middle Eastern history and American diplomacy, he had worked as a State Department historian and intelligence analyst. In 1989, he joined the State Department's Policy Planning staff and became a primary member of the U.S. negotiating team, working closely with six secretaries of state on every Oslo agreement, including Camp David in July of 2000. He traveled constantly, visiting the leaders of Israel, the Palestinian Authority, Egypt, Jordan, and Syria. There were times when he would return from Jordan and less than twenty-four hours later be on a plane to Tel Aviv. Once he told me he was going to London for a conference when, in reality, he left on a secret trip to Israel under an assumed name.

Having him gone so much was difficult, especially for my younger brother. When he was seven, Danny wrote a letter to my dad's then boss—Secretary of State James Baker—asking him to please fire my father.

(Danny swore he would never waste his time with Israelis and Palestinains, but halfway through college switched his focus from astrophysics to the Middle East.)

Our dad's stories fascinated us. There were tales of midnight dinners with Yasir Arafat. The chairman had quite an affinity for my father and would often beckon with his shaking staccato English, "Aaron, come eat from my plate." There was the time during the Hebron negotiations when my father, a tape measure in hand, physically recorded the width of a particular road in the Jewish Quarter of Hebron under the gaze of angry Israelis and Palestinians. And my favorite: the tale of a bothersome fly on Air Force Two that Secretary of State James Baker caught with his bare hands and deposited for inspection on my father's legal pad.

Many of my father's stories were not amusing. I listened to him talk about terrorism and bus bombings. I remember his account of Arafat's compound after Israel Defense Forces (IDF) destroyed most of it in March 2002. I remember scanning TV footage of Yitzhak Rabin's funeral for my father, feeling not only sad but terrified that someone would try to commit a terrorist attack because of the number of world leaders gathered in one place. I was always worried about my dad's safety, but I was adept at forgetting that he was away. I focused on school, my friends, the play I was in, the school newspaper. And I was extremely proud. My father's job made me feel special. I knew that no matter how bad the situation became, my dad traveled to the Middle East to try and fix things. He was the eternal optimist.

Meanwhile, my mother was also working for Middle East peace. One spring day in 1993, John Wallach—a neighbor and family friend—announced his desire to bring Israeli and Palestinian teenagers together for a summer camp. My mother thought the idea was a bit loony, but John had a knack for making the impossible happen, so she signed up to help. During the years that my father was riding around Gaza in FAVs (fully armored vehicles), my mother was meeting with congressmen and ambassadors, fund-raising and garnering support for Seeds of Peace. She knew absolutely nothing about lobbying or congressional appropriations—her background was in social work. With incredible determination, she was in there with the best of them: heading downtown to Capitol Hill with the morning Metro rush, finding congressional champions, even testifying before Congress. In the end, a significant appropriation came through, funding much of Seeds' follow-up work in the Middle East.

Since politics was big in my family, it's not surprising that as a kid I ardently, fervently, *loathed* politics. Politics were *so* boring. At dinner, on the weekends, at parties, my parents talked about nothing else. Politics were a source of embarrassment, especially when my father came into my Hebrew school and attempted to educate a class of ten-year-olds about the Israeli-Palestinian issue. The lesson went something like this: "The Gaza Strip is (a) land occupied by Israel in 1967; (b) a kind of outdoor mall; (c) a kind of steak . . . Anyone? Anyone? Bueller?" Yes, I was proud of my father, but like all daughters, I wished he would just leave me and my classmates out of what I saw as his obsession.

To spite my parents, I refused to read the newspaper. Most children lose their television privileges for talking back. I, on the other hand, was forced to read *The Washington Post.* On a family trip to the Antietam Battle Field, I was nearly grounded for refusing to get out of the car. In my book, history and politics were one and the same. What did I care about some big field of grass? What did I care about the world?

Seeds of Peace changed all that. The participants traveled to Washington every year after the camp ended, and because of my mom's involvement, I attended their events at the White House, the State Department, and Congress. I showed them around my school, and slowly, I began to see that what my parents were doing actually affected people—people my own age. Not to mention that I found this particular group of kids to be great fun. Sure, they were interested in politics, but they were also energetic and drawn together by a common purpose. At sixteen, having graduated from a girls' camp full of upper-class, white, Jewish kids, I went to Seeds of Peace as part of a small American delegation. I was hooked. I returned to camp the following summer and later attended the Seeds of Peace International youth conference in Villars, Switzerland, where 130 Seeds alumni engaged in mock negotiations covering the seven Oslo final status issues. I was on the Jerusalem committee—perhaps the most sensitive and volatile. I was up every night until three a.m. debating, arguing, sometimes crying, and generally fighting to help my group reach an agreement. More than once I wondered, "*This* is what my dad does for a living?"

When I was old enough, I went on to join the Seeds of Peace staff as a camp counselor. I spent three summers living in the bunks, mentoring kids, and teaching them drama and creative writing. During and after college I traveled to the Middle East to visit my friends and campers from Seeds. Before the second intifada began, I was fortunate enough to collect a few stories of my own: being kissed and *blessed* by Arafat, giving speeches before Madeleine Albright and Queen Noor, and shaking hands with the late King Hussein of Jordan. And of course, there were my interactions with the "Seeds"—sharing meals with their families, traveling through their communities, smoking shisha (a water pipe with flavored tobacco) with their friends. I realized I'd been completely drawn into my parents' world.

I am continually baffled by the diversity of experiences, people, and ideas I encountered by the age of twenty-three. Chevy Chase, Maryland, has no checkpoints or bus bombings. I grew up with privilege, which meant that I didn't have to take the bus anyway, because there were usually one or two sport utility vehicles at my disposal. I went to a small, liberal private school where most people were well off and at least forty percent of the student population was Jewish. I attended Hebrew school classes twice a week until my confirmation at sixteen. The mantra there was simple: "Israel is great and as for the Palestinians—what Palestinians?"

I fully internalized what I learned at Hebrew school. I felt tremendous pride in being connected to Israel: this tiny country that repeatedly kicked the butts of any attacking army. My first trip there was at the age of thirteen, just after my bat mitzvah. In Jerusalem's Old City, I asked my parents to buy me an Israel Defense Forces T-shirt: army green with the IDF crest in gold. I wore that shirt all the time. I felt much cooler than the wannabe tough kids at school strutting around in their Redskins and Raiders jerseys. Israel was the classic underdog and it was my home team. I didn't wear the shirt because I hated Palestinians. The truth is, I never thought about the Israeli army in relation to Arabs. Wearing that shirt was extremely naive, especially for the child of a State Department negotiator, but the armies that Israel kept defeating were an amorphous, undefined vision in my head. I never thought about who they were or what their motivation might be. All I knew was that they didn't want Israel to be there. To me, these Arab nations seemed childish. Israel was so small. Couldn't they just nudge over a little? Make some room for the Israelis?

Nor did religion greatly influence my connection to Israel. Religion was important to me, because celebrations like Passover or Shabbat brought my family together. I never thought about God, and I knew little of the Bible. The holy sites were of abstract importance. I learned at Hebrew school and from the movies my parents showed me before going to Israel (such as *Exodus*) that Israel was a "homeland for the Jews." I was Jewish, therefore Israel was important to me. Though the prospects of needing to flee Chevy Chase, Maryland, were incredibly slim, Israel was my safe haven, should I ever need one. But mainly, Israel was my badge of distinction. I liked the fact that my family had played—and through my father was continuing to play—an important role in something that distinguished us from everyone else. Something that made us a little bit famous. How many other kids had photos of their great-grandparents and grandparents standing with David Ben-Gurion and Golda Meir? How many daughters got to see their fathers on television sitting behind George Bush and Mikhail Gorbachev at the 1991 Madrid conference, an event that opened the door for Israeli-Arab cooperation? Of course, no one other than my mother, my brother, and myself saw him in those shots; we were the only ones who could recognize the top of his head.

So my fascination with Israel was mostly glitter and lights. As a child and young adult, I had no substantive knowledge about the country, its history, or the political circumstances of its creation. In keeping with my apolitical attitude, I lacked any real ideology about the place. I had the same basic and ignorant attitude about the Arab world as I did about Israel. I had a vague association between Arabs, the Middle East, and terrorism. Some of this had to do with details I picked up from my father's books about the PLO, snippets of his experiences visiting Iraq and Saudi Arabia, and my own cloudy conception about what the Middle East was really like. On that 1993 family trip to Israel, I was afraid of getting into any taxi cab ahead of my parents, because the driver might try to kidnap me. I'm not sure I assumed all the cabdrivers were Arab, but I had a clear association in my head between the Middle East and kidnappings. I suspect this idea came from a movie my father had recommended to me around that time called *Not Without My Daughter.*

In this film, Sally Field plays the American wife of an Iranian man who convinces her to spend two weeks in Iran with their small daughter. From the minute the family arrives in Iran, the audience is made to feel Field's great estrangement from her husband's homeland. His sudden devotion to religion, the skepticism of his traditional family toward a Western wife, and the restrictive nature of the society as a whole toward women combine to push Field's character to the fringes. The seemingly loving relationship between husband and wife deteriorates as Field's husband informs her that he has decided to remain in Iran permanently—with their daughter. According to Iranian-Islamic law, the father has sole rights over the child, but Field refuses to leave the country without her. Braving domestic violence and the Islamic authorities, mother and daughter escape Iran to the American embassy in a neighboring country. The credits role over the image of an enormous American flag waving in the wind. This final shot has remained vivid in my mind since I first saw the movie. Even at the age of thirteen, the symbolism of the flag was perfectly clear: America equals freedom, the Middle East equals authoritarianism.

I didn't have any context to understand what I saw in *Not Without My Daughter,* and it became a central image in my definition of Islam. Now I realize that that movie has more to do with Islam's vision of women, and with Iran specifically, than an indictment of the religion as a whole. I had always thought: Middle East, Islamic, Arab. This couldn't be further from the truth. In fact, the world's largest Muslim country isn't even in the Middle East. It's Indonesia. Of the five countries in the world that have the highest Muslim populations, not a single one is Arab. Iran's ancestors are Persians, not Arabs, and they speak Farsi, not Arabic.

Fortunately, my misconceptions about the Middle East did not translate into actions. I did not feel consciously afraid when I met an Arab or Muslim person for the first time. Though I remember many of the American campers at Seeds of Peace feeling uncomfortable around so many foreigners, I was intrigued as opposed to intimidated by their strangeness. I learned to feel comfortable around people from a wide range of cultural and religious backgrounds. Still, even today, I am aware of retaining many stereotypes about Islamic and Middle Eastern culture. These aren't issues I think about when I'm with my Arab and Muslim friends, but I can never completely forget them while traveling in Palestinian and other Arab cities.

As you can see, I grew up much more sheltered and, frankly, more ignorant than you might expect given my parents' pursuits. Coming from a privileged background meant I had little conception of the difficult realities that many people in the world face on a daily basis. Seeds of Peace opened me up to these realities and taught me to take an active interest in the world beyond "Jen." It put a practical face on what my family had been telling me all along: you have to leave the world a better place than you found it. To my great-grandparents and grandparents this meant supporting the formation of an independent Jewish state after the Holocaust. My parents have also devoted themselves to improving the world, but they have expanded their views regarding the nature of the contribution they want to make. For them it is no longer enough to simply support a Jewish state as my grandparents did. My parents know that a Jewish state under constant threat is not what their elders envisioned. So the more recent family photos include Yitzhak Rabin and Ehud Barak as well as Yasir Arafat and King Hussein; it is working toward a just solution for *both* peoples—Israelis and Arabs—to which my parents have committed themselves so that a Jewish homeland can exist peacefully.

This has not been easy work for my parents. Throughout his career, my father received hate mail ranting that his work on the so-called peace process would ultimately bring about Israel's destruction. People asked, had my father forgotten his family's commitment to Eretz Yisrael, the Land of Israel? A group of protestors called him a Jewish Benedict Arnold. My own grandfather was appalled by the fact that I'd sat at the same table with Arafat. He called Arafat a murderer and wanted me to call my book "Arafat Exposed." As numerous as these accusations, there were just as many attacking the U.S. government for being a tool of Israel and the Jews in general. Through most of the 1990s, the U.S. peace process team included four Jews—Dennis Ross, Dan Kurtzer, Aaron Miller, and Martin Indyk. For many people, this was proof of the conspiracy between Israel and the United States for world domination.

In truth, my parents' Jewish identity never interfered with their work in conflict resolution. Perhaps they were compelled to take up this work in the first place because of a spiritual or historical connection to Israel, but in the business of peacemaking, you could call them neither "pro-Israel" nor "pro-Palestine."

I wrote *Inheriting the Holy Land* to get this idea across: As individuals, we are much greater than our religions, our nationalities, and our ethnicities. These are defining categories, but they are not unyielding. My work with Seeds of Peace has shown me how diverse one individual can be, and what's more, what a great capacity we have to expand our perspectives. Because even when I returned home to Chevy Chase, where I grew up, I saw how frighteningly close the Israeli-Palestinian conflict was to my life. I live thousands of miles away from the violence of Gaza and Tel Aviv; I ride the bus and never wonder whether someone might detonate a bomb inside of it; and I have never seen a tank parked outside my home or waited hours at a checkpoint to get to school. After I lived among Israelis and Palestinians, I realized how much I took my freedom and security for granted. Even after September 11, 2001, I did not see how precious these qualities were and what my life would be like without them. Israelis, Palestinians, and many others in the Arab and Islamic world know this absence too well. For them, oppression and insecurity are daily life. When these people look at U.S. foreign policy, they see the most powerful nation in the world acting against the ideals of democracy and freedom it claims to cherish. Many of these people are calling the United States hypocritical. Some, as we have already seen, are acting on their words.

Nothing is more important to American national interests than helping Israelis and Palestinians to reconcile. It's not only that we are a vital third party, but that our national security depends upon a solution that satisfies both peoples. This is largely because the conflict's outcome has direct consequences for how the Arab and Islamic worlds view the United States today and how generations of young Arabs and Muslims will treat us in the future. I am not implying that the United States is embroiled in an epic conflict with Muslims and Arabs, but I do think we need to take an honest and critical look at who we are as Americans and to question so-called truths we've been taught about other nations. I want to act in my country's national interest, but I don't want to do it blindly. As Uncle Ben tells Peter Parker in the movie *Spider-Man,* "With great power comes great responsibility." The United States certainly has great power, but it is not physical and monetary might alone that has propelled us to superpower status. It is our democratic foundation, our values of free thought and expression, our openness. Herein lies our real strength. So then, how do we use this strength responsibly? I believe we must lead by example. Not by spreading our values, but upholding them, especially in our conduct abroad.

In this sense, my advice to Israelis and Palestinians about experiencing and appreciating diversity also applies to Americans. No person on this earth—no Israeli, no Palestinian, no American—is an isolated entity. As nations, we are even more closely connected. So working for one's national interest means thinking internationally, or at the very least, thinking outside ourselves. I've seen what happens to societies that don't, and it's frightening.

The young Israelis and Palestinians you will meet in this book have learned to look beyond themselves and to see that they are a significant piece in the global puzzle. It hasn't been easy for them. A Jordanian friend of mine once said that to make peace, you have to go to war with yourself. This often means struggling against the ingrained ideas of your own nation, ethnic group, or religion. This doesn't mean forgetting your home. The young people of *Inheriting the Holy Land* have embarked on a truly national quest. They are eager to experience the diversity outside their nations in order to build stronger societies inside them.

I feel the same. Living in the Middle East and learning from these extra-ordinary young people has reinforced my American identity. My loyalty to my country was born at home, but the necessity—in fact, the urgency—I feel to act on behalf of that loyalty was created only on the road from Gaza to Tel Aviv. I hope this book will encourage other Americans to act on their loyalty as well.

FROM MAINE
TO THE
MIDDLE EAST

An Unusual Friendship

I t was the largest Star of David I'd ever seen suspended from someone's neck. I was in Maine for the first day of the Seeds of Peace Camp 2003, and the bus carrying the Israeli delegation had just opened its doors. I was there to observe and select some of the Israelis and Palestinians who appear in this book. I wanted to include both the students I knew from my years as a camper and some of the new kids who were attending Seeds of Peace in the middle of the second intifada. One by one, they were getting out, catching their first glimpses of the lake. And suddenly, there it was: a Jewish star the size of a silver dollar swinging over a blue T-shirt. "Now that's what I call bling-bling!" someone behind me said. It was true; I'd seen plenty of Israelis strutting their stars down the camp road, wearing their chains like rappers, though this one was the most eye-catching. "So you're a tough guy?" I silently asked the skinny kid with the outrageous star. "This is Seeds of Peace, not South Central."

That was before I knew Omri, before he knew me, and before I had any insight into his politics.

Omri, fifteen, is dark and skinny with large, searching eyes. He is Israeli to the core and clearly has the jewelry to prove it. The six-pointed Star of David (which he got as a promotion from his favorite Israeli rapper) is both a Jewish symbol and a national Israeli emblem. Omri also wears his father's army tag, which he keeps in a dark green canvas pouch. For him, the tag symbolizes his love of the army. He swiped it from his father's dresser one day and was afraid his dad would get angry. Instead, his father was honored. I imagine this scene: Omri pulling up his shirt, showing off the tag on his bony brown chest, perhaps puffing up to look more manly. I imagine the pride in his father's eyes.

One afternoon in the camp dining hall, I asked to see the tag, and Omri placed the silver rectangle on the table with great care, like a jeweler appraising his diamonds. For Omri, Israel is forever.

Omri is a Mizrahi Jew—a Jew of Middle Eastern descent. His mother was born in Turkey and his paternal grandparents are from Yemen. His family was part of the Jewish community that flourished throughout the Arab and Islamic world. Many of these Middle Eastern Jews were deeply integrated into their respective societies and had been for decades. The events of 1948, however, came as a revolution for these Jewish communities, as it did for the entire Middle East.

From the end of World War One until May of 1948, a British Mandate had governed Palestine. The British made various unsuccessful attempts to map out a viable political future for the Arab and Jewish communities in Palestine. In 1947 the United Nations suggested a partition plan that would divide Palestine into separate Arab and Jewish states with Jerusalem as an international district. Despite a great deal of internal opposition, the Jewish leadership endorsed the plan. The Arabs, however, rejected it, saying they opposed the Jewish claim to a state in Palestine.

When the 1947 partition plan failed, Britain withdrew its forces. The Jewish community in Palestine declared the independence of the State of Israel, and the next day, armies of Egypt, Syria, Lebanon, Transjordan, and Iraq attacked the nascent Israeli state. The Israelis were highly organized in comparison to the uncoordinated Arab forces, and though the Arab soldiers outnumbered the Jews, Jewish forces had the upper hand in some of the most strategic battles. By the war's end, Israel had signed cease-fires with each country. These were armistice agreements, not treaties; the Arab countries refused to acknowledge Israel's legitimacy.

Israel captured all of historic Palestine *excluding* the Gaza Strip, which remained part of Egypt, and the land west of the Jordan River, today known as the West Bank. (Israel did not capture the West Bank and Gaza until a second Arab-Israeli war in 1967.)

The war of 1948, which Israel calls its war of independence and the Arabs call al-Nakba, "The Catastrophe," resulted in the creation of over 700,000 Palestinian refugees. These were Palestinian Arabs who fled to Egypt, Jordan, Lebanon, and Syria as a result of Jewish-Arab hostilities. Some of these refugees fled believing they could return to their homes at the war's end; others were intimidated into leaving by reports of Jewish atrocities. Many of these stories were fiction, but others, such as the infamous massacre of Arab civilians in the village of Dir Yassin, were true. Finally, the Jewish forces forcibly expelled Arabs whose land was necessary to build a contiguous Israeli state.

After Israel declared its independence, the Israeli parliament, the Knesset, passed the Law of Return, which grants full Israeli citizenship to any Jew in the world. The law is highly offensive to Palestinians, because it allowed masses of Jews to immigrate to Israel while 700,000 Palestinian-Arabs who had been living in Palestine for hundreds of years were uprooted from their homes. For most Jews, however, the Law of Return embodies the very meaning of a Jewish nation.

After the war of 1948, Mizrahi Jews like Omri's family were in need of a safe haven. When Israel defeated the five Arab armies, the Arab and Islamic nations either expelled their Jewish communities or made their lives increasingly difficult. The Law of Return made Israel the obvious destination for these Arab Jews, though not always the easiest. Until the mid-1950s, Israel was dominated by Ashkenazi Jews—Jews of European descent. They were highly skeptical of and even outright discriminatory toward the new immigrants, who seemed much closer to Israel's Arab neighbors in terms of custom and appearance. Israel's intense desire to acculturate the new immigrants as "Israeli"—by teaching them Hebrew, putting them in the army, and instilling in them a connection to Eretz Yisrael—has largely paid off. Despite remaining divisions, including cultural differences and a sizable socioeconomic gap between the majority of Israeli Mizrahim and Ashkenazim, today Jews of Arab origin have all but lost their former national allegiances. In fact, their communities consistently vote in large numbers for the right-leaning parties that advocate rigid policies toward the territories and the Palestinians.

Omri's parents and grandparents have passed much of their distinctive culture on to him: the food they eat, the music they enjoy, and the way they practice Judaism. Omri says that if an Ashkenazi Jew were to attend his father's Yemeni synagogue, he would hardly understand a word of the service. But as a second generation Israeli, Omri is completely integrated into Israeli society. I have never heard him refer to himself as an Arab Jew or call himself culturally Arab. Neither does he feel part of a separate ethnic group. Omri is Israeli and Jewish. To him, the Arabs are a people apart. This includes Israel's own Arab population—those Palestinians who did not flee Palestine in the 1948 war and to whom Israel ultimately granted citizenship.

Omri told me about the tension between Bat Yamis (the Jews who live in Omri's neighborhood of Bat Yam) and the Arabs from the neighboring city of Jaffa. According to him, an Arab man murdered a Jewish girl at the Bat Yam bus stop in 1996. In retaliation, a group of Bat Yamis went to the city limits near Jaffa and started burning Arab cars and smashing windows.

"That's why the kids, and actually me and my friends, don't like those kinds of people." Omri paused and then decided to clarify, "The Arab people."

Omri went on to say that every year on Yom Kippur, the Jewish day of atonement, the Arabs from Jaffa come to Bat Yam with discmen and cigarettes. "They are very disrespectful," he said scornfully. "And they paid for it."

They paid for it. The way he said this, it sounded like the Arab world had collectively insulted Omri's mother.

"How did they pay for it?" I asked.

"Five years ago on Yom Kippur, they came with a jeep and started to honk the horn. And we are not allowed to drive on Yom Kippur. And people just flipped the jeep into the water," he said, as if this were a casual occurrence. "So this is where I come from. The city where almost everyone is rightist."

For Omri, it seemed, being "rightist" was a badge of honor. Having tough, uncompromising opinions about the Arabs made him feel tough—perhaps made him feel more "Israeli" and less an Israeli with Arab roots. Not that Omri is ashamed of his heritage or that his feelings about Arabs are all a show. The stories he told me were very real, and they did cause him pain. But I began to wonder if there wasn't something slightly exaggerated about Omri's "rightist" pride.

At the same time, this pride is a source of strength for him. Omri's parents are divorced. During the months I spent in the region, he was living in Bat Yam, a lower-middle-class suburb of Tel Aviv with his mother, who works in a sunglasses store. His father does part-time gardening and electronic jobs in wealthy Tel Aviv suburbs. Omri's home is a modest apartment in a crowded Bat Yam neighborhood where every street and building resembles the next. There was rarely a time when I didn't drive in circles trying to find it. The neighborhood is rich with tropical plants and trees, and the gray-colored apartments are livened by clothes hanging out to dry. But the sidewalks are dirty, full of pigeon and dog droppings. Omri says the parks are local gang hangouts. One afternoon, Omri and his mother returned home to find their apartment burglarized. Now Omri's mother blasts music when she goes out in order to throw off potential thieves.

Omri's room is a small corner space with a dresser, a bookshelf, and a narrow bed. He has decorated his door with bumper stickers: "Oslo Is Proof: Don't Give Them a Country"; "I Am a Patriot"; "Don't Give Terror a Country"; and "Achud Leumi," the logo of Israel's National Union party. They advocate "transfer," the removal of Palestinians from the West Bank and Gaza to Israel's neighboring Arab countries. Omri's CD collection is full of Subliminal, the highly nationalistic rap artist who some people consider a racist. The cover of one album, *The Light from Zion,* depicts a muddied hand gripping a Star of David. The fingers curl up out of blackness, clenched in anger. In a song called "Hope," a reference to Israel's national anthem Hatikva, "The Hope," Subliminal rhymes in sharp, forceful Hebrew: "Another soldier coming back covered in the Israeli flag / Blood and tears falling down / Strong nation, we won't leave / Cause no motherfucker can stop Israel." Another song is entitled "Beladi," which means "my country" in Arabic. Beladi is also the name of the Palestinian national anthem. "Zionism is in our blood," Subliminal raps in "Beladi," but he goes on to say that "the Jews respect Islam and Christianity / My throat is not thirsty for blood . . . I put down the Uzi and pick up the microphone / I'm dreaming of peace but I get good-bye."

On one visit to his home, after we had met at camp, I asked Omri about the racist accusations against Subliminal.

"It's not true!" Omri was quick to defend his hero.

"But I've heard that people shout 'Death to the Arabs' at his concerts," I said.

"I went to his concert," Omri replied. "And there were forty thousand people there. And the whole room started shouting this. And Subliminal told them not to say it."

"Did you say it?"

"Yes."

Knowing Omri's politics and his feelings about Arabs, especially before Seeds of Peace, I wasn't surprised that he had participated in this type of anti-Arab tirade. And yet I simply could not picture this fifteen-year-old I had come to know so well standing among a mass of people shouting racist slurs. I asked Omri if he would do it again or if he could remain silent while forty thousand other Israelis screamed.

"I won't do it now," he said. To prove it, he showed me his screensaver.

It was a photo from Seeds of Peace: the wide grassy field leading down to the bunkline and, through gaps in the buildings, slivers of lake.

"That camp, it did something to him!" Omri's mother, Sima, whispered a few minutes later when Omri went to the bathroom.

"He's really that different?" I asked.

"In some ways he's just the same; in other ways, you'd hardly know it was the same Omri." At that moment, Omri appeared around the corner with a skeptical look. Sima winked at me and popped back into the kitchen.

As Omri searched the Internet, I began thinking about my first real conversation with him. We were at camp and I had persuaded him to skip general swim in return for "illegal" phone privileges. Campers were not allowed to use the phone during activities, but I promised to cover for him. I wanted a chance to talk to the boy who boasted the fanciest bling. We chose a table at the back of the dining hall overlooking the lake. Perhaps it was the tranquil setting or the gentle wind, but suddenly, realistic, hard-nosed Omri was talking about transfer the way romantics speak of lost love.

"It was my dream," he said, his large eyes drifting across the lake.

"Your dream?"

"Since I was a boy, I dreamed that the Arabs would be transferred away from here."

"You mean from Israel?"

Omri emerged from his reverie. "That's what I wanted, but I know it's not going to happen. You can't just take three million Palestinians and throw them in other countries. But"—and now he looked straight into my eyes—"it was like a dream for me. I voted for the Achud Leumi [National Union] party in the last elections."

"I thought the voting age in Israel is eighteen," I said, thinking about how National Union was one of the most extreme parties in the Israeli parliament. They believed the Jews rightfully owned all the land between the Mediterranean Sea and the Jordan River, and that the Arabs should be forcibly kicked out.

"It is," Omri announced.

"Then how could you vote?"

"My mother voted for the one I chose."

Many Israelis and Palestinians will tell you that if they had one wish, it would be to wake up tomorrow to find the other nation gone. Vanished.

But I'd never known any Seed to believe in transfer as seriously as Omri or to try to make this wish come true.

"Omri, why did you come to Seeds of Peace?" I asked, wondering why any kid who wanted the Arabs to disappear that badly would agree to live with them for a month.

"I didn't lie to get into Seeds." He grew defensive. "I said very rightist things. My principal interviewed us and asked us what we thought about the conflict and what was our way to peace and *he* heard very rightist things. When they interviewed us with kids from all over the country, I *also* said very rightist things. And then there was a phone call and it was my principal and he said, 'Seeds of Peace wants you to go.' " Omri sounded like he was still surprised about this. "My father and mother told me, 'Listen. They say they want you. It doesn't matter if you're rightist or left wing. Whatever you said to them, they want you. They want Omri.' Even though"—he paused to make sure I had gotten the message loud and clear—"I said rightist things."

"But why did you apply in the first place?"

Omri shrugged. "I just wanted to see if I could get in."

Of course. I'd known Omri for only a few days, but I already knew to expect nothing less from him. He thrived on challenges, and Seeds has a highly competitive reputation. Any school in Israel could nominate students, but they could send only two or three to compete against hundreds of others nationwide. I also knew that many kids on both sides of the conflict apply to Seeds without the slightest intention of making friends with "the other side." They want the opportunity to prove to those *Palestinian terrorists* or those *Israeli war criminals* that they are right. But in Omri's own words, going to Seeds of Peace still meant he had "to sleep in the same room as Palestinians, and play with Palestinians, and cooperate with Palestinians, and swim with Palestinians, and do *everything* with Palestinians."

How could a boy who hated Arabs so much that he wanted them exiled from their homes live in such an environment? Even after he decided to attend Seeds, some Israelis in his delegation told him to tone down his opinions or the Arabs in his bunk would kill him the first night of camp. And Omri had replied, "Relax, I'm not going to fight anyone. I'm just going to kick some . . ."

"Kick some what?" I ventured.

"Kick some ass over there!"

He sounded like a macho movie fighter, but I was sure—at least ninety-nine percent sure—that he was joking.

"You know the Israeli delegation came to camp first," Omri told me. "And the counselors asked us to clap when the Palestinians came and to give them a warm welcome. And that was a very hard thing to do. Because we were thinking about how most of them might have contact with terrorists and how their fathers might be in Israeli prisons and how the Palestinians don't want to live peacefully with Israelis. And I understand the Palestinians, because I was exactly like them."

Only later did I realize how complicated this statement was. Omri was admitting to me that he'd changed. In the past he didn't want to live peacefully with the Palestinians. Now he did. On the other hand, Omri seemed to suggest that despite his change, the Palestinians were the same as they'd always been: a people who didn't want peace. Still, this contradicted the fact that less than a week into camp, Omri's closest friend outside his own delegation was Mohammad, a Palestinian.

I asked Omri if it was difficult for him to have a Palestinian for a best friend.

"I'm not looking at this guy as a Palestinian," Omri explained. "I don't call him Mohammad, the Palestinian. I call him Mohammad. I can see his personality from my coexistence group [also called coex, the daily meeting where kids wrestle—often in tears and anger—with history, politics, and identity]. I can tell he wants peace. And coex aside, he's a very nice boy—a nice kid. We always laugh together. We enjoy being together."

"Do you think you can enjoy being together when you go back home?"

Omri looked down at his hands, examining his thin fingers. "This is the question I now ask myself. If I should go home and say, 'I've got Palestinian friends. I should chill out, and I should calm down.' " Omri paused as though waiting for the answer. Finally he decided, "No. I cannot do it. My nation is more important to me than Mohammad."

Clearly, you could take Omri out of Israel, but you couldn't take Israel out of Omri.

"I'm not going to hate Mohammad," Omri continued. "He still was my friend for three weeks. And hopefully, he'll be my friend when we go home. But I don't think I'm going to change my opinions or change my way to peace."

"What's your way to peace?" I asked.

"Okay, that's politics now." Omri seemed eager to plunge ahead. "Do you know that in the Palestinian Charter in the sixth paragraph, it says that

Israel does not exist? How can I make peace with someone who says Israel should be destroyed to make a Palestinian nation?"

The Palestinian Charter proclaims the ideals and goals of the Palestinian national movement and was drafted in 1964 alongside the creation of the Palestine Liberation Organization. The PLO is an umbrella group of Palestinian political factions, and its longtime chairman was Yasir Arafat, head of the nationalist Fatah party. Among the central tenets of Fatah and the other PLO organizations was a policy of armed resistance against what they considered to be the illegitimate Jewish state. This resistance took the form of attacks by Palestinian militants along the Israeli-Jordanian and Israeli-Lebanese borders, the hijacking of Israeli aircraft in 1976, and the murder of the Israeli Olympic team at Munich in 1972.

I told Omri that Arafat had indeed removed the articles in the Palestinian Charter calling for Israel's destruction.

"No, no they didn't." Omri sounded as certain. "In the Oslo agreement, part of the agreement was to take this clause out. And Arafat says, 'Ya, I'm going to do it as soon as I can.' But I'm still waiting."

In fact, the Palestinian Legislative Council had removed the clause calling for Israel's destruction, but it took them until 1998, five years after Arafat and Rabin formally signed the principle of mutual recognition. The summer of 2003, while Omri and I sat in the Seeds of Peace dining hall, the original charter still appeared on the PLO Website.

"And I'm not saying that peace is just on the paper," Omri continued. "You have to change the minds of people. The Palestinians are not thinking about peace. They are going into the street with Israeli flags burning. You know the lynching that was two years ago? A man came out of the window and shows his hands with the Israeli blood. I have a picture that says, 'Can you shake his hand for peace?' "

I have seen this photo, taken in October 2000, two weeks into the second intifada. A young Palestinian man stands at the open window of the Ramallah police station, displaying to the crowd below his bright red palms and a victorious smile. The man with the bloodied hands and others, including Palestinian police, had stabbed and beaten two Israeli soldiers to death. Afterward, one soldier was thrown from the window and the other dragged through the city. An Italian camera crew caught the entire event on tape and Israeli television broadcast the footage nationwide. In response to the murders, the IDF destroyed the Palestinian police station. Later, the Palestinians claimed they couldn't adequately fight terror because Israel had destroyed their police forces.

I asked Omri if he thought a lot of people in Israel were still turned away from peace.

"I still don't think this peace is going to work. Israelis and Palestinians living together."

"And you still believe this? Even after being at camp and your friendship with Mohammad?"

"I said in coex today, 'If my father tells me since I was one-year-old that the sky is orange, I will say, "The sky is orange." ' You know the menorah of the holy temple? The Palestinians believe the menorah is a sign of war, that the Star of David symbolizes a star from the sky and that means we want to conquer all the world. I was in shock when I heard those things. Their education system is just confusing them. You cannot educate those kids like that and expect them to think that peace is something that could happen."

"And what about you?" I pointed to the Jewish star around Omri's neck. "How were you educated about the Palestinians? What did your parents tell you?"

Omri said he arrived at his opinions by himself, though he told me his father had explained to his stepbrother that there are good Arabs and bad Arabs. "And if my father is saying this," Omri considered, "then probably most of the fathers and most of the families are saying it."

Later I learned that Omri didn't talk to his father much about Seeds of Peace. It was fine to spend one summer in the program, his dad said, but beyond that Omri was wasting his time.

General swim was almost over, but I had to ask Omri outright: Had he changed since he'd been at camp?

"I moved a little bit and I didn't want it to happen," Omri said, fiddling with his Star. "I wanted to stay with my opinions. The same Omri as before. But when you've got friends from the other side, it makes you a little bit confused."

Like Omri and his necklace, I noticed Mohammad's feet before I saw his face. They were walking down the camp road: metallic silver sneakers reflecting sunlight like laser beams. They looked like part of a superhero getup; shoes like these could be a dangerous weapon on the basketball court. In the store, they would have screamed "showoff," but not on Mohammad's feet. This fifteen-year-old Palestinian from Jerusalem's Old City was soft-spoken and modest. When I asked him how he came to choose such flashy footware, an embarrassed smile seized his face. He didn't know, he said. He just liked them.

One look at Mohammad's smile and you knew he was everybody's friend. You knew he was a "great kid," the highest honor Seeds of Peace counselors could bestow upon a camper. Of course, all the kids were great, but to be a "great kid" you needed an extra special spark. "Silver Shoes Mo," as I took to calling him, had it.

With his secret weapon shoes (which enabled him to outrun and out-jump his peers in most sports), Mohammad was half of that summer's dynamic duo. Like any true superheroes, Omri and Mohammad defied all the odds. On top of their ethnic, cultural, and political differences, their personalities were like day and night. Omri was loquacious and self-assured. Mohammad was private. The one thing they shared, however, was a love of basketball. They were as committed to the game as they were to their own countries. In fact, you might say that basketball became the boys' new nationalism. It divided the Seeds of Peace camp, not by Arab and Jew, but by those to whom basketball was sacred and those to whom it wasn't. When it came to basketball, Omri and Mohammad played for the same team.

Omri and Mohammad also spent most of their off-court time together. They were assigned the same activities, put on the same color games team, and were forced to spend an hour and a half every day in the same coexistence session.

I asked Mohammad about coex. Did he and Omri fight?

"Everybody fights in coex," Mohammad said. "But it doesn't affect our friendship. We leave coex in the coex room."

"But Omri's politics are pretty severe. That doesn't bother you?"

Mohammad said he liked confronting Omri. "If he's my friend," Mohammad said, "it's easier to face him, even if he's right-wing. Everyone has political views that are critical to his own side. But camp is important because your enemies may be closer to you than your friends at home."

I asked Mohammad how this could possibly be true, but it was clear enough to him: Camp had given him a unique experience that was unlike any he had ever had with his friends in Jerusalem. They wouldn't be able to understand what he went through at Seeds, but Omri would.

"How do you think your friends and family will react when they hear about Omri?" I asked, remembering that Mohammad had just called Omri the "enemy" even if he no longer felt that way about him.

"Some will say that you shouldn't have friends from the other side." But Mohammad assured me, "I won't listen to them."

"So you'll keep your relationship with Omri going when you get home?"

"Absolutely. Yes." He answered without a second's hesitation. "I don't know about him, but I like Omri as a person and not as an Israeli." Which was exactly what Omri had said about Mohammad. At the same time, I knew there was a lot Mohammad *didn't* know about Omri. I remembered Omri's words: *My nation is more important to me than Mohammad.*

I put these thoughts aside and asked Mohammad if he would take Omri to meet his friends in the Old City.

Mohammad admitted that such introductions weren't a good idea. "His friends won't accept me as Palestinian and as his friend. My friends won't accept him as Israeli and as my friend."

"Would you introduce him to your parents?"

"It's not a good idea for him to visit the Muslim Quarter with his Star," Mohammad said, as though asking Omri to remove his necklace wasn't a possibility.

It occurred to me that with a quick costume change, Omri would look right at home in East Jerusalem. Remove the Star, exchange the basketball shorts for tight-legged jeans, gel the hair, and he could easily pass for one of those skinny Arab youths smoking cigarettes outside the Old City walls. And Mohammad wouldn't have to change his appearance at all to blend in around Bat Yam. With his rolled-up sleeves and relaxed smile, Mohammad looked more the product of Mediterranean beach culture than the Muslim Quarter. Stick him in an Israeli high school and he'd be an instant heartthrob.

But I knew that neither boy belonged in the other's environment.

"When I first saw the Star," Mohammad told me, "I thought, he's a racist and he doesn't like Palestinians. And maybe he felt the same way about me."

Like Mohammad's shoes, Omri's Star was *his* secret weapon. But it was one of the many things the boys would never be able to share. Indeed, Omri was even more worried than Mohammad about going home to his friends.

"We all support you and we want you to have fun," one of Omri's friends had said to him before he went to Seeds of Peace. "Go and represent us with honor. But *please!* Don't . . . come . . . back as a peace man. As the one who thinks that peace is over everything and that we should give back all the settlements. Don't do it!" And Omri told his friend, "You *know* that I won't."

But now, Omri was having doubts. "When I get back to Israel," he told me halfway through the summer, "I am really worried that I will disappoint my friends."

A week before their camp session ends, I let the boys cut the line at dinner and grab their pizza from the staff side of the dining hall. They pile on slice after slice, and balancing their plates over cups of red bug juice, push through the screen doors with their shoulders. They follow me to an empty picnic table.

I cannot help but think that soon they will be back home, Omri in Bat Yam and Mohammad in East Jerusalem: neighborhoods at distinct odds with each other. I want them to confront this issue face-to-face: What will happen to their relationship in the Middle East?

At first the boys are awkward with the question. They chew on their pizza in silence. Then Mohammad swallows and says, "For my side, I have no problem being your friend even if we go back home. But do you share the same feelings?" He looked at Omri across the table.

"Of course," Omri says with a full mouth. "Only because of you—one person—I have changed. You have changed the way I think about the Palestinians. I didn't think that my best friend at camp outside my delegation would be Palestinian. Maybe American or Greek, but *not* Palestinian. I didn't believe that it could happen."

"I am going to tell you what." Mohammad's face grows serious. "The first time I saw you, you were wearing the David Star, and I thought you didn't like Palestinians at all. And after we had activities together our friendship became bigger and bigger, and I find that you have the same brain that I have and that we can be friends."

I know the conversation is just getting started, but this exchange sounds like a cheesy Seeds of Peace advertisement, not a genuine heart-to-heart.

"You know, I was so . . ." Omri fumbles for the right words. "Look," he says, "you know that I am a right-winger. You changed the way I think. I see people like you who want to be friends with us. But I don't trust Palestinians as a nation."

A shadow crosses Mohammad's face. Omri does not see it. He is studying the crusts on his plate.

"Does it matter to you," I ask Mohammed, "that Omri says he can't trust Palestinians as a nation?"

"No," he says, but his voice rises defensively.

Again, Omri seems not to notice Mohammad's discomfort. I am looking at him, hoping he will raise his head, catch his friend's eye. Instead, Omri continues explaining just why he can't trust Palestinians as a nation. There's a mother who lost her son to terror, he says. And when Prime Minister Sharon came to pay his condolences she told him to stop the violence. "She didn't say, 'I want revenge, I want to kill them.' " Omri is clear. "And this is the difference between my nation and your nation. In your nation, if they lost someone, they want to go explode. That's why we are called the Israel Defense Forces and not the Israel Attack Forces. We don't kill innocent people!"

I expect Mohammad to jump up and swear that Palestinians do not kill innocent people, that Omri is generalizing and being grossly unfair. To my surprise, he doesn't dispute the accusation, but defends his fellow Palestinians who are compelled to use violence. "Imagine if someone takes your land," he confronts Omri. "Imagine if someone kills your brother or—"

"Or your best friend." Omri stops Mohammad in his tracks.

"What do you do?" Mohammad asks, trying to make Omri acknowledge that he could call for revenge.

"I can understand you. I can understand those people who explode in the bus and killed those people. But just because I can understand them doesn't mean it's okay."

"I don't agree with them either," Mohammad says, quietly, though hardened. "But I just want to tell you how I live. When I came to the camp I needed a passport. So I went to the Ministry of Interior. Do you know where it is? It's in East Jerusalem. It's a disgusting place. It's the most disgusting place in all of Jerusalem. There are bullies. They want money. You have to wait twelve hours under sun and rain to get your passport. I stood in my turn from seven in the morning until ten in the evening to enter. That really pissed me off."

"Is it from the Israeli government?" Omri asks, and I can see he's not eager to hear the response.

"Ya!" Mohammad exclaims. "And I saw Israelis go inside and they go out in ten minutes. And that pisses Palestinians off, and it influences their actions."

"But it's not my fault." Omri shakes his head.

"It's your government's fault!"

"It's not my government's fault," Omri retorts. "It's *your* government's fault and I'll tell you why. We give the Palestinian Authority millions of dollars every year. Millions! And do you know what's going on with that money? It goes to Arafat's pocket. It goes straight to him. That's why he's one of the ten richest Arabs in the world. *We* give you money that should make your life better, but your government doesn't give it to you."

I can't argue with Omri about Palestinian Authority (PA) corruption. The European Union used to give the PA money for general finances. So much of it disappeared that they decided to fund specific projects, to make sure there are tangible results. According to *Ha'aretz* (a newspaper often called Israel's *New York Times*) Arafat's wife, Suha, reportedly received an allowance of $100,000 a month. French police investigated the transfer of 11.5 million dollars into her French bank account. When the United States pressured Arafat to reform his government in 2003, he appointed Salam Fayad, a former World Bank professional, as finance minister. Palestinians claim Fayad is one of the few noncorrupt members of the Authority. Though Fayad has made great strides in organizing Palestinian Authority finances and making their accounts more transparent, he spoke of his job as a Sisyphean task.★

According to Mohammad, there is nothing he or any other Palestinian can do about this corruption. It's Israel's responsibility, he says, to give the Palestinians a real state. But Israelis don't want to give up the land.

"What about Camp David?" Omri throws back.

"What about it?"

"Ehud Barak gave ninety-nine percent of the territories. He said, just take it. And Arafat didn't take it."

Mohammad is not convinced. "The ninety-nine percent did not include the settlements or Jerusalem. Imagine what Jerusalem means to each Palestinian and each Muslim. It is a holy place and sacred place. And if you were me, you wouldn't surrender it."

In fact, Barak agreed to concede all of Gaza and ninety-one percent of the West Bank to Palestinians. This was more than any Israeli prime minister before him, but not the ninety-nine percent that Omri professes.

★*Ha'aretz,* August 6, 2004.

I am surprised that Mohammad says nothing about Jerusalem being his home. I wonder whether Omri has thought about this fact. Does he know how close Mohammad lives to the al-Aqsa mosque, the third holiest site in Islam? But before I have a chance to interject any questions, I hear Omri saying:

"We won't give up Jerusalem. Jerusalem is joining the Jewish people since they came into the world. It's where the holy temple was. We have proof—the Western Wall."

"That's the point," Mohammad breaks in. "You want—"

"If you have Jerusalem—" Omri presses on. "Not Jerusalem, but if you have something—this pizza—and it means a lot to you and I want to take it, would you give it to me?"

"I cannot give it to you," Mohammad answers. "I can share . . . but I can't give it to you."

"Jerusalem is not a place that we can share. It's our *dream*, Jerusalem. It's our dream. We can't give it up. That is why in the Independence War the brave soldiers who shot people, when they saw Jerusalem, when they saw the Wall—the Western Wall—they took off their hats and they started to cry. You know it was a dream. You have this holy place and after people took it from you, you took it back. You know how much you would feel. When you finally have what you want?"

I understand the root of Omri's emotion. I was startled to learn that after Jews won the 1948 war and declared an independent state, the eastern part of Jerusalem—where the Jewish, Muslim, and Christian holy sites are—remained in Arab hands. It was not until Israel captured East Jerusalem in the war of 1967 that Jews were able to call the Western Wall, the remaining structure of their holy temple, their own. For Jews this was a watershed, perhaps as important as achieving a Jewish state in the first place. Today, the Israeli government claims Jerusalem as its capital, though the international community calls the capital Tel Aviv.

"Don't you think that it is also the Palestinian dream?" Mohammad asks, disbelieving. "They have holy places to go to. They have been living there since the beginning of the religious ceremonies. You just can't do your dream that someone else dreams about also."

This, of course, is the problem. Adjacent to the four quarters of the Old City is the Temple Mount, what the Israelis call Har Ha-Bayt and the Palestinians call the Haram al-Sharif, or Noble Sanctuary. This space is religiously and nationally sacred to Israelis and Palestinians, Muslims and Jews. And it literally overlaps. The Al-Aqsa mosque and the Dome of the Rock sit directly on top of the platform supporting the Western Wall, the last remaining wall of the Second Temple. The structures are inextricably linked, just like Israelis and Palestinians themselves. Even though their holy places are so closely connected, and even though these boys have become so attached to each other, each seems to be in his own separate world.

"We can't let it go, we can't let it go," Omri mumbles over and over, despite his friend's continued protestations. "I'm not saying that you can't go and pray," he finally confronts Mohammad. "I know Jerusalem is special for Muslims and for Christians. So you can still go and pray, but it is in our hands."

But Mohammad says he doesn't trust the Israeli government to be in charge of the holy sites. Omri says he doesn't trust the Palestinian government either.

"I just want to tell you that Palestinians aren't as you think them," Mohammad says, frustrated. "Maybe you have been told that they are so aggressive that they want to take the whole land and that they want to throw the Israelis into the sea—"

"I saw it with my own eyes," Omri says. "The necklaces show it."

Though Omri's Star of David offends many Arabs, kids in the Palestinian delegation wear necklaces with charms shaped like historic Palestine— or, depending on whom you ask, the land of modern-day Israel. The tiny maps are red, white, and green: the colors of the Palestinian flag. Palestinians call the map "Palestine," referring to the land before 1948. To Israelis, the necklaces signify the Palestinians' desire to eradicate Israel.

"*You* understand the necklaces wrongly." Mohammad is suddenly fierce. "The necklaces mean that my home as it *used* to be was the whole Palestine, but that my nation is within 1967 borders. You have to understand that not all Palestinians are as you think them."

Omri does not respond. The last ring of the activity bell melts into the air and with it the argument. The boys aren't looking at each other. It's as though the three of us are frozen. I realize with a start that they are going to be late to coexistence. I tell them to hurry, I'll clear the table. "See ya later, Jen." They get up and jog away. They're off to another hour and a half of the same discussion. The same disagreements. I see how easy it is to forget that so much is hidden behind the hugs and high-fives, behind the late-night gossip in the bunk and talk of girls. Mohammad had told me that their arguments don't interfere with their friendship. That no matter what happens in coex, they walk out as friends. They can get up from the table and run off together as they just have.

I also know, from being in those sessions myself, that Omri and Mohammad are generally respectful to each other. They do not scream or attack. They listen to each other better than a lot of kids. Better than many adults. But is that good enough to make a difference in their understanding of each other? At camp, they have no choice but to run from a difficult discussion to a fun activity. They have no choice but to be together. At home, however, they won't have such opportunities, especially because Mohammad lives in Jerusalem and Omri lives near Tel Aviv. It's only a forty-five-minute drive, but these boys are teenagers. They have school, friends, basketball practice, and little time for trips to other cities. Their parents are especially overprotective when it comes to issues of security. I feel a sense of urgency for Omri and Mohammad. Time is running out for them, and if they don't tie up all their disagreements before they go home, the tie that binds their friendship will simply snap when they step off the plane. Of course, when it comes to one's nation, one's history, one's very sense of self, there are no neatly tied knots. All of my Seeds of Peace friends who attended camp with me and are now young adults have stopped hashing out these issues of Jerusalem, the Holocaust, the intifada. They know complete reconciliation does not exist. And for them, it's okay. They have years of friendship to fall back on. Their friendships are as much a reconciliation as winning an argument. Mohammad and Omri don't have that—at least not yet. Perhaps they will. But they have to stick together, and for some reason, I don't trust their vows to do so.

The boys are well into their coex session by now. It is a peaceful evening up here in Maine. It will be warm tonight, even after lights out. I will help the counselors put their kids to sleep and then sit with them on the dock, watching the stars and satellites flicker over the lapping water of Pleasant Lake. For a couple of hours I will be consumed with my friends' crushes, as well as job complaints—anything that is not about the Middle East. And most of us will easily forget that for 160 sleeping teenagers, the Middle East is inescapable. This is what Omri and Mohammad will struggle with when they wake up the next morning, when they return home, and perhaps for years to come: the inescapable realities of friends and family who do not understand the boys' friendship, teachers who give them only one side of history, and conflicts beyond their control.

I take my time gathering the cups and silverware. By every appearance, Omri and Mohammad haven't left much behind: paper plates and pizza crusts, a few drops of bug juice. But there is a silence in their wake—full of heaviness and too much unsettled.

Our Dream, Jerusalem

It's mid-August 2003 and I've come to Jerusalem to continue research-ing my book. I want to follow up with Omri and Mohammad and reconnect with my old friends from Seeds. I've also been conducting in-terviews with Israeli and Palestinian religious, social, and political leaders to get their assessment of the conflict. On this particular night, I'm out to dinner with my father (who's in Jerusalem on a business trip) at his favorite fish restaurant. Getting inside the restaurant is a bit of a proce-dure. Though I've gotten used to having my bag checked and my body wanded at most restaurants, here it's even more complicated. You must first ring a doorbell, get buzzed through, then have your bags and body checked, then walk through a small lobby, then pass through a second door, and only then enter the restaurant. Seem a bit paranoid? Welcome to Jerusalem.

Midway through our meal, we hear the first sirens. My stomach sinks. I pause mid-bite. I look at the fish and wonder: Is it appropriate to eat this piece of fish, now that I know there has been an explosion somewhere in the city? The sirens grow louder. They fill the room, echoing over our dinner plates. I decide to finish my dinner. My father and I pause between bites, listen, and speculate. I look around the room to see how others are reacting. From the look of the other diners, it's just a normal evening.

This bus bombing in August 2003 shattered a summer-long calm and ended the *hudna,* or cease-fire, agreement between the Palestinian Au-thority and Hamas. I don't think Israelis put much faith in the *hudna* from the beginning. For them, it was like the sensation of being followed. You feel danger creeping along behind, but when you turn around, you see only shadows: harmless in themselves, but ominous still. I took to laughing at my father when he was still working at the State Department. "We've negotiated a cease-fire," he would announce. "Great, Dad. You better start working on the next one right now." Where cease-fires are concerned, they're made to be broken.

So the August bombing was no surprise to the Israeli public. But for the recent Seeds of Peace graduates—like Omri and Mohammad—the event was a test. These kids had a lot at stake: friendships, newfound ideas of tolerance and respect, commitments to communication, and most important, the realization that they were not beholden to the hatreds of their nations, that they could be strong as individuals.

The previous summer there had been no terrorism while camp was in session, but when one Israeli graduate got on the airplane to go back home, the newspaper headline read: *The first 24 quiet days have just finished. Big terror attack today in Tel Aviv.* "And you could see," this young Israeli explained, "that the Israelis became Israelis again. They became *themselves* again."

This comment echoes a feeling of many Seeds' kids that camp is a dream. Israelis may make Palestinian friends and learn to see Palestinians in a new light, but these experiences hide what is real: home and one's national identity.

After the August 19 bombing I called Omri to see how he was doing.

"I'm pissed off" was the first thing he said. "I want to scream bad things, but I don't, because I'm a Seed. I feel really confused and I don't know what to do; I'm a Seed but I'm also an Israeli." It was exactly what the Seeds of Peace graduate from 2002 had said.

I asked Omri if he had talked to Mohammad.

"I don't have much to say to him right now. His nation hurt me. I don't need to call him." Omri sounded exasperated. "I'm really confused."

Omri hadn't heard from Mohammad, but his Palestinian friend Eman had called after the bombing. Hamas was responsible for the bombing, she'd reminded Omri, not her.

"I'm sure Eman is sorry," Omri told me. "But I'm not sure the Palestinian people are sorry. There were 100,000 people at Abu Shanab's funeral"—Omri was referring to a militant Israel had recently assassinated—"and they said, 'We'll flood Israel with blood.' I saw it on the news. We have a very serious problem." He sounded like Israel's security chief addressing the prime minister. But he continued as the fifteen-year-old I knew best.

"Now I got really sad because this didn't happen for a long time. Then we saw this explosion. It's blowing up everything we had there."

"And what did you have there?"

"To live side by side."

There was a song at my old summer camp called the Unity song. I remembered the lyrics: "Side by side, hand in hand, we are working together . . ." Silly words, I thought, in the context of this very real and very hard reality.

"But I feel I should still be in Seeds of Peace," Omri continued, further reflecting his struggle to reconcile his Seeds experiences with his current life. "We knew the bombing would happen. I didn't waste my time in Maine. I'm going to talk about camp in my school. It will be a real challenge, but I want it. When I went to Seeds, I wanted war. It sounds crazy, but it seemed like the only way."

"I've been filled with hate. Killing and *revenge.*" I imagined Omri's hands clenching like those raw fingers on the cover of the Subliminal album.

But then he softened. "I'm only a kid, not powerful like the guys in the government. But one day maybe people won't be killed. My Palestinian friends are against those killings."

I wanted to point out the reality of his beliefs versus the idea of them. "Just a moment ago you said that you can't talk to Mohammad because his nation hurt you. It seems that you're treating Mohammad more as a Palestinian than as a friend."

"I'm not treating Mohammad as part of a Palestinian nation." Omri was adamant. "I'm looking at him as a friend, not as a Palestinian. I really wanted him to call. I was surprised that he didn't."

I, too, was surprised that Mohammad didn't call after the bombing. Knowing how involved he was with Seeds—how he came to the organization's Jerusalem Center most days after school and was constantly writing to Seedsnet, the SOP listserv—I would have thought he'd reach out to Omri.

It turns out that Mohammad was very close to the bombing, because it happened near the Old City. He was on his way back home from playing basketball when he heard the explosion. It took him two hours to get home, because police had closed off the streets.

"I think it's wrong to kill innocent people," Mohammad said, when I reached him and asked his opinion about the bombing. But he sounded conflicted. "They shouldn't have done this bombing, but what else can Palestinians do?" I assumed he meant what else could Palestinians do for protection. I knew Mohammad was against suicide bombings in principle, but he was also angry at how weak the Palestinians were compared to the IDF. "This stuff will happen," Mohammad continued, "even when we are Seeds. We have to accept that we are in a conflict."

"Did you call Omri after the bombing?" I asked.

"He didn't call me," Mohammad replied.

I had always assumed there was a kind of unwritten Seeds of Peace post-suicide bombing or postmilitary action etiquette: Palestinians called Israelis if Israelis were targeted and vice versa. I'd seen it happen often enough in the past. But two months after camp, Mohammad and Omri had hardly communicated. I was beginning to think my intuition about their relationship falling apart had been correct.

"You didn't want to see if Omri was all right after the bombing?" I pressed Mohammad once more, hoping he might show some emotion for his friend.

"We didn't need to talk about it," Mohammad said. "Omri knows how I feel about the bombings."

I wasn't so sure he did.

It's much harder being a Seed now than when I attended camp. Those who participated in Seeds of Peace in the summer of 1997 (I was seventeen and a second-year camper) call it the Golden Summer: the year of the strongest friendships and the tightest bonds. According to the initial Oslo timeline, permanent status talks were due to happen the following year. It was clear to all of us that these talks would be postponed. The Oslo process was having serious difficulties. Yitzhak Rabin had been assassinated by a fanatical Israeli Jew in 1995 and the current Israeli prime minister, Benjamin Netanyahu, was implementing his side of the Oslo interim agreements at a snail's pace. Yasir Arafat and the Palestinian Authority seemed to be moving in a similar fashion when it came to security cooperation and terror control. In essence, both sides were shirking their commitments. This made life for ordinary Israelis and Palestinians uncertain and difficult. In order to distinguish between Palestinian territory that was under Palestinian political sovereignty, and territory that was still controlled by the IDF, Israel had established a system of ID cards and checkpoints. For Palestinians, this meant that movement and transport between their cities and towns—and between Palestinian territory and Israel—was more difficult now than before Oslo began. After a security breach, Israel closed down the checkpoints, effectively trapping Palestinians inside their cities. Though the Oslo process had led to international investment and a strengthening of the Palestinian economy, restrictions on movement were starting to have a seriously negative effect on the economy and on Palestinian morale. Palestinians also saw Israel's continued settlement construction in the West Bank and Gaza as a means of undermining the peace process.

For their part, Israelis weren't feeling very secure. Extremists on the Palestinian side were not giving up their fight against a two-state solution. There had been suicide bombings every year since the Oslo process began, with four bombings between February and March of 1996. There had already been one in March of 1997.

Still, at Seeds of Peace, we shared a general feeling of hope. Oslo was moving slowly, but it was moving. Then, halfway through the summer, two Palestinian men dressed as ultra-orthodox Jews entered the open-air Mahane Yehuda market in Jerusalem and blew themselves up. Never before had such an extreme act of violence on either side occurred while camp was in session.

I remember the day well and how it started out like any other. Friday morning before the wakeup bell, I put on my headphones and went running. That same morning, men and women in Jerusalem went to Mahane Yehuda to buy food for the Sabbath. Nearly one hundred people in the market were hurt in the blast, a handful losing their lives. Though I was nowhere near the bombs, I felt their impact. After breakfast, 150 Israelis and Arabs sat together chatting and joking, waiting for the announcement we'd been told John Wallach would make. Probably something about an award Seeds of Peace had won or some big media opportunity. John stood up before us, his face white as putty. "Today a terrible thing has happened . . . something that will test each and every one of you." One quiet wail went up even before John had finished speaking, and then another. I was sitting on the floor of the Big Hall in a crowd of these Middle Eastern teenagers, feeling as though we were all sinking into quicksand. I was entirely unable to comprehend what those around me were feeling. There was little chance I knew anyone who was killed or injured in the bombing, little chance that my friends or family members might be somehow hurt in the likely military retaliation that would follow. I had never been more aware of my identity as an American. So I sat still in my ignorance, feeling afraid.

Then a remarkable thing happened. A Palestinian boy stood up in the middle of the room and said, "I want to say that this is a horrible thing that happened. And I want to tell all my Israeli friends and all the Seeds that I did not wish this to happen. I am sorry for what these people have done."

And then an Israeli girl, her eyes red from crying, got up and looked at the Palestinian boy. "This wasn't your fault. I know it wasn't your fault, and I am sorry, too."

And then one by one, kids began to stand and express themselves, their anger and their empathy. Because they *could* empathize with one another— these Israelis and Palestinians—better than I or anyone else in the world. They shared the common experience of battering one another and of being battered. In this moment, they were drawn together, wrapped in that common shroud of death but also in the same green T-shirts of hope.

Camp activities were canceled for the rest of that day. Facilitators spoke with their coexistence groups and the kids were encouraged to sit with one another and talk, to take it easy. I spent most of the day alone, now and then listening in on conversations. I knew this day of rest wasn't for me.

Since 1997, both suicide bombings and Israeli military actions have taken place during the summer. Since the second intifada began in 2000, it has become impossible to stop camp for every action; there are simply too many. Now the focus is on resilience. The kids are allowed to call home, but activities continue. Just as Israelis and Palestinians push on with their daily lives, so do the Seeds of Peace campers. That's how they get through each day. There are few bold, public displays of empathy. The intifada has hardened everyone. Perhaps out of allegiance to their communities at home, they feel such overt touchy-feeliness is no longer appropriate. Still, they have learned to take their intense emotions and put them into the work they do at camp: what we at Seeds call the "J-O-B." But as I saw with Omri and Mohammad, continuing the J-O-B in the region, away from the supportive camp environment, was a different story entirely. Mohammad said he didn't call Omri because Omri supposedly knew how he felt about the bombing. More than this, Mohammad said he feared the two of them would fight about other issues if they began talking about this one.

The second bombing to occur while I was in Israel took place a month after the August bus explosion. I was in a Jerusalem taxi when Israeli radio broadcast one of the Hebrew words I knew all too well: *pigua*. It means bombing or explosion. I rolled down my window and listened anxiously.

No sirens. Where was it? What city? I bombarded the taxi driver with questions, but he grumbled and switched off the radio. When I reached home, I ran inside to check the news. Nine soldiers killed and thirty people wounded outside Tzrifin army base. Hamas claimed responsibility. I breathed a tired sigh—I didn't know where the Tzrifin army base was, but I knew it wasn't anywhere near me.

It was a callous thought, but I was exhausted after a long day. I'm sure Israelis were upset regardless of where the bombings took place, but I could put the event out of my mind if it wasn't in a major city where people I knew were more likely to be. It was out of my control, anyway. Just like Israelis and Palestinians, I had learned to keep a degree of detachment if I wanted to accomplish my research. Now all I could think about was my quiet apartment, my large couch, and a book to take me far, far away. I stretched out and soon enough had forgotten where I was.

One moment and a dozen things happen: my heart slams into my ribs, the walls seem to shake, and above all else, *the sound*. A neat, compact *pop*. It could be any number of things: a firecracker, a thunderclap, a helium balloon bursting open, but I immediately know it is none of these. My eyes fill with tears and I wipe them away. After that they stay dry.

In the distance I sense something. It feels like the vibrations that come before a train: imperceptible at first, but growing distinctly louder, piercing the silence, shrieking toward my apartment. The sirens rush upon my street, my house, and then fly past.

The ambulances stop two blocks away at the Café Hillel on Emek Refaim, the central boulevard running through my neighborhood. I don't know it then, but seven people have been killed instantly. Among them are the head of emergency at Shaare Zedek hospital; his twenty-year-old daughter, who was to be married the following day; and a young Palestinian waiter. Fifty more people are wounded. My phone begins to ring. A friend: Where are you? Are you all right? Jenny, don't go over there. Sometimes there are two bombers—the second one waits for the emergency crew.

Go there? Why would I do such a thing? To get the "real" experience? So I could put it in my book? Disgusting. Besides, the camera crews are doing a fine job. I flip from CNN to BBC, to Israeli channels One and Two, to Sky News. I am bombarded with images: people lying in their own blood, medics carrying the screaming and wounded to ambulances, sirens and shattered glass. After a minute, I realize that every channel is playing the same ten-second clip, recycled over and over.

"The temptation to go live has become so pressing," I remembered one of Israel's top journalists telling me, "that the media [today] shows bodies of Israelis killed even before the families know. This is a sin that goes against the legacy of Israeli media," he had said. "We are all predators. We can't restrain ourselves when we see a good picture of a dead body."

Well I could, so I switched off the television. I didn't feel angry or sad. Just worn-out, as though I'd returned home from some long and harrowing journey. I wanted nothing more than my bed.

I waited a day and a half before I decided to visit the bombsite. As I left my apartment, I noted how normal everything appeared. Emek Refaim, the street on which the attack had taken place, was full of people shopping, talking. Simply living. It was like any other sunny day I'd spent walking through my neighborhood. I realized that Jerusalem is not as frightening as it seems from the United States, perhaps because we get only the most dangerous sound bites. Here, I felt perfectly at ease being out and about two days after a bombing. Still, I knew that this feeling of apparent normalcy is exactly what my parents feared when I announced my decision to come to Jerusalem. During weeks of quiet, I didn't always think about "keeping my head down," as my father called to remind me nearly every day. I had passed Café Hillel a number of times and always thought to myself what a tempting target its floor-to-ceiling windows and unguarded patio would be. *This place is asking for it,* I thought each time. Yet a few weeks before the bombing, I agreed to go there with a Palestinian friend. Even as I was sitting on the patio, eating my sandwich, I was thinking, *Why am I eating here? This is so stupid.* It was a perfect Jerusalem night with a light breeze and my food was delicious. But it was a facade.

I was pretending to be in a normal city, but I wasn't. A place isn't normal if you (usually) feel compelled to scope out a restaurant's "fortifications" before you decide to eat there. A place isn't normal if dinner could mean death. To my mind, it showed a great deal of resolve and stubbornness that so many Israelis refused to give in to fear. As one Israeli Seed said of the terrorists, "If we don't go out, that's how they will win."

On my way to see the remains of Café Hillel, I passed Café Aroma, which I took to calling the Starbucks of Israel. Aroma is Hillel's main competitor. This morning, the one on Emek Refaim was dark with a large cardboard sign taped to the window: *Café Aroma sympathizes with the fami-*

lies of the victims of Café Hillel. As I was taking a picture of the sign, I saw a woman walk up to the door and try the handle. Finding it locked, she peered in the window, then tried the handle again. Can't you read the sign? I wondered. Do you need your espresso that badly? The woman stood dumbly outside the locked door. I imagined she was trying passwords to get in—Open Cappuccino! Let me in Latte!—but she eventually moved on. Later I wondered if I'd been too hard on this woman, who only wanted her caffeine fix. There were so many bombings. Life couldn't stop for each one.

The same went for Café Hillel. It was less than forty-eight hours after the bombing and construction workers were already making repairs. There was nothing left of the horrible images I'd seen on television. Nothing to gawk at. Makeshift walls had been erected around the shop, the debris cleaned from the streets. A light police presence, a few journalists, and a flower shrine next to the sidewalk were the only reminders that this was a bomb site. Otherwise you'd have thought the café was simply undergoing renovations.

Café Hillel reopened a few weeks later with a stylish metal fence and a row of flowerpots as its new fortification. Behind the replaced glass windows, the café was always packed. Though they say lightning rarely hits the same place twice, I never went back. I know that Hillel's shining new face is a symbol of resilience, but I couldn't help think of the café as a scar, marring the city like a dozen others around Jerusalem.

A Tourist in the Old City

Mohammad showed up freshly showered for our first afternoon together in the Old City—so fresh that there were still water streaks on his neck. His carefully gelled hair glistened in the August sun. "Hello!" he said eagerly and flashed two rows of perfectly white teeth. He opened his arms in welcome. I leaned in carefully, not wanting to disturb his hair, and got a strong whiff of aftershave. In the Arab world, scented bodies and stiffly spiked hair are the cultural marks of adolescence. At camp, after seven a.m. wakeup, you can always detect a haze of synthetic sweetness about the Arab boys, mixing strangely with everything natural that is Maine. It wouldn't be Seeds of Peace without the confluence of these smells.

I pulled away from Mohammad and looked him over. He was wearing basketball shorts and a matching sleeveless jersey, silver lined with blue. The silver sneakers sparkled on his feet.

"Ah, Silver Shoes!" I exclaimed. Mohammad hated to be called this and frowned, but I couldn't help myself. "I won't do it again," I promised and fought off the urge to tousle his hair. He showed that wonderful smile. "So, we're going to see your place?"

"Hmm?" he said, like he was asking a question. "Let's go." I followed Mohammad up the hill toward Lion's Gate, the closest entrance to his home in the Old City. When we arrived at the gate, I was disappointed not to see any lions. I suppose I'd been expecting something grand and majestic, à la the New York Public Library. After scanning the arch of the gate, I located two small figures carved into the wall on either side of the gate, facing each other. Time had eroded the lions and their edges melted into the massive stones around them. Lion's Gate has two other names. The Christians call it St. Stephens Gate after the first Christian martyr, who they believed was stoned to death there. The Arabs call it Bab el-Maryam, according to their belief that Mary was born inside.

Lion's Gate is rarely visited by tourists. It lacks the craze and color of Damascus Gate, the main entrance into the Arab souk, or market. On most days, the area outside Damascus Gate is a moving sea of bodies and sellers hawking cheap goods, clothing, and vegetables. There is a constant jostle of limbs, and everything, down to the foodstuffs, seems to sweat under the boiling sun. Lion's Gate was not only shaded by its narrow entrance, but I saw few people other than old women selling grapes and a couple of Israeli soldiers. Mohammad and I walked by them and passed into the Old City, where the high walls shielded us from the sun. The streets were narrow and made of large, pale-colored stones, commonly called Jerusalem stone. The smell was cool and damp, though an intermittent garbage stink trailed behind us. It was cleaner here than the area inside Damascus Gate, but not that clean. We walked on, stepping over dark puddles and discarded trash.

The few adults we passed gave me short, strange looks. The children were less inhibited and looked longer. I knew that observant Muslim women covered their arms and neck, even their hair. Though it was probably all right for tourists to wear T-shirts (I had already changed my usual tank-top for something that covered my shoulders), I put on my long-sleeve shirt anyway. I was about to meet Mohammad's parents. I wanted to make a good impression.

Steel doors lined the streets at regular intervals. The stiff metal set into the stone walls made the doors seem more than shut; it made them look impenetrable. A few of these doors were open enough to reveal stairs leading up into dark, hidden homes. I was eager to peer up these stairways and see the families inside, to unlock the life of this place. There was so much hidden within the Old City's walls, I thought, as there was within Mohammad. Of all the young people I was following for the book, he remained the most closed. I wondered if he would fully open his mind and let me in.

To my surprise, the door to Mohammad's home was open. He led me up a staircase, through a short cramped hall, and then out into an equally small courtyard.

"This is my house." He waved his hand as though brushing away a fly. "We'll go upstairs to my uncle's home. There's more room there."

"Can I just look around a little?"

"Let's go to my uncle's," he repeated, and rushed ahead of me up the next flight of steps to let them know we'd arrived. Three small children— his cousins—scooted past us on the stair. His two brothers were both in university and no longer lived at home. His sister was married and lived with her husband outside the Old City, in another East Jerusalem neighborhood.

The second set of stairs led to a balcony cluttered with chicken coops.

"Let's go." Mohammad urged me away from the chickens and into his uncle's home. It consisted of a rectangular sitting room lined on three sides with couches, two narrow bedrooms, a bathroom, and a kitchen. The walls were lined with shelves displaying neon-colored knickknacks. I spotted a hula dancer and a Barney dinosaur. Cages of canaries hung from the ceiling. The decor seemed unusual, but I felt that it would be inappropriate to ask about it.

I shook hands with Mohammad's father, Abdullah, and with his mother, who went to prepare the tea. Mohammad's uncle could not shake my hand because he had just cleansed himself for prayer. There were more cousins sitting on the couches, including little girls in white communionlike dresses and black patent leather shoes who stole sheepish glances in my direction. They wore pastel hair clips, ruffled socks, and sparkles on their eyelids. Just after I sat down, one of Mohammad's teenage relatives arrived home from work. Seeing his great aunt, he knelt before her and applied a dozen lightning-quick kisses to the back of her hand. I had never before seen such a skilled and reverent greeting.

Abdullah began to relate the family's history. Mohammad's great-grandfather, Abdullah's grandfather, was born in this house. The great-grandfather and grandfather worked as head assistants to the director of the Al-Aqsa mosque. So this mosque, the third holiest sight in Islam, was an integral part of Mohammad's family history. Though Abdullah didn't work for the mosque (he taught high school English) his connection to it had largely shaped the family's movements over the last ten years. Shortly after Mohammad was born, Abdullah decided he wanted to move the family to the West Bank in order to give them a higher standard of living. He built a house in al-Ram, close enough to Jerusalem so the family could still visit the Old City and attend services at Al-Aqsa. When Israel began issuing separate ID cards to West Bank and Jerusalem residents, Abdullah moved the family back into the Old City. It was a smart idea. Since the second intifada had erupted, West Bank residents were largely prevented from entering Jerusalem. If Abdullah and his family had stayed in the West Bank, they may not have been allowed back to their ancestral home and to the mosque. Jerusalem residents could go into the West Bank, but Mohammad rarely did so. The al-Ram checkpoint is known for long lines and fighting between Israeli soldiers and Palestinians. More than this, it is a humiliating experience to pass through the checkpoints, searches, and ID checks. Though Mohammad had essentially grown up in the Old City, he still believed his home was al-Ram.

A bit later, after we had talked about the family, Abdullah took me and Mohammad outside to the balcony. It overlooked a small wooded area, and I was surprised to see trees growing in an area I had assumed was entirely stone. An asphalt path ran through the grove in the direction of the Haram al-Sharif, known to Arabs as the Noble Sanctuary and to Jews as the Temple Mount. The gold-capped Dome of the Rock mosque where the Prophet Mohammad was said to have ascended to heaven as well as the Al-Aqsa mosque were just visible between the leafy branches. Until this moment, I'd had no idea that Mohammad lived so close to the mosque.

Children in blue T-shirts walked along the path toward the Haram walls. Only then did I remember that today was the Al-Aqsa Children's Fund Festival sponsored by the Islamic Movement. The Movement, which had political, religious, and social components, headed Islamic activities for Arabs in Israel. I'd read that over twenty thousand children had participated in activities over the previous months: religious quizzes, mosque drawing competitions, and collections. The Islamic Movement would use the money to finance transportation of Muslims from all over Israel to Al-Aqsa for Friday prayer. The festival was also intended to help sponsor Waqf (the charitable trust that runs Muslim holy sites) activities in Arab towns throughout the region. The festival's theme, Al-Aqsa Is in Danger, marked the thirty-fourth anniversary of a deranged Australian tourist setting fire to the mosque. This year's festival was a show of solidarity against what the Islamic Movement considered current threats to the Al-Aqsa mosque. These included Israel's recent arrest of Islamic Movement officials suspected of collaboration with terrorists and Israel's decision to allow non-Muslims on the Haram.

Before the second intifada began, Israel allowed people of all faiths to visit the Noble Sanctuary. I myself had been inside the Dome of the Rock three times between 1993 and 2000. After Ariel Sharon's visit to the Haram in September 2000, and the outbreak of the intifada, Israel banned non-Muslims and, at times, Muslims under the age of forty from entering the Haram in order to prevent riots. After three years Jews and others were again allowed to visit the Haram mosques. The Islamic Movement, like most Palestinians, believed they were the rightful guardians of the Muslim holy sites. It was not Israel's place, they believed, to dictate who could and could not enter the Haram. The Islamic Movement did not trust Israel to keep the Haram peaceful and safe for worshippers, especially after Sharon's visit, which Palestinians considered a blatant provocation.

As we stood on his uncle's balcony, I asked Mohammad what he thought about taking me to see the al-Aqsa Children's Fund demonstration, now that I was allowed to visit the Haram.

"No!" He exclaimed as though he feared I would leap over to the Haram at that very moment. "You can't do that!" His eyes shone with urgency. The situation was so tense, Mohammad explained, that a foreigner would not be welcome there.

A deep voice rose from the Haram and echoed over the trees. It was exultant, fierce: *"Allahu Akbar!"* *"We are ready to sacrifice. God is great. Thanks to God!"*

We are ready to sacrifice, I whispered to myself. To Allah, of course. But how? Through acts of peace or those of war? It could mean many things, I thought, as the next *"Allahu Akbar!"* resounded. I considered how these words bring intense fear to so many people and great joy to as many others. And what did the sounds bring to the thousands of children now on the Haram? If I were a small child, such sounds would frighten me, but these children had grown up listening to these prayers. The call that sent a shiver through my arms would be as natural to them as their mother's lullaby.

We are ready to sacrifice! The voices soared and died like wind.

"You cannot tell a child to kill himself for religion," Abdullah said, divining my thoughts. "Look at those two children." He motioned to two small figures walking between the trees. A taller child held the hand of a smaller one. "What do they know about sacrifice?"

"What about the young bombers?" I asked. "Those who are not yet twenty years old?"

"I don't know." Abdullah's attention seemed elsewhere, and I wondered if he was avoiding the question.

I took a last look at the Haram. The sun was low in the sky and the wind was picking up.

"Jen, it was nice to meet you." Abdullah extended his hand. I hardly had a chance to thank him before Mohammad was leading me away from the balcony, the mosques, and this sacred, volatile heart of Islam.

Mohammad's home was like many houses in the Muslim Quarter of the Old City; the rooms were situated off a central courtyard, meaning you had to go outside in order to get from one to the next. Mohammad's courtyard was nothing more than a small uncovered space with stone floors and walls. Two people standing next to each other with their arms outstretched could probably touch doors on either end.

After I begged Mohammad to see his room, I was allowed into the literal box, which until this year he had shared with two brothers. Beds lined three of the walls. A desk with a computer was squeezed diagonally into the corner. This, I thought, was where Mohammad stayed up all night instant messaging his friends. I imagined him sitting in the glow of the screen, his brothers' dark forms behind him, turned to the wall to cut out the computer glare. Now the screen, like the room itself, was dark.

"Don't you want something to eat?" Mohammad seemed eager to leave his home. I couldn't tell if he was embarrassed by its small size or whether he really was stretching the limits of Old City tradition by having a Western stranger here. Or perhaps—and this was an option I did not want to admit—he did not trust me enough to fully let me into his world. I told myself to be patient, not to push Mohammad, and that hopefully trust would come in time. Though I met with Mohammad many times over the next six months, I never again visited his home.

On the way out of the house, I peeked into the kitchen, also the size of a closet. Also dark. Then we were back in the city streets, walking away from the steel door that Mohammad shut with a clang behind him.

On our second trip to the Old City, Mohammad took me to eat *kenafe,* a hot dessert of orange-colored pastry layered over sweet cheese and drenched in honey. The café was fluorescently lit, and the air was sweet and hot. You had to really like *kenafe* to tolerate this place, and fortunately I did. Mohammad ordered two Cokes, and we took our sugar-loaded trays and found a table at the back of the café. I poured myself a full glass of water from the cool metal pitcher on our table, and we began to eat. After a while we got onto the issue of Hamas. It was shortly after the August bus bombing, and the lack of communication between Mohammad and Omri weighed on me.

"He knows how I feel about the bombings." Mohammad reiterated his reason for not calling Omri after the attack, but I remained uncertain.

"Hamas is a resistance organization," Mohammad said, chewing. "Without this organization, Israel won't stop doing ugly things in the Palestinian territories. Because the United States supports Israel, no one else will tell Israel to stop. When Israelis see their relatives and friends killed, they see that their government is indirectly supporting these attacks. And this will force the Israelis to make sure their sons don't do ugly things to Palestinians."

"But after so many suicide bombings, Israelis aren't having the reaction you describe," I responded. "In fact, it seems that every time there's a Hamas bombing, it causes the IDF to conduct more operations in the territories."

If Israeli media wasn't so biased, Mohammad said, the Israeli public would not support such operations. He told me his theory that the Israeli media (which portrays Arabs as terrorists) has influenced U.S. policy toward the Palestinians. The United States would act differently, he believed, if they better understood the Palestinian perspective. "What did the United States say about Palestinians after September 11?" he asked me then.

"The news I watched said that Arafat condemned the acts. But they also showed images of Arabs celebrating and"—I knew Mohammad was waiting for this answer—"some of the Arabs shown were Palestinians."

Sure enough, he immediately said the celebrations had nothing to do with 9/11, and to him, this proved that the U.S. government was trying to convince Americans that all Arabs really were terrorists. Later, I learned from a Seeds of Peace graduate in Gaza City that many Palestinians did indeed celebrate after 9/11. I was not surprised by this confirmation. The Palestinians had quite a few grievances against the Americans, especially when it came to U.S.-Israel relations. I was also not surprised that Mohammad would deny that such celebrations took place. It's quite possible that he witnessed nothing of the kind. Moreover, I knew how badly Mohammad wanted to portray his nation as peace-loving. The idea of Palestinians dancing in the streets over the deaths of thousands was entirely contrary to the image he held of his own people.

"Why did 9/11 happen?" he asked me, pushing his *kenafe* away, looking a little sick. "Why did those men sacrifice their lives for this? I don't support it, but the ones that did the action had a reason for sure: The United States is pro-Israel; it is not doing justice, not giving Palestinians their rights, and it is fighting against the Islamic religion."

Such a barrage of grievances, I thought, listening to him. I didn't believe all of these reasons were true, and I certainly didn't believe they were legitimate excuses for killing thousands of innocent Americans. But how was I supposed to explain this to a young man whose environment had convinced him otherwise? I acutely felt my national identity as both separate from and closely intertwined with this conflict. "It's true that the United States gives Israel a lot of support," I told Mohammad, "but is it America's responsibility to give the Palestinians their rights?" It was true that the United States had come to the aid of other oppressed nations around the world, but the Israeli-Palestinian conflict wasn't as simple as one nation victimizing another. Palestinians lack certain rights partly because Israel's security is at risk. U.S. negotiators have always believed that achieving a secure Israel and an independent Palestinian state was something both parties had to work out together—with America's help, but not by its imposition.

"And why do you think the United States is fighting Islam?" I asked Mohammad, addressing his last criticism.

"I heard these things from TV," he said. "But I agree from my own point of view. I don't hate the United States. I hate the actions of the U.S. government. I hate their policy." He pulled the *kenafe* back toward him and took a bite. "Is it true that all Americans think all Palestinians are terrorists?"

I tried to explain that Americans, like Israelis and Palestinians, get their opinions from a variety of sources, and that some are better educated about the Arab world than others. I told him there was a strong stereotype about Arabs being terrorists, reinforced by media and movies, but also by acts such as 9/11. Mohammad finished his *kenafe* and said nothing.

"What do you think about the Israeli cabinet's vote to expel Arafat?" I asked. The Israeli cabinet had recently voted to force Arafat out of the territories in an effort to depose him as head of the Palestinian Authority.

"It will never happen," Mohammad replied. "The Americans wouldn't let it."

"Because you think Israel does everything the United States says?"

"Yes!" He was emphatic. But then he leaned across the table, and whispered, "Why does Israel always follow the United States?"

I was stunned. Mohammad had been spouting such strong convictions about the United States supporting Israel against the Palestinians, and yet here he was admitting he did not know why. I wondered how long he'd been carrying this question around, looking for someone who wouldn't embarrass him for his ignorance.

"I think the United States and Israel have a close relationship," I said. "But I'm not sure Israel does everything the United States says. The United States has been critical of Israel's settlement policy, and yet Israel continues to build the settlements."

Mohammad wasn't satisfied and raised the opposite question of America following Israel's demands.

I told him that there was indeed a Jewish lobby in the United States that worked very hard to get congressional representatives to support pro-Israel policies. "But no one lobby group is able to control the government," I made clear to him. "The Jewish groups in America are often successful because they are so well-organized and unified around the cause of supporting Israel."

"What about the Arab lobby groups?" Mohammad wanted to know.

"Well, I think the Arab community in the States could make the U.S. government listen to their concerns, but they are too fragmented. Everyone has a different nationality, different interests and beliefs. The fact of the matter is that the Jewish community has taken up support for Israel as its central cause. The Arab community has not taken up support for the Palestinians in the same way." I felt bad having to articulate this to Mohammad, because I knew how two-faced the Arab world could be toward the Palestinians. They trumpeted the Palestinians' plight as their main criticism of Israel and the United States, but they had done little to help the three million Palestinians under Israeli occupation and the millions of refugees in Lebanon, Jordan, and the occupied territories. Though today, Palestinians in Jordan have full citizenship, in 1970, Jordan's military killed nearly three thousand Palestinian civilians in an attempt to root out PLO leadership there.* Today Palestinian refugees in Lebanon are denied citizenship, work permits, and basic rights. Historically, Palestinians have felt abandoned by their Arab brothers.

I did not go into any of this with Mohammad. I was already feeling as though I were giving him a lecture, and I felt uncomfortable answering his

---

*William L. Cleveland, *A History of the Modern Middle East* (Boulder, CO: Westview Press, 1994), p. 331.

questions. I believed the truth of what I was telling him, of course, but what if he went home and repeated my answers to his father? Would Abdullah accuse me of filling his son with American propaganda? Mohammad wasn't through with his questions, though. Was it true, he wanted to know, that if Bush didn't support Israel, he would lose the next election? By Mohammad's reasoning, if the Jews controlled the U.S. government, then they would refuse to vote for Bush unless he helped Israel fight the Palestinians. I explained to Mohammad that the majority of Jewish voters are Democrats. So Bush's policy toward Israel probably wasn't strong enough to swing the entire Jewish vote.

"Did you vote Democrat?" he asked eagerly, as though worried I would be on the "wrong" side of the political spectrum.

"Yes. But I also don't think most Americans choose their government based on its policies toward the Middle East."

"They don't care about foreign policy?" Mohammad looked genuinely hurt.

"It's not always that," I said. "But America is a big country, and people don't always pay attention to what's going on in the outside world. People have to make a living, put food on the table, and provide for their families. I'm sure you understand that."

Mohammad seemed surprised to hear this, as though he'd assumed most Americans were intently following the Israeli-Palestinian conflict (even if it was through biased media channels), because that's what the Israelis and Palestinians were doing. To think that Israeli-Palestinian politics could be so removed from a person's life was an alien concept to him.

"I'll tell you something that my dad thinks," I started the conversation back up. "He believes that Republican presidents tend to be tougher on Israel than Democrats. Republicans are the ones who have put pressure on Israel to dismantle the settlements. But after 9/11, Bush won't lift a finger to help any nation seen to be supporting terrorism. This means he won't pressure Israel to do something that rewards the Palestinians." Then I added, "You might not consider suicide bombings to be terrorism, but George W. Bush certainly does."

"Do *you* think what Hamas does is terrorism?" Mohammad asked.

"I certainly don't think it's defense," I answered him. "I don't think blowing up buses or cafés has helped protect Palestinian civilians or improve their situation at all."

"Are you done with your *kenafe?* You didn't finish it." Mohammad suddenly seemed bored. Or maybe he wanted to avoid an argument.

We stepped into the crowded street. Mohammad was taking me to buy a *tabla,* a traditional Arab drum. I needed his assistance because in the Old City there were two prices for everything: the tourist price and the Palestinian price. All prices, even the Palestinian ones, were negotiable, and I had not yet learned the art of haggling. We hadn't gone two feet when he pointed to a young man and woman walking ahead of us. "They're Jews," he said.

I had noticed the couple was speaking Hebrew, surprising because you didn't find many Jewish Israelis spending time in the Muslim Quarter these days. The mayor of Jerusalem had told me that one of the reasons the streets were dirtier in the Muslim Quarter of the Old City than in the Jewish Quarter was due to the Jewish inspectors' fear of going into the Muslim areas. I'd been going to the Old City for weeks now and felt highly conspicuous but rarely unsafe. Of course, the Old City was known to be dangerous at night, but that applied to all the quarters, not just the Muslim one.

"Why did you point those people out to me?" I asked Mohammad.

"Because," he said sourly, "I wanted to show you that they are free to walk here like anyone else."

But how free did Mohammad feel here, I wondered? Even though he could probably follow the streets and alleys of the Muslim Quarter in his sleep, I had the sense that he didn't feel quite at home. "It's hard living there," Mohammad had told me at camp. "The houses are small. There is great humidity. And nothing to do but watch TV and play on the computer. Maybe read." Mohammad admitted that he didn't have any close friends in the Old City. And even if he did, what could they do together? There weren't parks for playing sports, and there wasn't enough room at his house to invite people over.

Mohammad was itching to go back to al-Ram. He talked about it the way elderly Palestinian refugees speak of their homes in Palestine before 1948: the freedom, the space, the beauty. Everything the cramped and cluttered Old City of Jerusalem was not. Clearly, this was not where Mohammad felt he belonged.

"It must be hard not to have anyone your own age here," I said.

"There are some cousins," he told me. And then he offered up a rare personal admission. "One of my cousin's friends thought I was a tourist. I was so angry that he said this about me." Even now, there was hurt in Mohammad's eyes, as though some truth upon which he had always relied was suddenly revealed to be a lie.

"I think you can find a good drum here," he said, entering a shop with a variety of "ancient" knickknacks and two-shekel religious memorabilia, all of it cheap tourist junk. I stood patiently while Mohammad spoke with the shopkeeper. The air was heavy with dust and the smell of imitation leather. The man brought out a small clay drum—more of a souvenir than a serious instrument. I tried to signal Mohammad to tell him that I wasn't interested, but he was already bargaining with the shopkeeper. When the man opened his mouth, he revealed crooked teeth and breath smelling stale with Arabic coffee and nicotine.

Mohammad turned to me. "He says eighty shekels for this."

"For this? Is he kidding?" Eighty shekels was about twenty dollars. This drum wasn't worth eighty cents. "He wanted one hundred." Mohammad looked dejected.

"Let's try the next guy," I said. Mohammad thanked the shopkeeper and we left.

"Are you all right?" I asked once we were back in the street. Mohammad looked so sad I thought he might cry.

"He gave me the tourist price," he said.

"It's because you were with me," I assured him. "It didn't have anything to do with you.

Mohammad said nothing, but he didn't look the least bit convinced. He longed for al-Ram; he didn't want to be a tourist in the Old City. Moham-mad's need for a place to belong, his obvious dismay at not belonging any-where, would become a familiar refrain for me as I continued my journey.

INESCAPABLE
IDENTITIES?

The Textbook Debates

The night before my meeting with the Palestinian minister of education, I learned my first serious lesson about the Middle East: Identity,
and perceived identity, is inescapable. Of course, I'd known this all along,
but I had never confronted it personally. I saw myself as an outsider in this
world of Israelis and Palestinians. Labels and judgments were for them,
not me.

I was so detached, in fact, that I had the following conversation without
a hint of personal anger or indignation. I was in Ramallah, staying with
Reem, a sixteen-year-old Seeds of Peace graduate. We were talking about
her budding career as an actor. Her first production had been at school,
The Merchant of Venice.

The Merchant of Venice, I thought? The one where the characters spend
half their time berating a Jewish moneylender? Had we been elsewhere,
I'd have given no thought to the choice of play. Anti-Semitic or not, it is a
great work of art. But we were in Palestine, and I had heard too many
tirades about the anti-Semitic nature of Arab education. I could not ignore
my curiosity for the sake of political correctness. I asked Reem what she
thought.

"Well, we were talking about that guy, what's his name?"

"Shylock?"

"Ya. People were saying that he was very greedy and no one liked him.
And we were saying how Jewish people control everything. They always
control and they're always," she gave a nervous laugh, "foxy."

"Like deceitful."

"Ya." She began to fiddle with her fingers. We were sitting cross-legged on her bed, face-to-face, talking as though this were a late-night gossip session. I could tell, however, that Reem was uncomfortable having this conversation with me. We were two friends, but we were also a Muslim and a Jew. I urged her on and assured her that she wasn't going to hurt my feelings. "This year at camp," Reem continued, "I was talking to an American guy about Jewish people. And he admitted that Jewish people have control of everything. And I think it's true, because you go everywhere and Jewish people have very good positions in the world. Like the States. Even Morocco. Everywhere. In the government and most of the employment places in the world."

"Do you have some specific examples?" I asked.

"We were talking about Wal-Mart and how so many people know about it and how it's very famous in America. And how it's Jewish. It's for Jewish people. It's a Jewish company."

"You mean that it's owned by Jews or that only Jews go there?"

"No. The owners are Jewish."

"And what do you think that the owners being Jewish means about the company itself?" I tried to sound casual.

"No, no, no. I don't mean anything." Reem wasn't buying my detachment for a second. "We were just giving examples of how people get control, but I like that. I wish that everyone can be like the Jewish. This shows how educated they are. They stick together because they want to achieve something. This is very good."

I later learned that Wal-Mart is owned by the Waltons, the wealthiest family in America. And surprise—they're not Jewish.

When I mentioned this conversation to Reem's father, Muhsin, he shrugged and said, "Even if the Waltons were Jewish, why does it matter?"

This was exactly why I liked Muhsin. He was a history professor at Birzeit University, highly educated and dispassionate. He'd received a Ph.D. from Princeton. The stereotypes and identity politics that abounded in his society did not fool him. To Muhsin, people were individuals, and I was one individual he trusted. Which was why the evening before my interview with the Palestinian minister of education, I was staying over at his home and joining his family for their Ramadan *iftar* (the nightly breaking of the fast during the forty days of fasting). After dinner we relaxed in the family room with holiday sweets and a Syrian soap opera. I felt like part of the family.

During a commercial, Muhsin asked me about my upcoming interview with the minister and my opinions about Palestinian textbooks. I offered up my findings candidly. At first, Muhsin said nothing, but his face clouded with disappointment, as though I were a student who failed to meet his high expectations. Then he said, "I am worried, Jen, that you are looking at the Palestinian textbooks from an Israeli-Jewish perspective. And I am concerned that you are looking at the Israeli textbooks from that same Israeli-Jewish perspective."

For some reason, my immediate reaction was embarrassment. My face grew hot, and my stomach fluttered. My fingers shook as though I'd been caught stealing. I composed myself and curtly explained that I was trying to be conscious of my biases. I was approaching my research, I said, with the same impersonal eye that I'd approached term papers in college. But explaining didn't help. Muhsin was distant for the rest of the evening, and the next morning, as I was leaving to see the minister of education, he said, "I think you're doing too much research for your book, Jen. If you had a real background in this conflict, you wouldn't have to do so many interviews."

I was furious. Both at Muhsin for his patronizing words and at myself for being so naive. Muhsin had prejudged me after all, but I had also prejudged him, thinking him to be so objective, so free from his surroundings. The precious detachment I'd used as a barrier between myself and Reem crumbled in the face of Muhsin. Reem was a teenager, and despite her experiences with Seeds of Peace, I expected her to be somewhat susceptible to the opinions and stereotypes of her peers. More than that, I could tell that she was already questioning some of her stereotypes about Jews. Unlike Reem, Muhsin had spent more than a couple of summers in the States. He had spent years there. Unlike Reem, he was not a student of history but a teacher, someone supposedly trained in the art of objectivity. Above all, he had welcomed me into his life and into his home. Then suddenly he was saying that my identity—or my identity as *he* perceived it—prevented me from being a fair researcher. I had an "Israeli-Jewish" perspective; I could not be trusted.

I believed it was impossible for me to look at anything from an Israeli perspective, because I wasn't Israeli. And what was the connection between my religion and my ability to do impartial, academic research? Muhsin had no idea what kind of connection I had to Israel, religiously or otherwise. He simply assumed that as a Jew I must have the type of connection that would skew my judgment. I understood what my father was up against all those years in the government: "No wonder the United States is pro-Israel," half the critics said, "its negotiating team is full of

Jews." Or from the other half: "No wonder the United States loves the Palestinians; Aaron Miller is a traitor to his religion, a Jewish Benedict Arnold." To my family, these were empty accusations. We knew my father's work as a member of the U.S. negotiating team had nothing to do with his faith. His allegiance was to the United States.

Muhsin hurt me, but he taught me that in Palestine as in Israel, nation and religion aren't name tags to stick on and discard as you please. I think this is precisely why Palestinians get so defensive when outsiders question their education system and school texts. Ever since the Oslo accords gave the Palestinian Authority control over its educational system, Palestinian education has been as much about instilling a sense of Palestinian identity in students as about teaching them language and math. Palestinians see the attacks on their presentation of history and religion as synonymous with attacking their right to have a national sense of self. Take Mohammad's feelings of displacement. He did not consciously blame Israel for making him feel like a tourist in the Old City, but he did blame the occupation for keeping him from his real home, al-Ram. As long as Mohammad lacked a secure place to call home, he would continue to feel that his identity was threatened. It's similar with racial and ethnic minorities in the United States who criticize a history curriculum dominated by white males. They want schools to teach a more multicultural curriculum in order to legitimize their voices and unique identities. When it comes to history education, Palestinian educators have never had a voice; from the Ottomans, to the Jordanians, to the Israelis, other nations always controlled their curricula. Only in the early 1990s were the Palestinians finally given the freedom to teach their own history and culture.

Now that the Palestinians have been given this chance, critics claim their lessons are anti-Semitic, incite students to violence, and deny Israel's existence. It's true that stereotypes and biases about Israelis and Jews are prevalent among Palestinian youth. My conversation with Reem about *The Merchant of Venice* revealed as much. But I think it's an oversimplification to blindly blame the Ministries of Education in Israel and Palestine for the negative lessons they instill. So much of the Israeli-Palestinian conflict is rooted in these societies' refusal to acknowledge each other's historical narratives and, therefore, their right to exist. I had set up my interview with the minister of education because I wanted to understand the root of this refusal—and to see how Israelis and Palestinians might work toward acceptance.

After the 1948 war, Egypt assumed governance over Gaza and Jordan assumed governance over the West Bank. Palestinian students in these areas were taught the Egyptian and Jordanian curricula, respectively. When Israel occupied these territories in 1967, it assumed responsibility for the civil administration of Palestinian life, including education.

The Israeli Civil Administration (Civ Ad) education department was responsible for building and maintaining Palestinian schools, hiring teachers, and distributing textbooks. While the Civ Ad didn't interfere with the overall Jordanian and Egyptian curricula, it removed material that seemed hostile to Israel and the Jewish people. The Civ Ad's program of school administration and textbook censorship continued until 1994, when the Oslo accords granted Palestinians more control over their civilian affairs.

In 1994 the newly formed Palestinian Authority faced the enormous responsibility of creating a new and independent curriculum for Palestinian students, and the following year, it created a Curriculum Development Center to do so. Meanwhile, Palestinian schools continued to use the Egyptian and Jordanian books previously censored by Israel. Within a year or two, however, the Palestinians began buying uncensored books from Egypt and Jordan.

In 1996 the Curriculum Development Center published its report, six hundred pages of harsh criticism directed toward all aspects of the existing educational system. Nathan Brown is a professor at George Washington University who has extensively researched the new Palestinian curriculum. In his paper "Democracy, History, and the Contest over the Palestinian Curriculum," Brown called the CDC's report "the most stinging and detailed indictment of existing education in Arab countries and the most radical reform proposed by an official body since universal education was introduced."* According to the CDC, Palestinian pedagogical methods failed to excite and motivate students, instilled a blind acceptance of authority, and did not teach democratic and humanistic values. In short, the report concluded that Palestinian education did nothing more than force students to memorize information and regurgitate it on state-administered exams.

The CDC report advocated an overhaul of the existing educational system. First to go should be the division of high school students into science and humanities tracks. Placement in these two fields depended upon an

*Source: http://home.gwu.edu/~nbrown/.

examination score, with higher scores eligible for science and lower scores for humanities. If a student received a high score but preferred to study humanities, he or she would most likely feel pressure to enter the more difficult, more prestigious science track. The CDC understood that knowing numbers was not equivalent to having brains, and they were wary of perpetuating these superficial divisions between students. Moreover, students in one track had only minimal exposure to the subjects in the other. The CDC advocated an interdisciplinary curriculum in which teachers would integrate a variety of subjects into their lessons.

Second to go, said the CDC, should be the Tawjihi, or final examination. This exam, which tested high school seniors on four years' worth of knowledge, stood directly at odds with the CDC's vision of a democratic approach to education. Students taught only how to memorize would not learn to express themselves or communicate with their peers. The classroom was a microcosm meant to prepare students for the broader community they would enter as adults, but the Tawjihi did not reinforce that concept.

Third, if school was meant to prepare students to be active community members, then its subjects should be relevant to the students' environment. Otherwise, the CDC feared, students would not understand the complexity of the world in which they lived.

It's important to note that the Curriculum Development Center worked with great autonomy from the Palestinian Authority. Its curriculum development team was composed mostly of Palestinian academics, educational reformers, and field specialists, and not government employees. As Brown notes, the committee collected the opinions of teachers and students by contacting them directly, as opposed to going through the Ministry of Education. When the CDC finally submitted its recommendations in 1996, the far-reaching criticisms shocked the ministry. The government's curriculum planning team ignored many of the CDC's suggestions, keeping the tracking system as well as the Tawjihi. In 1997, the Palestinian Legislative Council ratified the new curriculum.

The Ministry of Education also created a new Curriculum Development ment Center, very much under its authority, to oversee textbook production. Books were written by subject specialists and then submitted to the ministry for approval. New books were to appear in schools each year, beginning with the 2000–2001 school year. They would be introduced two grades at a time, beginning with grades one and six and followed by grades two and seven, and so on. As the Ministry of Education produced new books, the Jordanian and Egyptian books were dropped from the curriculum.

The finalized curricula written by the new government-run CDC does integrate some of the first Curriculum Development Center's recommendations into textbooks. Brown cites the introduction of civic education as a new subject, and lessons about human rights and democracy as examples. An eighth-grade civic education book asks students to hold mock trials with kids playing the roles of judge, attorneys, and jury.

The books also include themes of gender equality. Some illustrations depict men cooking and an exercise asks students whether they think it's justified for a father to ban his daughter from sports because she's a girl. One book quotes the Koran saying that when a father dies, the son should receive twice the inheritance of the daughter. The text then questions the student as to the reasons behind this law and whether he or she thinks it is fair. An exercise like this is particularly controversial, not only because it forces the student to confront elements of gender inequality in Islam, but because it openly questions a religious dictate.

Other elements in the books suggest that one's observance of Islam is a matter of personal choice. Illustrations show women wearing the *hijab* (an Islamic head covering) working side by side with women who do not cover their hair. They also depict women wearing a variety of clothing styles, ranging from traditional Islamic and Palestinian dresses to more modern fashions like pants and blazers.

Overall, however, the books are not progressive in terms of religious education. Muslim identity and belief in God are fundamental to the curriculum. Exercises require students to repeat: "I am a Palestinian Muslim." Koranic verses and lessons appear throughout most subjects. Religion is a mandatory subject for all students, with Christians and Muslims learning their respective holy texts. In most schools, students learn religion not as an intellectual pursuit but as an unquestioned belief system. For this reason, many Palestinians are unhappy with the images of gender equality and the critiques of Islam that appear alongside the more traditional lessons.

This idea was further explained to me one afternoon at Checkers, the single American fast-food restaurant in Palestine. Reem's cousins manage it. She took me there in the middle of the week after school, and the place was jumping. A large sign at the door exclaimed "Grand Re-Opening!" This Checkers had been shut down for a year after Israeli tank fire, aiming for the adjoining Palestinian Authority offices, destroyed it.

Reem and I ordered sandwiches and Cokes and chose seats by the window. Checkers is on the third floor of a small shopping center and overlooks Ramallah's bustling city center. When I mistakenly called this area "downtown," Reem said I better be careful or I'd give away my American identity. "You think *that's* going to give me away?" I teased. "How about my hair, my accent, my clothes?"

Perhaps Reem thought I'd feel at home here—in the next best thing to McDonald's this side of the Jordan River. But American chain or no (I'd only seen a single Checkers in the United States), I felt distinctly foreign surrounded by so many uniformed school kids and *hijab*-clad ladies.

After lunch, Reem and I joined her father and his friend Shafi, a high school teacher and textbook author. Shafi explained that in 2002, the Palestinian Authority trained educators how to teach lessons about democracy, equality between the sexes, and questioning religion.

"Many teachers don't like the idea that the books are promoting equality between men and women," Shafi said. "Some teachers also don't like the fact that the books are questioning the Koran. Many teachers are religious, and they don't accept an idea that comes from the West."

"Most Palestinians believe these lessons are a corruption of Palestinian, Arab, and Islamic culture," Muhsin agreed.

Most Palestinians? I wondered. Many of Checkers' patrons were wearing religious garb, and they didn't seem bothered by this infiltration of the West. They were, after all, all up here in fast-food heaven, great symbol of the United States, happily munching their hamburgers. I had to wonder how many of the educators who rejected the new curriculum also came here for an after-school bite. It seemed to me that as "American" as Checkers may be, it had still become a small part of Palestine.

Months later, however, I was given a new perspective on this issue. Mohammad and I were at Café Aroma on the Hebrew University campus in Jerusalem. He felt comfortable meeting me there because the university has a joint Arab-Jewish student body and is on the east side of the city, where the majority of Jerusalem Arabs live. Still, we could have mistaken our location for downtown Tel Aviv. Café Aroma was full of young women wearing their hip, hip-hugging fashions. In the middle of our conversation, Sean Paul's "Get Busy" came on the speakers: "Woman get busy, just shake that booty nonstop . . ."

The environment was a fitting backdrop for our conversation—if not a cynical comment on it. Mohammad, you see, was explaining his views on appropriate standards for women. Women weren't fit to hold positions of power, Mohammad was certain, because they were controlled by emotion instead of intellect. He could not imagine a woman driving a car, let alone running the government. Moreover, he believed that Palestine should be an Islamic state; forcing women to cover their hair and bodies was the only way for a society to prevent rape and murder. I asked him why this was so, and Mohammad replied that men look at women in sexy clothes and are unable to restrain themselves. I pointed out that this statement contradicted his previous one about men acting according to intellect and women by emotion, but Mohammad didn't seem to understand the flaw in his reasoning.

I admit, it was difficult to hear such ideas from him. I had never seen him display any sexism toward female campers or counselors, and I wondered how exactly he had come by these ideas. Were they from his father, his teachers, his general environment? I remembered the former imam from the al-Aqsa mosque telling me that a Muslim woman should cover her hair only if she is "convinced" by Islam. At first, I was reassured to hear such open-mindedness from an Islamic leader. But then the sheikh's wife had interrupted: If I wore the *hijab,* she told me, I would go to heaven for eternity. If I didn't, she looked me in the eye, I would "burn, burn, burn."

Later, a religious Seeds of Peace graduate named Tamara, a university student studying to be a pharmacist, said her decision to wear the *hijab* was a pact between her and God, and her independent choice.

"But what about people who believe Islam is restrictive to women?" I asked.

"It's the silliest thing I've ever heard," she said, disbelieving. It was the way some people interpreted the Koran, Tamara explained, that made it repressive. Though Tamara certainly would have taken Mohammad to task over his assertion that women couldn't hold positions of power, I know she would have agreed with him about the importance of modesty. She most certainly would have criticized the Sean Paul song and the immodest, sexual flaunting it represented.

For Tamara and Mohammad, religion is integral to daily life, and they welcome it as part of their schooling. More than this, neither one sees it as something that should be questioned and critiqued. Except Tamara would certainly claim that Mohammad was misinterpreting some aspects of Islam. And vice versa. In studying Palestinian education, I learned that the schools aren't dealing with this contradiction. According to Shafi and Muhsin, the traditional forces in Palestinian society have made broad-based reform of religious education impossible. Even the original Curriculum Development Center avoided concrete proposals about religion. The question, then, is how to keep the curriculum relevant to students' lives—to not offend their ideas of faith and belief—while still challenging them to consider a more diverse spectrum of perspectives on what religion means in theory and practice.

This question applies to all areas of Palestinian education. The curriculum must depict the students' environment honestly, but it must also challenge students to see outside the confines of this environment. In other words, if you want to educate for democracy, critical thinking, and questioning of authority, you can't ignore these values simply because they are not dominant in society; you must push students, but you have to avoid pushing them away. The United States faced these challenges in the late nineteenth century over teaching evolution. Today, there is a similar debate in the more conservative school districts about teaching sex education and AIDS awareness. Where is the middle ground between preaching abstinence and handing out condoms?

The Palestinian curriculum has begun to work toward this balance, though the books blatantly overemphasize certain ideas such as Palestinian nationalism. In his report Brown observes that in the Palestinian textbooks, "Every school is pictured flying a Palestinian flag, homes have pictures of the Dome of the Rock, classrooms have nationalist slogans on their blackboards, computers display Palestinian flags, a school bus carries the name Palestine School, Jerusalem is mentioned in any possible context, and even children playing soccer wear the jerseys of the Palestinian national team. And this is only the books' *visual* display of nationalism. They also ask children to repeat 'I am from Palestine' and 'My nationality is Palestinian.' The students read nationalist writings when studying Arabic, copy nationalist slogans while practicing calligraphy, and count Palestinian flags while learning arithmetic."*

Sami Adwan, professor of education at Bethlehem University and one of the researchers who analyzed the new curriculum for the European Union, explained the root of this nationalism in the Palestinian texts.

"The Palestinians are a nation without an identity," Adwan told me. "This identity has been shattered by the Ottomans, the Jordanians, the Is-

---

*"Democracy, History, and the Conflict over the Palestinian Curriculum." Paper presented at the Adam Institute, November 2001. Source: www.geocities.com/nathanbrown1/.

raelis. We've developed a culture of silence. I grew up studying textbooks that didn't relate to myself or my society. When we come to look at textbooks, we are moving toward ourselves."

For the first time in their history, the Palestinians have a chance to formally teach their children who they are as a society. Nearly every conversation I had with Palestinian educators, politicians, and journalists revealed that this society stands upon a single, dominant foundation: national unity in the struggle against Israeli occupation. Teaching youth a strong Palestinian identity is, in itself, a method of resistance, because it creates a generation of young people who can stand up and shout "I exist" when everyone is telling them they don't. This is wonderful in the sense that it empowers youth growing up in the least empowering circumstances. It is problematic, because in the current political environment, young Palestinians tend to confuse "I" with "we." A young person might feel empowered to stand up and declare him- or herself as a Palestinian, but not necessarily as an individual.

As a teenager, if someone asked me to define myself, "American" might not have appeared at the top of my list. Ask most Palestinian kids who they are, and "Palestinian" will be one of the first, if not *the* first, response. Because I don't perceive a threat to my national identity, I have the freedom to disassociate myself from this identity. Palestinian youth don't have this luxury. They don't want their friends to call them unpatriotic, but more than this, they *want* to show solidarity with their nation. So in implicit ways (like the numerous images of the Palestinian flag) and explicit ones (repeating "I am Palestinian"), the textbooks educate for identity as much as for knowledge.

The Palestinian minister of education, who looked to me as if his entire life is a perpetual bad day, probably wouldn't agree with my assessment. He told me that Palestine is like any country in the world. "We don't talk about national issues more or less than anyone else," he said. "We're not trying to make our children crazy about being Palestinian. We just want kids to love their country, their culture, and Jerusalem—to be good citizens. It's just like in the United States. The way people talk about the Fourth of July."

"And what about the Israeli accusations?" I asked. "What you call nationalism, others may call anti-Israel or anti-Semitism."

The minister sighed like a deflating balloon. These accusations were completely unfair, he said. He told me they had come from a right-wing group, the Center for Monitoring the Impact of Peace (CMIP), whose research on Palestinian textbooks has become the main source for anyone studying Palestinian education. According to the minister, the CMIP studies were biased and inaccurate. The whole purpose of this organization, he believed, was to defame the Palestinian Authority. But the minister said he wasn't concerned, because the European Union had decided there was no truth in the allegations against the Palestinian curriculum. I wondered if the EU and the United States had interpreted the CMIP reports differently, because if the Europeans called the Palestinian curriculum harmless, some members of the U.S. Congress had expressed the opposite reaction after reading the reports.

CMIP has conducted studies of the new Palestinian Authority textbooks as well as the uncensored Jordanian and Egyptian books used throughout most of the Oslo years. They also have separate projects reviewing Israeli, Syrian, and Saudi Arabian books. The Palestinian Authority claims the reports are biased and, in some cases, outright falsified.

CMIP analyzed all the textbooks used in Palestine to determine whether they met United Nations Educational Science and Cultural Organization (UNESCO) criteria for accuracy in facts, dates, and maps; the objective and honest presentation of political disputes; the absence of prejudice; and the teaching of freedom, international cooperation, and peace. The reports are English translations of the texts, which were originally written in Arabic, and are grouped by topic, with a short summary and conclusion. They present little analysis. Professor Brown, an open critic of the CMIP, told me the translations are highly accurate, but that the reports can be misleading in their presentation.

I visited the CMIP offices in Jerusalem to get its side of the story. Upon my arrival, I was surprised to find the Arabic textbooks locked up in two gigantic safes.

"Are you worried about someone stealing them or ransacking your office?" I asked Arnon Groiss, author of the Palestinian textbook reports.

"It was very difficult for us to obtain some of these books," Groiss said as he worked the locks.

"What do you mean 'difficult?' "

"Well"—he opened the door revealing rows of tall, skinny readers—"let's just say that the Saudis did not give us their schoolbooks with open arms."

"So how did you get them?"

"I can't tell you that," Groiss said curtly, and selected what we needed from the safe. He closed the door and checked to see that it was secure. Who is this guy, I wondered? Was he a textbook spy? Did he go on covert textbook operations? I imagined him hiding behind a potted plant, nabbing books out of some Saudi Arabian teachers' lounge. We left the safes behind and sat down to discuss the books.

Here is my main criticism of CMIP: Its reports do not always clarify whether the quotations they cite come from the new Palestinian Authority textbooks or from the Egyptian and Jordanian books used prior to 2000. In fact, the material that Israel and the U.S. Congress call so blatantly offensive—that the Palestinian books equate Zionism with Nazism— appears in an eleventh-grade *Jordanian* text. Zionism is the movement in support of a Jewish State in Eretz Yisrael, the Land of Israel. In a unit on racial discrimination, the Jordanian text states that "the clearest examples of racial discrimination in the world are Nazism and Zionism." The book was published in 1998, years before eleventh-grade Palestinian books were even written.

I do not want to ignore the fact that the Palestinians allowed this book to be taught in their school system—in 2003 it was still in use in some schools—but nothing like this quotation appears anywhere in the books *they* have authored. Similarly, nowhere in the new Palestine Authority books do any words call for Israel's destruction. This kind of incitement simply does not exist. While there are illustrations of bulldozers demolishing houses and armed soldiers, it's the real-life versions of these pictures that truly influence students. I asked Yohanan Manor, CMIP co-director, point-blank if he thought these images or anything else in the Palestinian books incited students to violence. He said no. Both he and Groiss admitted that the new PA books are a huge improvement over those in other Arab countries.

At the same time, the Palestinian books are much more nationalistic than most countries' school texts. They are full of references to Jihad: including poems about martyrs, literature about fighting oppressors, and historical events that emphasize religious-national resistance. For example, a 2002 eighth-grade Arabic-language book contains a poem called "Palestine." An excerpt reads, "Kiss a martyr fallen on the ground of Palestine / Who for her sake has called God and been martyred. Palestine, youth will redeem you / Praise be upon the redeemer and the redeemed. Palestine, many bodies keep you away from us / We have only the choice of life or the choice of death."

Jihad is never discussed in a modern-day context. There are no references to Hamas or any other current militant Palestinian organization. It would be an overreaction to think that students who read these poems are suddenly filled with a desire to blow themselves up on a bus or even go into the streets and fight. The Ministry of Education should not exclude important historical events from its history curricula because they involved violence, but the fact that Jihad has an overwhelming presence throughout the texts cannot help but stir up students' emotions about the conflict with Israel. In Palestinian society, there is already a general acceptance and solidarity with those who die or kill themselves in the fight against Israeli occupation. Jihad's place in the curriculum reinforces this. While one book talks about Gandhi and nonviolent resistance, the texts do not prioritize these values overall; the Palestinian curriculum does not advocate war, but neither does it emphasize peace.

Despite this, some Palestinians feel the books are too bland in their depiction of national suffering. The minister of education told me he is being pressured to make the books more political. Sami Adwan echoed this: "Between forming an identity and reflecting reality, it's very difficult. So students are accusing us of duping them."

Indeed, the Palestinian books are highly inconsistent. As Brown notes, they are firm on issues of national consensus, like Jerusalem as the Palestinian capital or Israel's responsibility for the refugee problem. But contested issues, such as borders or appropriate methods of resistance, are treated ambiguously or ignored. I saw firsthand how awkward the Ministry of Education was about these contested issues.

While talking with one Palestinian educator, I pointed out a lesson for the first grade entitled "The Shape of Palestine." The text at the bottom of the page reads, "So that students will be introduced to the shape of Palestine, and be able to distinguish it from other shapes." In the center of the page is a large outline of the area that *was* historic Palestine and is *now* Israel, as recognized by the United Nations. Dotted lines within the map indicate the West Bank and Gaza, but the names are absent. The word "Israel" does not appear on the map.

"The borders of Palestine are not yet decided," the Palestinian educator told me. "How can we draw borders that don't exist? So we draw the shape of Mandatory Palestine" (meaning Palestine as it looked under the British Mandate).

I pointed out that neither this map nor any other in the books indicate that "The Shape of Palestine" refers to Mandatory Palestine. "If you don't know this, as I'm sure a six-year-old doesn't, you can only assume that the map represents modern day, and therefore negates the existence of Israel."

"But the borders are not yet defined," I was told a second time.

"This map outlines the West Bank and Gaza," I said, "but these areas had no special significance in Mandatory Palestine. Moreover, if the West Bank and Gaza are not marked by name, what is a first-grader going to think they mean?"

"Look," the educator said, exasperated, "I'd like to know how Israelis draw the borders of *their* maps. Can they do it? I don't think they can."

True, it is difficult to accurately represent the outlines of Palestinian territory with the question of borders still unresolved. And how *do* you explain the current political situation to a six-year-old? How do you teach him or her a sense of national identity and pride when you can't even show her where her country is? In this, the Ministry of Education is facing an incredibly difficult challenge. And the Palestinian books do not entirely exclude Israel. A recently published text for the eleventh grade discusses the Oslo accords, including the idea of mutual recognition.

However, as long as the Palestinian curriculum sidesteps sensitive issues or presents vague and contradictory material to students, it will reinforce the skepticism and distrust children already feel toward Israel. More than this, such a curriculum presents children with an oversimplified picture of the world in which they live. Those concerned—myself included, I will admit—would rather tell the children their land is disputed. It's no secret to young Palestinians that Israel is a neighbor in conflict.

The Ministry, however, seems to insist on avoiding this reality.

I saw a startling example of this outside a school in Ramallah. Dima, a ministry employee, was taking me on a tour of Palestinian public schools. I had tried to go on my own, but the ministry insisted that I be chaperoned. The morning Dima took me to the Al-Hashimiya Secondary Science School for Boys was cold and nasty, though even sun would not have altered the school's industrial appearance. The buildings were boxy, their outside walls scratched and scraped, and their windows barred. A concrete courtyard was strewn with trash and dotted with dark puddles. Clouds bore down on us as we searched the school's perimeter for the front door. There wasn't a light or sound coming from the place; for all we knew, it was deserted.

As Dima and I walked across the expanse of concrete, I noticed a series of posters on a far wall. Some were peeling, but the idea was clear enough: They were photos of martyrs. From this distance, the vertical AK-47s on each side created a filigreelike border, the Dome of the Rock a bright halo above the heads of the deceased. But even as far away as I was, something else caught my eye. I squinted. Between the martyrs' faces was a shadowy image I couldn't quite make out.

"Dima," I said, "can you tell me exactly what these posters say?" She gave no response. "Dima?" I asked again. Still no response. I stepped closer to the wall, but I couldn't bring myself to approach it directly. I felt as though whatever was lurking in that poster might leap out at me. I craned my neck. What was that ghostlike shape hovering behind the martyrs' faces? Was it just my imagination? I began to think that the artist had designed his poster with such a guessing game in mind. Yes, I decided, there was definitely something there—a face. I had seen that long, thin nose and bony chin, those glassy eyes and malicious smile somewhere before. But where? I looked closer. Long white hair, straight as bone, hung down on either side of the head. What I thought I saw, I realized with surprise, was the traitorous Wizard Saruman as he appeared in the latest *Lord of the Rings* adaptation. Then it hit me: This wasn't some fictional character. Between the martyrs was the ghostlike image of Sheikh Ahmed Yassin, the spiritual leader of Hamas. What I had mistaken for Saruman's hair was really the sheikh's head covering.

"Dima," I asked a third time, "do you think you might come over and tell me the names of the men in these posters?"

"Which posters?" she asked, looking straight at them.

"Those." I pointed to the wall. "Over *there*."

"Those were men killed in the intifada," she said, as though she couldn't be bothered with my pestering.

"I know," I said, aggravated, "but who's that man in the middle?"

Again, there was no answer. She'd begun walking away.

"It looks like Ahmed Yassin," I finally suggested. "But I'm not sure."

"I suppose it's him," she mumbled. "It's really too small to tell." And that closed the conversation.

I couldn't believe that a grown woman, an educator, had tried to deny what was right in front of our eyes. If she was so embarrassed about the Hamas posters, as I suspected she was, why couldn't she be honest about it? If she thought it was wrong for the school to allow them, as I hoped, why not say so? Did she worry that I would go home and write up some story about how school principals were encouraging their students to become terrorists because of a couple of Hamas photos? What really bothered me was the fact that if I had said to Dima, "I know you're not encouraging Palestinian kids to join Hamas, so how can you permit these pictures on school property?" she probably would have come up with the same list of excuses I'd heard her give on other occasions: *We're under occupation. We can't ignore the students' daily reality.* Rather than confront the issue, she would sidestep and avoid it.

It seems to me, however, that if the Palestinians really want to accept the students' daily realities, they have to accept that Hamas is vying for the hearts and minds of their children. The education provided by the militants is largely extracurricular—the lessons students see and absorb *outside* the classroom. I agree that school textbooks will not change students' minds about the occupation, but in the area of education, I see the ministry as Hamas's main competitor. It is not Hamas but the schools that can empower students to be strong, independent thinkers; the schools that can educate young people about the complexity of a modern, globalized world; and the schools that will ultimately prepare students to deal nonviolently within Palestinian society and in the international arena. These lessons and not those of violence build strong societies and leaders. It seems to me that if the Ministry of Education exposes students to selective realities, such lessons will fall flat. Palestinian teachers have so much potential, but so many of them seem overwhelmed with pessimism. They feel they cannot change the situation, so why try?

I fear that this is the main difficulty with Palestinian education. It isn't that kids are being taught to hate Israel. The real issue is the pervasive ethic of avoidance. Educating for independent thought and personal accountability has taken a backseat to national identity. I was stunned when Mohammad asked me, over plates of *kenafe,* why Israel blindly followed the United States. Now I realized how big a leap it was for a student who had never been encouraged to question, to ask for an explanation of Israel's motives.

Like their Palestinian counterparts, Israeli educators are growing increasingly frustrated over the criticism of their textbooks.

"This is the end of apologies," Professor Israel Bartal told me. Bartal heads the committee tasked with designing the next high school history curriculum for state-run secular schools. (About eighty percent of Israel's population attend secular state-run schools, and twenty percent attend state-run religious schools.) Bartal is known as a leftist in Israel, but obviously not *that* leftist.

"As an Israeli and a Zionist I don't have to put the Palestinian narrative on an equal level," he said. "Not because it's not legitimate, but I totally disagree with my colleagues on the left who put a question mark on Zionism, Israel, and even the Jews. Who questions whether the United States or France is legitimate? So why ask it about Israel? We don't have to give reasons for why we are here."

There is hardly a nation-state that developed without the conquest or displacement of another population. Consider what early Americans did to a continent of Native Americans. More than that, the colonists had to fight a war against Great Britain to prove their legitimacy as an independent nation. Two hundred years later, few people call the United States illegitimate, though if the Native American population had been larger and stronger this might not be the case. But Israeli history, like Palestinian history, is being taught in the middle of a bitter conflict. There is a reinforcing relationship between what kids learn in school and what they see around them. It seems to me that Israel will raise a more rational, open-minded generation of leaders if its schools work to counteract the negative, violent images of conflict.

Bartal agreed with this. "I do want kids to keep an open mind," he told me. "I don't want terror to force Israeli kids to act in the same way as the Palestinians." At the same time, Bartal said he didn't want young Israelis to lose their sense of national identity.

Israel has experienced a great deal of rope tugging over its history curriculum. The debate is exactly as Bartal described it: how to balance the country's Zionist raison d'être with the inclusion of other, possibly counter, narratives. Should the curriculum be Israeli and Jewish-centric or taught through the lens of universal humanism? The former approach was criticized for being xenophobic, the latter for failing to give students enough knowledge and pride in their culture and nation. To further complicate matters, there have been numerous Israeli ministers of education from the Oslo years through the present, each with a different idea about what the curriculum's focus should be. Constant changes at the ministry have prevented a uniform policy. With the outbreak of the second intifada, the stakes skyrocketed. Criticizing Israel's history could turn students into what Bartal calls "extremists on the left": those anti-Zionist Jews who question Israel's very right to exist.

There has been a backlash against this kind of thinking, especially because it runs contrary to the value of national pride that has dominated Israeli education for so long. Indeed, Israelis have not taught Israel "like the French teach France," as Israel Bartal claims. As in Palestinian society, the conflict has forced Israeli educators to overcompensate—in this case, to teach a nationalism that often instills an attitude of national and cultural superiority. This attitude was most prevalent in Israel's first few decades, but has not disappeared. I asked the supervisor for state-run religious schools in Jerusalem to address the criticism that the government's program of religious education taught students to hate Arabs. The supervisor, who asked not to be identified by name, looked at me as if my question was entirely beside the point.

"How would you as a white American compare yourself to black people?" he asked, flashing a sympathetic smile. "Or how would a white American compare to Hispanic society? White America doesn't like to be Spanish while the Spanish or the blacks like to be white. Everyone wants to belong to the best. I'm talking about general American values: education, integration, the right to vote, progress, freedom of speech. I see these as basic American values that white people have carried out. Of course other sectors of society would like to imitate those values."

Ah, yes, I thought. These were *white* values, every one of them. I gripped my chair to avoid falling out of it.

"An Arab is looked at as inferior because he unfortunately represents a culture that is behind. We try to teach Arabic in schools, but we haven't succeeded because Arabic is seen by Israeli society as representative of inferior society. This is how the United States looks at Mexicans. You look at Mexicans differently from Canadians. I've never said that it's right, but you shouldn't be surprised."

In fact, I was shocked. I knew that people held these opinions, but I had never heard anyone express them out loud. Even though I knew there was truth in the supervisor's assessment of how many white Westerners treated nonwhite, non-Western people, hearing him say in total seriousness that blacks and Hispanics aspired to be white left me speechless. To me, it was as absurd as saying that Arabs wished to be Israeli. Arabs might want to achieve some of the things Israelis have—their military power, their developed economy, their international standing, and even the Israeli system of government. But to emulate Israeli culture? To view Hebrew as superior to Arabic? I thought the supervisor might be joking, but I doubted it.

Israel's state-mandated history curriculum for religious schools reflects the supervisor's attitude much more implicitly than explicitly. One is more likely to find these values expressed outright in the semi-independent ultra-orthodox stream where a small minority of students study. These schools receive government subsidies, but their curriculum and textbooks are privately developed and taught. When I asked a prominent official at the Ministry of Education about the ultra-orthodox approach to teaching history, he replied, "This group doesn't look at the practicality of history. They don't use today's criteria to judge whether the Bible is a racist book."

As for the majority of Israeli schools, where eighty percent of Israeli youth study, the Bible is taught from an academic or cultural, as opposed to a faith-based, perspective. More than this, the history curriculum for these schools is undergoing a process of revision that is meant to balance Israel-centric and universalist positions—to help students keep "an open mind," as Bartal desires. The new curriculum will be based upon an integration of Jewish and general history. As students learn Jewish and Israeli history, the curriculum will orient these events within a broader world context. From what I saw, the current interim curriculum seems to be making a good attempt at this new orientation.

"I won the war," Bartal told me. "The new history curriculum will not surrender to the terminology of the extreme left wing or right wing. There is no one history, and writing history can be changed. In democracies, history is rewritten all the time. So books should be rewritten all the time."

Because Israel has an open market for textbooks, the education system allows for the continued rewriting of history. Academics write most books, and in theory, schools can use any books they choose. The majority of schools, however, teach only the books the Ministry of Education formally recommends. These are texts the ministry feels reflect the values of its history curriculum and which will best prepare students for the statewide exams, which resemble the Palestinian Tawjihi. By subsidizing its recommended list, the ministry gives schools an added incentive to use these texts. Even so, some of the most popular ministry-"approved" books are some of the most progressive, and a few have drawn intense criticism from the Israeli parliament, the Knesset. Knesset members fiercely attacked one book for challenging a fundamental Zionist myth. Another book caused such great controversy that the Knesset banned it from schools.

Israeli education has come a long way since the state was founded. Professor Eli Podeh, author of *The Arab-Israeli Conflict in Israeli History Textbooks, 1948–2000,* believes that Israel's history curricula and textbooks have passed through three stages since 1948. According to Podeh, the first and to a great extent second stages (1948 to mid-1970s and 1970s to mid-

1990s, respectively) were "approached entirely within the context of the Zionist struggle against the Arabs."★ The supervisor for state-religious education exemplified this attitude clearly enough.

"The Palestinians suffer from the same problems we did," Podeh told me. "If the role of their books is to inculcate national identity and attachment to the land, then their books must be very nationalistic. It happens during the first stages of building a state. Perhaps the current Palestinian books should be compared to the first generation books in Israel and not the third."

The first- and second-generation books largely ignore the Arab presence in Palestine and portray the land as empty when they discuss the first wave of Jewish immigration there in the late 1800s. The maps include Jewish and mixed Arab-Jewish areas, but entirely omit Arab areas. The books even show photos of uninhabited land to demonstrate this point. Similarly, the first- and second-generation books avoid the term "Palestine" and "Palestinians," because they don't want to legitimate a Palestinian national identity or land claim. "Eretz Yisrael" (the Land of Israel) and the "Arabs of Eretz Yisrael" are the preferred terms. Even those second-generation books that do acknowledge Palestinian nationalism explain it as a reaction to the Zionist movement. According to Podeh, the idea was to make the Palestinian movement seem "less authentic than the Jewish national movement."†

(I asked Israel Bartal if he believed the insensitivity of many current Israeli leaders toward the Palestinians stemmed from the misinformation conveyed in the first- and second-generation texts they studied growing up. "On the contrary," Bartal replied. "I'm impressed with how democratic and open-minded Israeli society has become. We didn't have to evolve in that direction.")

The third-generation texts still don't depict the early Arab settlements on their maps, but they invalidate the claim that Palestine was empty when European Jews first immigrated there. These books also acknowledge the existence of a Palestinian national movement; most use the terms "Palestine" and "Palestinians."‡ Certain textbook authors, whose books

---

★Eli Podeh, *The Arab-Israeli Conflict in Israeli History Textbooks, 1948–2000* (New York: Bergin and Garvey, 2002), page 32.

†Ibid., p. 93.

‡Ibid.

are popular with schools, are known to give a more thorough and balanced Arab perspective. A 1998 text gives what Podeh calls a "comprehensive analysis" of the development of Palestinian nationalism through the outbreak of the first intifada.* Similarly, historian Eyal Naveh's 1999 history text on the twentieth century challenges one of the central myths of the 1948 war: "the few against the many." As the 1954 curriculum states, the textbooks were to give students "knowledge of the Arab invasion [in 1948], the heroic war of the few against the many, and the armistice agreements."† In fact, this particular 1999 text states that Israel actually had the advantage in the 1948 war, because the Jews outnumbered the Arabs in specific strategic battles. Though this text came under heavy criticism for undermining the central myth, the ministry still put it on the list of recommended texts.

Despite a growing tolerance for Palestinian and Arab narratives, these perspectives are not integrated into the Israeli curriculum. Thus, few books go out of their way to challenge accepted historical norms or present the Arab perspective. Amos Yovel, who wrote the CMIP report on Israeli textbooks, told me that only two textbook authors use the word "expulsion" in reference to the 1948 Palestinian refugees. The majority of books say that the Palestinians fled hostilities during this period or were enticed to leave by neighboring Arab countries. The omission of "expelled" demonstrates a widespread unwillingness within Israel to accept the heart of the Palestinian historical narrative: Israel's forcible removal of Palestinians from their lands and its culpability in creating the refugee problem. This question is very touchy for Israelis because it is the prime anti-Zionist argument—that Israel built its nation by expelling an entire indigenous population, and therefore, the Israeli state is illegitimate.

In fact, both stories hold truth. Some Palestinians fled in response to local hostilities, believing they would return to their homes when the fighting ended; many fled fearing Jewish aggression; others were killed in raids by Jewish militants or were forcibly expelled by the official Jewish defense forces toward the end of the war.

If most Israeli textbooks are somewhat bland in their explanation of these events, the Palestinian texts present the other extreme. A 2001 Palestinian seventh-grade text states that the goals of the Jewish settlers were to "take over Palestinian lands and replace the original inhabitants in them,

---

*Podeh, *The Arab-Israeli Conflict in Israeli History Textbooks,* page 94.
†Ibid., page 93.

after having expelled and exterminated them." Israelis would be as horrified at the appearance of "exterminate" in the Palestinian books as the Palestinians would be at the omission of "expelled" in the Israeli books. Even if Israeli and Palestinian books are not inciting, their selective realities can be as offensive. A present-day example made this very clear to me.

Palestinian schools in East Jerusalem are under the jurisdiction of the Jerusalem municipality and not the Palestinian Ministry of Education. This means that Israel reviews and distributes all the Palestinian texts inside Jerusalem. While the Jerusalem municipality doesn't have an organized policy of censorship like the Civil Administration did, they do censor some material. The same seventh-grade Palestinian text that talks about "expulsion and extermination" goes on to say that as a result of the 1948 battles, "The Zionist terrorist organizations violently drove out thousands of Palestinians from their homes." In the East Jerusalem book, unlike those in the West Bank and Gaza, there is a blank space instead of the word "terrorist." Now the text reads, "Zionist   organizations." It looks like a typo. Something that would make a good bonus question for a pop quiz: "What is missing on page thirty-three?" But this omission is quite deliberate. The Jerusalem municipality had covered the word and reprinted the page.

Why did the Israelis delete "terrorist"? (I was surprised to find that "exterminate" remained untouched.) If this Palestinian book is referring to the mainstream Jewish armed forces (the Haganah) in general, then the term "terrorist organization" is historically inaccurate. If the book is referring to the Jewish resistance groups—the Etzel and Lekhi—that were not under the Haganah's auspices and indeed did commit acts of terror against the Arabs and British, then "terror organizations" is a fitting description. In fact, the book seems to lump all these groups together under the term "Zionist," thus giving Palestinian students a highly generalized and inaccurate picture of events.

The Israeli books do the same thing. They describe Arab operations against the Israelis in the 1930s as "terror acts," which is probably true in some cases and false in others. In particular, they call the group of Izz al-Din al-Qassam a "terrorist organization"—the *exact* term that the Palestinian books use. Sheikh Qassam was killed in 1935 while fighting against Jewish settlement in Palestine. His death sparked three years of Arab uprisings, termed the "Arab Revolt" by Palestinians and the Arab "events" by Israelis. The military wing of Hamas calls itself the al-Qassam brigades, but Palestinian as well as many Israeli historians don't consider Sheikh Qassam's group terrorist.

When the Palestinians deny or falsify Israeli history, they implicitly deny the Israelis' right to exist, and vice versa. Each side's fear of being declared illegitimate, which is to say being robbed of its identity, seems to motivate the censorship. Spending time in Seeds of Peace coexistence sessions where the kids hash out issues of history and national identity, I've seen the intensity of this fear. When the Seeds kids argue about what happened in 1948, they cease to be the fun-loving teenagers of the sports field but are transformed into full-fledged warriors, battling over no less than the preservation or destruction of the world—at least the world that comprises their nation and home. It's as though their lives depend upon convincing each other that their history is the right one, the only one. Look into their eyes and you understand what they fear: that if they can't prove this, they have no identity. They may as well not exist.

Forever a Citizen, Never Israeli

Yara, fifteen, is like a lot of Israeli girls her age: part responsible daughter, part drama queen. She loves showing off her hippest pair of jeans from the Jerusalem mall, matched with hoop earrings, a big necklace, and a fluorescent purse of blinding proportions. Her nails are like neon lights—pink, orange, or blue—flashing with each excited movement of her fingers. She wears her black hair in a ponytail or parted on the side. Her brown eyes are always smiling.

Yara attended Seeds of Peace as a member of the Israeli delegation. She lives in a Jewish town, has scores of Jewish friends, and attends a Jewish high school. But Yara is not a Jew. She is Arab and Muslim. Her mother's family is originally from Dabburiya, an Arab town in northern Israel. Her grandparents are among those Arabs who did not flee Palestine during the war of 1948. When Yara talks about her ancestors, she calls them Palestinian. So Yara is a Palestinian-Arab-Muslim-Israeli. Find this confusing? You're not alone.

For Yara and a million other Arab citizens of Israel, daily life is an identity crisis. This significant minority (about twenty percent of the population) lives in a country that proclaims itself—through its anthem, its flag, its very purpose—to be a Jewish nation. In recent years, it has become nearly impossible for many Arabs living inside Israel to identify as Israeli. Yet they remain in Israel. Their identity is so closely tied to where they live, they refuse to leave.

During the 1948 war, most of the Arabs living in Mandatory Palestine became refugees, fleeing or being expelled to Lebanon, Syria, and Jordan.

When Israel declared its independence in May of 1948, 150,000 Arabs remained inside the country. Many of these were internal refugees, meaning they'd lost their homes but had remained within the boundaries of the Jewish state. The new Israeli government found itself in a serious predicament: what to do with the sizable non-Jewish population inside this state that was founded for Jews? The war had vanquished the remaining Arabs, but the Israeli government saw them as a potential threat, a fifth column. Though they granted the Arabs inside Israel full Israeli citizenship, the government simultaneously put these communities under military rule. Technically, the Arabs had equal rights and protections under the law, but in practice their physical movement, occupational opportunities, and means of organizing were severely restricted until the mid-sixties. It wasn't until the 1980s that the Arab minority was able to organize politically and begin calling for its rights.

Since then, Israel's Arab citizens have seen substantial improvements. They move freely throughout the country, work alongside the Jewish population, have representation in the Knesset, and join the Histadrut (the workers' union) in large numbers. Arabs also have total freedom of worship including autonomy over their religious courts and places of worship.

Yet Israel consistently treats its Arab minority as second class and even as a national threat. Israel's Declaration of Independence, the document that grants all Israeli citizens equal rights, proclaims Israel to be a Jewish state where "it is the natural right of the Jewish people . . . to control their own destiny." Some call Israel an ethnic democracy because it gives preference to a single ethnic group. The Law of Return, the law allowing any Jew in the world to become an Israeli citizen, is the foremost example of this. Other inequities include the state's ongoing confiscation of Arab land under legal pretexts and the preference its quasi-governmental institutions (which largely control distribution of resources and services) gives to Israeli Jews. Because Arab citizens are exempt from Israel's mandatory armed service, they lose many socioeconomic benefits and opportunities open to those who do serve. Though the Israeli government understands the ideological conflict that mandatory service would present Arab citizens, the state continues to promote an "equal duties guarantees equal rights" policy. Finally, political parties that deny or question Israel's legitimacy as a Jewish nation are banned. This means that Arab parties cannot advocate repealing the Law of Return.

Before Seeds of Peace, Yara gave little thought to these inequalities or to her identity as an Arab living in a Jewish nation.

"Back at home, I couldn't see myself as any side," she told me shortly after she arrived at camp. "I saw myself alone."

After a few weeks at camp, however, this began to change. The other campers told Yara she had to pick an identity: Israeli or Arab.

"It was really hard," she said. "The Palestinians yelled at me, because I came with the Israeli delegation. They started calling me names like 'Sahyuneyyah,' which is Arabic for Zionist. Some of them came up to me and asked, 'Do you believe in God?' "

When Yara refused to answer, a Palestinian boy delivered the ultimate insult. "That's right," he told her, "the Jewish don't believe in God.' "

Even if Yara wanted to attend camp with the Palestinian delegation, she couldn't have. The governments select their delegations, so campers are grouped by citizenship as opposed to ethnic or national affiliation. Camp can be particularly painful for youngsters whose identities are mixed or for those who don't identify with their country of citizenship. Flag raising is one example. At the beginning of each session, the delegations raise their national flags and sing their anthems. Afterward, the entire camp raises the Seeds of Peace flag and sings the camp anthem. The ceremony is meant to celebrate the diversity of cultures and nationalities at camp, but also to acknowledge Seeds of Peace as a community in its own right. For many years, delegations were asked to stand as a group before their flag. Each summer I watched the Arabs in the Israeli delegation hide in the back, their heads bowed, as the Jewish members proclaimed their love for Israel: "In the Jewish heart, a Jewish spirit still sings . . . our hope is not lost, our hope of two thousand years ago."

For Israeli Jews, this anthem, called Hatikva, "The Hope," signifies the return of the Jewish people to their biblical homeland after thousands of years in exile. At its core, the song reflects the idea that Israel belongs to the Jews. Its melody is stirring and sad, and even Yara says she gets the tune stuck in her head. But Hatikva moves Israelis in different ways. For Israeli Jews, the song brings tears of pride. For Israeli Arabs, it produces tears of pain. They know the hope expressed in Hatikva is not for them; in their eyes, hope was crushed in 1948, the year Israel declared its independence. And even though most Jewish Israelis understand why the Arabs cannot identify with Israel's flag or its anthem, many in the delegation treat their Arab peers harshly for not singing Hatikva—or worse, for singing the Palestinian national anthem instead. These days, the camp tries to prevent the delegations from standing in groups when they sing in order to mitigate this tension.

Flag raising isn't the only problem. Every weekend, the Muslim, Christian, and Jewish campers hold religious services. These services are optional, but anyone can choose to watch. The Jewish kids wear white shirts to the Shabbat service as a show of unity. When Yara showed up in a white shirt, the Palestinians lashed out at her.

"I wanted to wear white," Yara explained, "because at the Muslim service the Jews came and took their shoes off out of respect. So I wanted to come and respect them as well as they respected my religion. But the Palestinians yelled at me: 'You're becoming one of them!' "

Strangely enough, the one person who didn't force Yara to take sides was the young man with the harshest views toward Arabs: Omri.

Intially, the two Israelis did not get along. Omri told Yara that he couldn't imagine touching an Arab kid let alone hugging one. Instead of getting mad, Yara told Omri about herself—and the experience of being an Arab citizen of Israel.

"And he got it," Yara said. "He's one of the kids I like most in the delegation. He said he knows it's hard for me."

Obviously, Omri learned something from Yara. For a boy who refused to hug an Arab, he had his arm around her often enough. But Omri's broader views about Israel's Arab citizens do not reflect his friendship with Yara. I asked Omri if he thought Israel gives equal rights to its Arab citizens. "They don't serve in the army," he said curtly, "so they shouldn't really cry that it's not equal."

"So let me ask you some provocative questions," I said.

Omri was expecting as much. "Okay," he agreed, "I'm used to it."

I smiled and pressed ahead. "The Arab citizens say that Israel discriminates against them because they're not Jewish."

"They don't have to be here" was Omri's harsh response. "If they don't like it they can leave. It's not that far—the other Arab countries." The fact that some of Israel's Arab citizens call themselves Palestinian offended Omri. He told one camper that if she wanted to be Palestinian, she should throw her Israeli ID in the garbage and move to Gaza.

I was taken aback by the callousness of this comment, and felt compelled to defend the girl. "But if she has been living in Israel as long as you've been there—"

Omri interrupted me. "I've been saying to all the Palestinian Seeds: You can't ask for something you lose. It's like a card game. Once you lose your cards, you can't have them back."

Omri seemed to be operating on a very one-sided standard of fairness. I knew the Israeli-Palestinian conflict was not a game in which two sides met congenially across a table and agreed to play each other. From the Palestinian perspective, the Zionists were a colonial force that conquered them. I decided to rephrase my question. "But isn't Israel a state for everyone who has Israeli citizenship?"

"The Arab Israelis can be Israeli citizens," Omri said, "but according to what *we* call Israeli citizens."

I reminded Omri that even if the Arabs did serve in the army, the Law of Return was still fundamentally biased.

"All right?" He sounded just like my argumentative younger brother: *So what's your point, Jenny?*

"Doesn't the Law of Return deny Arabs equal rights?" I asked.

"Ya, okay, I told you," Omri repeated. "It's a state for the Jews all over the world before it's a state for other people. The Israeli Arabs have maybe forty Arab countries. We have only one state for the Jews."

"And if those other Arab countries don't want them?"

"It's their problem. It's not my problem."

I couldn't help but feel disappointed with Omri's attitude, especially given his relationship with Yara. She claimed he understood her mixed identity, but I wasn't sure. Perhaps Omri sympathized with Yara as an individual, but not with her community—some twenty percent of the country. I could tell that the presence of such a sizable non-Jewish minority made him insecure. I knew that Israeli Arabs' calling themselves Palestinian, in the middle of an intifada, when many Israeli Jews saw Palestinians as a major threat, was bound to make Jews nervous. Added to this are Israeli Jews' fears, however remote, that Israel could cease to be a Jewish country.

Take it from the perspective of an American Jew. As a kid in Hebrew school, I learned the indispensability of a Jewish state. This was long before I knew that there were Arabs with Israeli citizenship, and even before I understood what the Israeli occupation was. The idea that Jews absolutely must have a safe haven was drilled into my head. Only at the age of sixteen, during my first summer at Seeds of Peace, did someone introduce to me the facts of *how* Israel achieved its statehood: The Palestinian refugees were uprooted from their lands and Israel's one million Arab citizens were guaranteed but not actually given equal rights. My initial reaction to these arguments was much the same as Omri's. If anyone tried to knock down my belief in the sanctity of Israel, I simply buttressed myself with more ingrained belief. Israel must be a *Jewish* state; tough luck if you don't like it. Over time, however, I started listening to my Arab friends. True, the Arab leadership in Palestine dismissed the 1947 UN Partition Plan that would have created separate Israeli and Arab states. It is also true that the neighboring Arab armies and not the Jews initiated the 1948 war. But to use Omri's own metaphor, it seemed to me that the Arabs living inside Palestine had the cards stacked against them. The Jews may not have intended to exile over 700,000 people and leave another 150,000 in highly unstable circumstances, but these were the consequences of creating an independent Jewish state.

After I allowed myself to accept this, I realized how shaky my own beliefs were. I was forced to question if the need for a Jewish state was great enough to justify the consequences that state had for so many Palestinians. And if the need was great enough in 1948, what about today? Would Jews around the world become threatened if a Jewish Israel ceased to exist? Many do believe that a Jewish Israel is the Jews' only real protection against religious discrimination and persecution. Even though I am far removed from the Holocaust and have never experienced anti-Semitism, I still feel a pang of fear when I consider not having a place to turn if the need arose. For many Israelis, the fear of another Holocaust remains a real issue. In the end, I have concluded that my personal insecurity is a product of history and not present-day reality. Perhaps a Jewish Israel was necessary to heal the wounds of the Holocaust, but it seems to me that despite the scars those wounds have closed.

I understand, however, that the desire for a Jewish state is not solely about Jewish need but about culture, religion, and history. Anyone who believes Israel is his or her God-given right will never question the legitimacy of a Jewish Israel. Even Jews who do not strictly believe in the Bible feel a connection to Israel. My parents, for example, are like a lot of Jews— agnostic, moderately observant, and passionately connected to Israel. They lived there for a year after they married and experienced the 1973 war— when Egypt and Syria launched surprise attacks on Israel during Yom Kippur, the Jewish day of atonement. They took my brother and me to Israel after my bat mitzvah in order to show us, firsthand, this country that was so much a part of our heritage. The timing was key. The trip to Israel, even more than the synagogue ceremony, was my initiation into the world of Jewish adulthood. I'm sure they bought me the IDF T-shirt I asked for without a thought to its political connotations.

My mother also visited me in Jerusalem during my research. She walked around the city like a boy-crazy teenager, a dreamy look in her eyes. She was in love. And this is someone who is highly critical of Israel's treatment of the Palestinians, who has been to Gaza and the West Bank, and who has no desire to use Israeli's Law of Return to become an Israeli citizen. Still, my mother seemed saddened by my inability to share her excitement and passion for Israel. I told her that too many Israeli taxi drivers had questioned why I, a Jew, would rather live in America than in "my homeland," Israel. I said I was sick of people—Israelis and Palestinians—assuming I felt an entitlement to Israel because I was Jewish. My frustration over these assumptions erupted one afternoon after the current finance minister and former prime minister, Bibi Netanyahu, called Israel's Arab population a "demographic threat" to Israel's future as a Jewish nation. I was on the patio of the King David Hotel in Jerusalem, arguing with my father about Israel's legitimacy. In my mind, he was ignoring the needs of Israel's Arab minority.

"Israel shouldn't be a Jewish country," I finally burst out at him. "If it's a state for the Jews, it's not a state for *all* its citizens." My voice had risen well above appropriate levels. Half a dozen people on the patio were trying not to stare. "I'll see you later," I said, and stormed out.

I'm sure plenty of people would brand me a radical left-winger and a self-hating Jew for that proclamation. I don't believe I am either. Just as I say that Israel should not be a Jewish country, I understand the connection that ninety-nine percent of the Jewish Israeli population feels toward their country. It is certainly not right for me, an American, to tell them what to do. It is their right to love their country and to want to protect the Zionist ideal—their belief that the Jews deserve a state in Eretz Yisrael. Moreover, young Israeli Jews have inherited Israel, its legacy, and the burdens of Zionism from their parents and grandparents. They are not responsible for the refugee problem, the discrimination against Israel's Arab communities, and the occupation of the West Bank and Gaza. The onus of this burden will fall on them, however, if the current leadership does not find creative solutions to fix these problems. I believe this solution begins with Israeli Jews confronting the difficult and painful situation of Israel's Arab minority. The Israeli government must implement the civic equality that its declaration of independence proclaims. As important, Israeli Jews must attempt to understand and eventually accept the connection Arab citizens have with Palestine.

Omri is absolutely right in saying that many Arab citizens of Israel identify more as Palestinian than Israeli. Though in the past, the Arab community might have identified as Israeli Arab or Arab Israeli, today such identifications are largely taboo. This is not to say that Arab citizens of Israel wish to move to the West Bank and Gaza, or even that they would move to an independent Palestinian state. On a practical level, they have a higher standard of living than Palestinians in the territories, and even as second-class citizens, Israel's democratic system allows them more representation and freedom of expression than they could have under the Palestinian Authority. But the Arabs won't leave Israel for ideological reasons as well.

I was surprised to learn that Yara lives in an entirely Jewish neighborhood. Even more shocking is that some people call her neighborhood a settlement. Yara's home is in Pisgat Ze'ev, considered a Jerusalem suburb by most Israelis. Until 1967, however, the land of Pisgat Ze'ev was part of Jordan, and therefore it is in the West Bank. Every morning, when Yara looks out her window, she sees the same view as the Jews in her neighborhood: dusty West Bank hills and the cinder-block buildings of the Shu'fat refugee camp. When I asked Yara's mother how a Palestinian family could possibly live in a settlement, her answer was clear enough. "This has been my land from the beginning," she said. "Why shouldn't I live there?"

Nardin, a twenty-four-year-old medical student, lives forty-five minutes north of Haifa in Arrabe village, her grandparents' original home.

"I will never leave the place where I was born," she told me when I visited her there. "It's my own right to stay. And if I move to the state that will be called Palestine, I will complete the evacuation of forty-eight."

Nardin is an intense young woman who observes the world through dark eyes beneath even darker lashes. Her movements and manner of speech are deliberate, often strained, as though she is constantly pushing against an invisible current. But the tone of her voice is still and deep, like that part of the ocean where little light shines.

"I define myself as Palestinian, Arab, Muslim, and female," Nardin said as we ate olives on her living room sofa. "I could say that I am a citizen of Israel, but this is so different from saying I am Israeli. I am not Israeli, and I will never be Israeli."

I asked Nardin if there was any part of Israel to which she felt connected.

"I am connected to the Palestine in Israel," she replied. By this she meant her village, her grandparents' land, and even to the old Arab houses in Haifa that are now inhabited by Jews.

This is exactly what so many Jewish Israelis fear. If Nardin isn't loyal to Israel, they might say, then what impetus does she have to obey the law? What prevents her from committing treason against the country? Though Arabs living inside Israel committed virtually no violence against Jews until the second intifada, since 2000 the Israeli secret service has uncovered a handful of suicide-bombing plots by Israeli-Arabs, as well as links between members of their community and West Bank militants, maybe even Hizbollah. I was sure neither Nardin nor the majority of her community was involved in such activities, but I wanted to know what it meant for her to be an Israeli citizen who refused to call herself Israeli.

"I can be loyal to the country that I'm living in," she said. "I will be a good citizen. I won't break the law. That's it."

According to Nardin, she has an obligation to uphold the democratic aspects of Israel but not its Jewish aspects. Most Arab citizens of Israel feel this way, including members of the national government. Nazim Budr, for example, was quite certain that Israel cannot be both Jewish and democratic. Budr is manager of the Peace and Equality Front, Hadash, which grew out of the Israeli Communist Party and, according to Budr, is open to both Arabs and Jews. His boss is Mohammad Baraka, who, in 2003, was one of eight Arabs in Israel's 120-person legislative body.

I met Budr in Baraka's Knesset office. It was on the top floor and looked more like a messy high school hallway—linoleum floors, scattered papers, piled chairs—than the spotless, carpeted corridors below. Unlike the other Knesset members I visited, Baraka's office was a single room with no reception desk. It was tidy enough, but far less professional-looking than the offices of Labor and Likud (the left of center and right of center mainstream political parties in Israel). Stickers, including one of a hammer and sickle, peeled from the file cabinet. There was a poster of Che Guevara on the wall and a framed photo of Baraka shaking hands with Yasir Arafat.

The decor is a testament to Hadash's communist roots. Budr said the party no longer subscribed to a stark communist ideology, though supporting the workers and the low-income neighborhoods are among its main principles, as well as supporting equal rights for Israel's Arab citizens.

"To be a Jewish state, Israel must keep the Arabs as a minority," Budr told me. "If we have basic rights to be elected, to bring kids into this world, then in some time, Arab citizens could be the majority." If this happens, Budr believed, and the Arabs elect an Arab-led government, the Jews will have two options. They must either accept a democratic state that isn't Jewish or a Jewish state governed by an authoritarian, nondemocratic regime.

This is exactly what Finance Minister Netanyahu meant when he called Israel's Arab population a "demographic threat." Yet Budr understands where Likud members like Netanyahu are coming from. They may be racist, he says, but at least they are open about wanting a Jewish state forever. Budr is more skeptical of the left-wing parties like Labor and Meretz, because they say they want full equality but act in favor of the Jews.

"It's painfully funny," Nardin said of the left-wing parties. Their members are all Jews, so they have no reason to support Arab-led legislation. According to one of Nardin's friends at the Knesset, the Jewish legislators passed a bill to build a hospital in an underprivileged Jewish neighborhood. When Arab legislators brought the same request for a hospital in a poor Arab neighborhood, the bill failed.

I asked Nardin why Arab Knesset members even bothered to work inside the system if they were so often defeated.

"Even if they fail to achieve," she said, "you have to try. Imagine if there were no members. We might lose most of our cases, but at least our voice is heard."

The Arab community has not been able to present a unified voice when fighting for equal rights. Their community is split into competing factions that Nazim Budr says have selfish interests. Arab city politics is a good example of this. I spent an afternoon in Taiybe, a city of forty thousand located in central Israel, about forty-five minutes from Tel Aviv. A sixteen-year-old Seeds of Peace graduate named Amira, and her twenty-eight-year-old history teacher, Amal, gave me a driving tour of the city. On our way there, Amal warned me: "Driving from Tel Aviv to Taiybe is like driving fifty years into the past."

By this comment, Amal meant the city's physical landscape, as well as its political and social culture. Taiybe is more of a small town than a city.

Its roads are dusty and lined with cars, but virtually empty of people. The pavement is crumbling. There is trash everywhere. More than once our car waded through nearly half a foot of standing water and sewage. Amal said she couldn't remember the last time she went for a walk. "We can open the windows," she said, "but don't blame me for the smell."

What struck me about Taiybe was that despite its sordid public space, it boasted large, beautiful homes, lined up one after another along the roadway.

"People just don't care," Amal said when I asked her about the phenomenon. "We could have fifty BMWs in this town and no road to drive on." She said that Taiybe has a wealthy population, but the people don't take care of their public space. Her sister's home is a perfect example. Amal's brother-in-law is a successful lawyer and built one of the most grandiose homes in the city: a glistening structure of white marble, furnished in leather. And yet it sits at the end of a dirt road, full of potholes, and across from a trash heap. Just as puzzling was the fact that on every other street I saw structures resembling the American White House. I asked Amal if my eyes were deceiving me. "The White House style is what everyone wants," she explained. "It reflects authority and power."

Maybe, but the "White Houses" looked silly sitting above so much sewage, which only reinforced Amal's point that Taiybe's political and social culture worked against the community's best interests. She explained that corrupt mafialike families control the town's local politics, and if you're not in cahoots with them, it's impossible to get elected. At the moment, the only group with enough support to challenge Taiybe's ruling family were the Islamists, but the national government did not want Muslim leaders assuming control over the city. They were wary of links between Muslim leaders in the region and terrorist groups. Amal said the Israeli Supreme Court had recently passed an order suspending elections to keep the current mayor in office.

Nazim Budr acknowledged the political corruption of the Arab family system.

"In fifty years," he said, "the Arab communities did not become modern like the Jewish." But according to Budr, the Jews were also culpable for the state of Arab politics. The government keeps the families fighting one another, he said, because this prevents them from struggling for equal budgets and for funds to develop the city. Budr believed this was why the Supreme Court suspended Taiybe's elections.

It is difficult to determine how much of the Arab community's second-class status is due to its internal conflicts and corruption and how much is due to governmental discrimination. Certainly there is a mixture. Nazim Budr said that when families control politics, people are not held accountable to the law. The percentage of Arabs who pay taxes to their municipalities, for example, is lower in Arab villages than in Jewish cities.

Amira believes her community simply doesn't care. "We're living here for a long time and the situation doesn't change," she said. "People don't feel that they belong to their town."

Amal agreed. "There's so much apathy on the town level. Everyone is trying to create his own bubble."

So the Arab municipalities have a double disadvantage. They don't receive the required tax money from their own population, and they consistently receive insufficient funds from the national government. Even though the law requires equality, in practice, Budr believes the Arab citizen gets sixty to seventy percent of what the Jewish citizen gets.

The first time the Israeli government confessed to discrimination against Israeli Arabs, Budr told me, "was under Rabin's 1992 administration. And they changed one very important thing: the amount of money given to minors. Before 1992, the Jewish family got more than double what the Arab family got."

Still, inequalities persist. When I visited Nardin's village of Arrabe, the faucets had been dry all week, because the municipality couldn't pay the water company. That evening on the news, a reporter interviewed citizens in the town who said the company would never have cut off water in a Jewish village. The screen then cut to an interview with a water company representative.

"Of course we would cut off water in a Jewish village if they couldn't pay," the representative said.

Nardin and her mother scowled at the television.

Many Arabs in Israel dream of a binational state. Instead of separate Israeli and Palestinian countries, they want all the people between the Jordan River and the Mediterranean Sea to live in one nation.

"One government and no boundaries," Nardin said. "For me this is utopia."

Nardin believes such a dream is impossible, and instead she advocates immediately giving the Palestinians a state. Arabs in Israel, she says, will never respect an Israeli government that denies the Palestinians in the territories their full rights.

Solving the Palestinian problem first has often meant putting Israel's Arab community last. Ehud Barak, former Israeli prime minister, was up front about his priorities when I spoke with him about the issue.

"I told the Arabs that we have three challenges: peace, equality, and integration. And I told them, this is the order of priority, because peace will change the context in which you are living." Though Barak did promise the Arabs concrete improvements, he did not deliver them.

"Even the correction of sewage in their villages will take five or six years," Barak told me. "And to correct other elements will take even longer."

I asked Barak why it would take so long to fix sewage.

"Assume for a moment that you want to build a house," he told me. "It can't take two weeks. Why? It can't. But I can promise you that in five years we will have done a great achievement."

But Barak was in office for only twenty months. "And in that amount of time," he said "you can't expect any kind of real project to be completed." According to Barak, the Arabs should have been more patient. Instead they collectively abstained from the 2001 national elections—one of the only unified political moves their community has taken in recent years. Barak lost the election to Ariel Sharon.

I asked Barak if he thought the Arabs' boycott was an overreaction.

"Ya!" Barak was empahtic. "They acted against their own interests. Unless they're happy with Sharon's government. But if they're not happy, they should blame themselves more than anyone else."

Barak and I both knew that the Arab community had abstained over much more than the lack of services. The deeper reason lay in a series of events that took place in September 2000, just days after the outbreak of the second intifada. These were the October riots, or Black October as the Arabs call it, confrontations between Arab citizens of Israel and the Israeli police that left thirteen Arabs dead.

The confrontations started on the road between the Arab town of Nazareth and the Jewish town of Upper Nazareth. Arabs said that Jews began throwing stones at them and trying to set fire to their homes. Using the loudspeakers atop mosques, the Arabs called to their community for help. Fighting escalated until the Israeli police arrived. In their attempt to quell the riot, the police killed two Arab men. The police claimed to have used tear gas and rubber bullets, but the Nazareth hospital reported live ammunition in one of the bodies.★

In the following days, more violence erupted between Arab and Jewish communities in northern Israel. The Arab leadership declared a general strike, and Arabs throughout the country demonstrated in protest of the Nazareth killings. In Arrabe, these were peaceful marches, Nardin's father told me, and entirely within the city limits. In other words, there was no opportunity for aggression against Jews. The morning of October 2, however, police came to Arrabe and allegedly shot at some Arab youths in the village olive groves. News of the shootings spread and families began going to the groves, looking for their sons, shouting at the police to leave the village, and throwing stones.

Nardin's younger brother, Asel, a seventeen-year-old Seeds of Peace graduate, found these events particularly upsetting. Asel felt a distinct connection to his Palestinian identity, but he was deeply committed to building bridges between Israelis and Palestinians. Now his community, which had rarely been involved in violence, was embroiled in clashes with Israel's police. More than this, the peace process had recently collapsed. Everything Asel had worked for was crumbling.

Nardin said her brother didn't think much about the meaning of Seeds of Peace when he first decided to go, at the age of fourteen. It was 1997, my second summer at camp, and Asel and I were assigned to the same table in the dining hall. My first impression of him was not positive, and I was sure his first summer would be his last. Asel was a pain in the butt. He had a restless energy, and he didn't listen. I remember one instance in which he came into the dining hall wearing a black sweatshirt with an Arabic slogan. I never found out what the words meant, but I remember some of the Arab kids at the table whispering about it. A counselor asked Asel to change his shirt. That was the rule at camp—everyone wore the same green Seeds of Peace T-shirt and blue Seeds of Peace sweatshirt. Asel refused. I remember him laughing at the counselor as though she were asking him to do a silly, inconceivable thing.

Nardin says her brother was always "nice, and sweet, and funny" as a kid, but she acknowledged that Seeds of Peace changed him. "He went back to camp different the second time and third time," she said knowingly. "That's for sure."

After his first summer at Seeds, Asel began to educate himself. He

★*Ha'aretz,* October 10, 2001.

wanted to learn how to reach people, how to affect them. Nardin said he used to read mountains of books about philosophy, education, psychology, history, and politics. Asel was only fifteen, and it wasn't as though a need for enlightenment ran in the family. Anger characterized Nardin's teenage years. "I thought to myself, 'What? I'm going to change the world? The community?' I'm not going to change it. I just have to live and get used to it."

Asel was never so cynical. With Asel, Seeds of Peace and what it represented were a daily commitment. According to Nardin, when her brother wasn't reading and writing, he was on the computer e-mailing and sending instant messages to his friends. His AIM (America Online Instant Messenger) name, Slider, even popped up on my screen now and then. He MC'd a talent show at the Seeds of Peace Center in Jerusalem and attended a youth summit in Switzerland where we had mock negotiations on the Oslo permanent status issues. That summit took place in 1998, my senior year of high school.

I have a photo from the summit of me surrounded by Seeds of Peace friends. Though we posed for the camera, the image has all the energy and life of a candid snapshot. A brightness bursts from the picture. It is an unlikely image, these Israelis, Arabs, and an American smiling as though peace had just broken out. As though we had something magnificent to celebrate, though really, we were just celebrating ourselves.

I have always loved this photo. It is a physical symbol of what Seeds of Peace means to me: a community of people who share an unmatchable connection. But the picture is more than that. It reminds me that I belong to something much greater than myself. Perhaps this is why when I used to look at the picture, I paid more attention to the group as a whole than to the individuals around me. I had it taped to my wall throughout my freshman, sophomore, and junior years of college, but I couldn't have told you who was sitting next to me in the photo. Then, one October day, I saw that person for the first time.

It was October 2, 2000, to be exact, just days after the second intifada began. It was the same day police came to Arrabe village. That morning I woke up in my dorm room, got dressed, and went to class. That same morning, Asel woke up and got dressed in his Arrabe bedroom. He choose a green one that depicted three miniature people holding hands: the Seeds of Peace shirt. Many of us in the Seeds' community agreed that it was a childish design. The little people resembled aliens, and the color wasn't exactly flattering, but Asel loved the Seeds of Peace shirt the way other kids love the jerseys of their favorite sports' teams. He had dozens of them. At seventeen, there was little hint of the fourteen-year-old boy who had once refused to wear the Seeds of Peace sweatshirt in the dining hall.

Later that afternoon, Asel heard about the alleged shootings and went to the olive grove. Asel's father, Hasan, saw his son arrive at the grove and sit down beneath a tree. As Hasan remembers, Asel was sitting in an isolated spot. A few minutes later, Hasan saw three policemen moving toward his son, and he called out. When Asel saw the men, he jumped up and started to run. Hasan said the police followed Asel, chasing him into the olive grove and out of sight.

Around four-thirty that afternoon, I was in my dorm. In Israel, the onset of fall had only just begun. The days were sunny and you wouldn't have needed a sweater. In Providence, Rhode Island, however, I was already wearing my winter jacket. The sky was a cold slate. I sat at my desk watching late afternoon slide toward night along that monotonous New England color spectrum of gray and darker gray. I'd been staring out the window a lot lately, wondering what use I was in a college dorm room when some of my best Israeli and Palestinian friends were living the daily turmoil of intifada. To make matters worse, my friends at school couldn't understand how I was feeling. I could tell that my depression over events thousands of miles away made some of them uncomfortable. It was eleven-thirty at night in Israel and Palestine, but I decided to call one of my Seeds friends anyway. He was an American, a fellow counselor living in Bethlehem. After a few rings, he picked up. I asked how he was.

"Actually," he said, "not too well."

"Why?" I asked, thinking nothing of it.

There was silence and then: "Asel's dead."

"Asel?" I asked, momentarily confused.

"Asel Asleh."

"What—"

"I don't know what happened," my friend said heavily. "I'm going to bed now."

I put the phone down, not sure what to do. I stared out the window for some time, as though nothing had happened. Then, for some reason, I felt compelled to turn around. On the wall in front of me was the photo from Switzerland. The person sitting next to me, with his arm around my shoulder, was Asel. I gasped. It was as though I'd seen a ghost.

Asel was horribly beaten and shot in the neck at close range. There is obviously more to the story, but no one, not even Asel's father, has learned the full truth. I asked Hasan why he thought the police murdered his son. Was there any way Asel could have been confused with the people shouting at the police or throwing stones at them? Hasan said absolutely not, because his son was nowhere near the other demonstrators. He called what happened a genocide.

"A genocide?" I asked, startled. "By definition?"

"You can take the tape of Israeli radio the same day they killed our children," Hasan told me. "The police were ordered to use any tool to separate the demonstrators and open the roads. That means kill them."

"But a genocide?" I asked again. Did Hasan truly believe the Israeli government was doing to its Arab citizens what Hitler did to the Jews in the Holocaust, or what the Turks did to the Armenians? Were the events of October 2000 comparable to those in Rwanda in the 1990s?

"I can repeat it as much as you want," Hasan answered. "A definite genocide."

"Meaning the systematic killing of a people because of their race or—"
Hasan was quite clear. "Because they are Arabs."

Ehud Barak called the October killings "a major tragedy." He told me the demonstrators should have been arrested but certainly not killed. Yet he also warned me to have no illusions about the situation.

"It was not a kind of demonstration that you sometimes have with labor coal miners or with the students at Kent University," he said. "This is a national upheaval that was encouraged by a highly extreme political leadership. The government didn't have any choice but to deal with it in an attempt to restore public order."

Israeli police have never fired on Jewish protestors. For them, riot control has always consisted of loudspeakers and, in rare circumstances, clubs and tear gas. The police who confronted the Arab demonstrators in villages like Arrabe were equipped with clubs and bullets. These included both live ammunition and rubber slugs, which are metal bullets coated in rubber and can be lethal at close range. They lacked less violent means of riot control. One policeman sent to the demonstrations said he was not asked to give warning but ordered to shoot stone-throwing demonstrators "with the intent to hit."* As it turns out, none of the demonstrators in Arrabe, including those who were throwing stones, were armed.

*Associated Press, February 19, 2001.

The Israeli government stated that only serious flaws in the police forces could have resulted in Israeli police shooting their own citizens. The Knesset established a special commission headed by Supreme Court Justice Theodore Orr to investigate the events of October 2000. The commission spent seven million shekels and three and half years compiling details and conducting hearings with police and witnesses. The eight-hundred-page report issued a sharp criticism of the Israeli police. It recommended an overhaul of the police's riot and demonstration policies, faulted its command structure, and partly blamed the police's excessive force against the Arab community on a culture of fear and hatred within the force toward Israel's Arab citizens. The head of internal security, as well as a handful of other high- and mid-level officers, were forced to resign. The Orr Report also criticized the Israeli government for not taking concrete measures to achieve civil equality for the Arab community, concluding that the community's second-class status was a main impetus for the demonstrations. Finally, the report leveled blame against Arab politicians, who were seen as inciting their community with anti-Israel rhetoric.

To those like Asel's father, the Orr Commission failed in its most basic task. No police officers were charged or indicted. According to *Ha'aretz,* police officers asked to testify at the hearings presented "conflicting testimonies" about how the thirteen Arabs were killed.[†] Not one of the police officers in Arrabe village assumed responsibility for Asel's death.

"None of those [police] who took the stand could explain or even guess how Asleh was killed or who pulled the trigger," *Ha'aretz* reported. One of the officers called it a "mystery."[‡] Hasan heard the police give their testimony. According to him, they said that one minute they were running after Asel and the next minute the boy was on the ground bleeding. The judge asked the policemen if they heard a shot and the police said no.

"But the judge didn't ask the police what distance they were from Asel," Hasan said, exasperated. "And one of the police said, 'Shimony was near-Asel.' And the judge didn't ask Shimony *why* he was near. It was a theater. What can I do?"

Hasan said he doesn't expect the Orr Commission's findings to accomplish any practical changes. "I know Israeli law and Israeli corruption," he

[†]*Ha'aretz,* June 7, 2001.
[‡]Ibid.

said. "There are two kinds of laws inside Israel, one for the Arabs and one for the Jews. But I must continue and not give up. I want to see the police inside jail. I hope I can reach the high court in the Hague. I hope I can do it."

Nardin says she doesn't have much energy to join her parents' fight. "It's difficult for you to work for something when you don't have much hope," she said. "You do the thing and you know you're going to fail." But Asel was amazing, Nardin said, because he never gave up the fight for justice or the fight for peace. "Asel believed that we should never forget where we come from, but he believed in forgiving and working together to find the best solution for both sides."

As she said these words about her brother, I realized that she was smiling. It was the only smile she showed all night, and it was gone in an instant.

A Different Kind
of Orthodox

When I was twelve, my Hebrew school offered an optional weekend homestay in the ultra-Orthodox community of Brooklyn's Borough Park. We were to leave Washington, D.C., Friday morning and return from New York on Sunday. The purpose of this trip was to expose us young Jewish ignoramuses to a traditional Orthodox Shabbat. I decided the excursion was a great idea, as it meant missing a day of school. We were to stay in homes in pairs of two, so I convinced my best friend Risa to accompany me. We were the perfect pair to spend a weekend of prayer and religious devotion. When we weren't heckling our Hebrew school teachers, we were taking thirty-minute "bathroom breaks," to munch candy and kosher pickles in the synagogue store. If there had been Jewish Juvie, I'm sure the synagogue would have locked up both of us.

This time, Risa and I agreed to behave. We wanted to see what a "real" Shabbat was like, and we wanted to impress our hosts by showing them what good Jews we were. We figured it shouldn't be too hard. Both our families kept kosher and celebrated the important holidays. I was already learning to chant Torah for my bat mitzvah the following year. But I was also nervous. I had the vague sense that, despite the short length of this journey, we were being sent away ill-prepared. The only guidance the synagogue had given us was a packing list that directed girls to bring "skirts of appropriate length" and "blouses that covered the arms." I owned few skirts, and my longest just brushed the tops of my knees. My mother assured me that I would be fine, put me on the bus, and I was off to New York.

Coming from our liberal, egalitarian environments, Risa and I were entirely unprepared for what we encountered in Borough Park: a community of women who were not allowed to read from the Torah, who wore wigs once they married, who stayed home to raise their many children instead of attending college, and who waited on their husbands and sons before sitting down to eat. Before Friday night dinner, everyone showered and dressed up. Risa and I were surprised to see our host mother appear in her house robe—so she could serve dinner and not dirty her good clothes, she explained. When Risa and I tried to show off our Hebrew by singing the Kiddish (the blessing over the wine), our host sister leaned over and hissed, "You *can't* let the men hear you sing!" To our young independent selves, this was blatant sexism. That these women could accept such a lifestyle was inconceivable when we were encouraged to do everything boys did.

When our host father inquired about our *fathers'* occupations we decided there was no longer any benefit to being polite.

Risa said something to the effect of: "My *mother* is a very successful lawyer and my dad is an AIDS researcher. What about you, Jenny?"

"Oh, well," I said in my most innocent voice, "my father works on the Israeli-*Palestinian peace* process. He spends a lot of time in Syria." My host father nearly choked on his chicken.

This experience planted in my heart a stronger bias against Orthodox Jews than any other group of people—stereotypes that today I still find difficult to shake. Growing up, I too often saw the *haredim,* the ultra-Orthodox, as the mold of a single person. This was mostly true when it came to Orthodox girls. I was secretly afraid of how closely connected we were, how easily I could have been born into their environment and made to dress in their clothes: dark skirts, white tights, orthopedic-looking shoes, tight-collared blouses. Clothes that seemed to come out of someone's attic.

I didn't understand how anyone could be happy attending a single-sex religious school or sitting behind a *mechitza,* the barrier in the synagogue separating the men from the women, so as not to distract the men in their worship. In my mind, the Orthodox girl was awkward, diffident, and one hundred percent complicit in dressing like a rag doll. Whenever I saw a girl like this on the street, I thanked God we were nothing alike.

This image was shattered when I met Sari at Seeds of Peace. Sari, fifteen, was one of the quieter members of bunk five. A kid who didn't seem interested in opening up to her counselors and who spent most rest hours reading or writing in her journal. I was secretly thrilled the afternoon I persuaded her to show me her photos from home.

"This is Yoav, my boyfriend." Sari handed me one from the pile. I noted that the picture was not on ostentatious display like those of other Israeli boyfriends. In the photo, Sari and Yoav stand in front of a green lawn, their arms around each other's shoulders. Yoav is skinny with closely cropped hair, a head taller than Sari. Sari is wearing a purple T-shirt with the neck cut off. The shirt has slid down over her left shoulder revealing a bright white bra strap and an angled collarbone. There is a freshness in her face, which, combined with the bra strap, gives the girl in the photo an air of maturity, as though she were in her mid-twenties instead of her mid-teens. The girl in the picture looked nothing like the tomboy in cropped red sweatpants across from me on the bunk bed.

"He's cute," I told her, but Sari snatched the picture from my fingers. She quickly turned over onto her stomach to hide her smile.

Later, when Sari told me she was Orthodox, I didn't believe her. "But look at how you dress," I protested. "And the photo of you and Yoav. Your *bra* strap is showing!"

Sari looked at me like I was nuts. "Not all Orthodox women cover themselves up and refuse to touch boys."

It was true that my image of what an Orthodox girl looked like, how she behaved, represented the strictest form of Jewish Orthodoxy. I knew people in the States who considered themselves "modern Orthodox," a less strict form of Orthodox Judaism, but Sari defied even my image of this group. Neither her appearance nor her behavior suggested my idea of the religiously observant females I saw on the streets of Jerusalem. She seemed too comfortable with herself, too open-minded, too relaxed to be Orthodox. And I had assumed that I would always know an Orthodox Jew when I saw one.

In fact, knowing what it means to be a Jew, Orthodox or not, is not an easy task, particularly in Israel. Only twenty percent of Israel's society considers itself religious, and only a fraction of these are ultra-Orthodox. Though Israeli Jews call Israel a Jewish nation, it is not a theocracy. Jewish law, in Hebrew "Halacha," has jurisdiction over a limited but important segment of personal law including marriage, divorce, and conversion. Most other laws are derived from democratic processes.

The majority of Israelis seem to be content with the limited reach of religion in their country and appreciate the cultural aspects of Judaism that are indeed pervasive. As Sari's father Aryeh, describes it, "Our holidays are national holidays. When you go to the supermarket, even if you're totally secular and ignorant of Jewish practices, the bottom line is, you're still buying special food for Rosh Hashanah. The newscaster is still saying L'Shana Tova, happy new year. It's not like January first."

Yet many feel that Jewish youth in Israel are ignorant of this special environment. According to Aryeh, who is the principal of a private school for secular and religious students, the public secular schools (where eighty percent of the population studies) do not teach their students enough about Judaism. Aside from the ultra-Orthodox, Aryeh told me, there is little organized religion in Israel. If you are not strictly observant, you are unlikely to be part of a religious movement, such as the Reform and Conservative congregations to which so many American Jews belong.

Israel's head Ashkenazi rabbi, Yona Metzger, lamented the situation. "For some young people, to enter a synagogue is the same feeling as to enter a church." Metzger shook his head. "Both are strange to them."

For Omri, however, this was not the case.

"God is *everywhere*," he told me one evening in Tel Aviv. We were sitting at a café in the center of a mall, and I watched in amazement as he tried to demonstrate this conviction by pointing frantically at the objects around us: the table, my coffee mug, his backpack, even the scantily clothed mannequin in the nearby window display. I detected God in none of these objects—in fact, I was not convinced such a force existed. But Omri had reason to believe. In junior high, he collided with another boy in a running contest and cracked his skull. He recovered, but only after months of painful surgeries. It was a wonder to everyone that he ever got back on the basketball court. "And it was God," Omri said, "who saved my life. My mother and I thank God every day that I'm alive."

Omri not only thanks God for his personal survival but for that of the Jewish people. According to him, the devotion of the ultra-Orthodox is the only thing keeping his nation from complete destruction. In contrast, the "Reforms," as Omri called nonobservant Israelis, are responsible for the suffering of the Jewish people throughout history, from the Holocaust to the second intifada. I was startled to hear this and asked him how the Holocaust could possibly be considered a punishment for nonobservance.

"In Europe, in the late nineteenth century," Omri answered with scholarly know-how, "the people married Christians and became more European than Jewish." This was clearly unacceptable to Omri, and he said he tried to obey all the things God asked of him.

But even as he spoke these words, Omri was displaying a lack of religious commitment. For example, he was sitting with a female in a café—something unmarried ultra-Orthodox teens and young adults would not do. More than that, this fifteen-year-old talked a lot about "Bat Yam" girls, the young women of his neighborhood.

"Now here, you see." Omri directed my attention to a group of girls walking toward us. It was a weekday afternoon and we were scoping out the Bat Yam shopping center. They were perhaps fourteen, their stomachs rising up from their jeans like skinny, taut strings. "The jeans are low—*very* low," Omri said of exhibit A. "Boys like the front of these jeans. They call it *the short way*."

"What do you mean 'the short way'?" I asked skeptically.

"It's the short way to what the boys are looking for."

"Ahh! Omri!" I shrieked.

"This is the way we live." He shrugged and pointed out a popular clothing store called TNT. "I don't like this store," he said. "The clothes aren't nice. They advertise their pants with the song 'How Low Can You Go.' "

"It's good to know you have standards," I kidded him.

"I want to do the things God tells me," Omri said, "but I can't change my entire lifestyle."

To ultra-Orthodox Jews, this exposing style—in fact, the very act of looking at it—is entirely unacceptable. At the edge of *haredi* neighborhoods, signs in English and Hebrew warn outsiders to respect religious custom and dress modestly. One afternoon, Sari and I were walking down the street near her school when we saw two religious boys coming toward us. They couldn't have been more than seven years old and were dressed in identical black pants and white-collared shirts, their *pe'ot* (long curls that grow in front of the ears) brushing gently against their cheeks. They were such a cute pair and I must have been staring, because the moment we met, the boys shielded their eyes with their hands. It was a bit of a shock to realize that these children saw Sari and myself (in our T-shirts and pants) as a threat to their faith. I couldn't think what they would have done had we been dressed like the girls in Bat Yam.

There's a part of Sari that understands these boys. When I connected with her in Jerusalem after camp, she gave me a tour of her wardrobe. The closet was a burst of color and stuffed with baggy pants and T-shirts. She wears skirts only on Shabbat and the Jewish holidays, but she dresses modestly compared to a lot of Israeli teens. She said she used to expose her stomach as an act of rebellion against her mother, but today she's relinquished the midriff of her own free will.

"Girls use their bodies for people to like them," she told me, "but I don't dress for guys to think I'm hot. I dress to look nice for myself. I only came to this conclusion in the last year. Maybe my religion had some influence."

Sari is an eighth-generation Israeli. Her father's family has deep Hasidic roots, reaching back to Rabbi ben Eliezer Baal Shem Tov, the founder of the movement. Though Aryeh has not always been an observant Jew, he and his wife, Dina, are now raising their three daughters in an Orthodox home. They keep kosher, meaning they never mix milk products with meat and have separate dishes for each; they strictly observe Shabbat, meaning that from sundown on Friday to sundown on Saturday they do not use electricity, drive, write, or do anything that the Torah considers to be work. The family attends an Orthodox synagogue, or shul, where men and women are separated by a *mechitza*. These are just the basics. Judaism is heavily rooted in law—much more so than Christianity and even Islam—and each tradition and holiday has its own rules to follow. It takes a lot of work and knowledge to be a practicing Jew. Looking back, it was Risa's and my lack of commitment to Judaism that caused the Borough Park residents to be so skeptical of us—and our inability to understand their devotion that gave us a negative impression of them.

These strictures have created a backlash against ultra-Orthodoxy in Israel. The ultra-Orthodox tend to have large families and little income, because Orthodox Judaism requires men to spend their time studying the Torah. In order to support such a lifestyle, the Orthodox receive substantial government subsidies. They are also exempt from army service, because the young Israeli state wanted to honor the tradition of religious study. The law was meant to be symbolic, but as the religious community expands, secular Israel has grown increasingly hostile to these Jews who neither support themselves financially nor fight for their country. Finally, the Orthodox exercise their political influence to expand the jurisdiction of Halachic law. Many Israelis see this as a threat to democracy, and a new political party has formed in response. Shinui, in Hebrew "Change," runs on a secular platform. It is the third largest party in the Knesset.

Living in Israel, the tension between secular and religious society is palpable. I witnessed it one afternoon in a *sherut,* a shared taxi, traveling from Tel Aviv to Jerusalem. I watched in astonishment as the taxi driver convinced an elderly man and woman to give up their comfortable single seats for two young religious women. When I asked the old woman, who was now crammed into the back of the van with three other people, why she moved, she shouted in a particularly obnoxious voice, "Because those two girls wouldn't sit next to a *man!*" In truth, I knew exactly why the seat swap had taken place, and what's more, I could have saved the old woman the trouble by volunteering to leave my single seat. Yet instead of doing the helpful thing, I simply looked on as the elderly couple was forced to evacuate. Like the old woman, I did not want to accommodate another's religious preference.

By the end of the drive, everyone in the van was feeling angry, indignant, and in my case, guilty. Perhaps a similar result would have occurred in any society where people feel as strongly about their personal space as they do their convictions. But this wasn't a confrontation between Palestinians and Israelis; this was between Jews. Even more puzzling, it happened in the one country created to unify the Jewish people. While Israeli Jews are supposed to be free from persecution and anti-Semitism, at times Israel seems to be a fractured society in which small communities threaten one another.

Even Sari, who has a unique facility to move between religious and secular communities, has felt this. On one occasion a religious man spat at her for wearing pants. On AIDS awareness day, an Orthodox man told her that "whomever put this upon himself should suffer from it."

"Is this what God wants you to do?" she asked me, still angered by the incident. "To not respect people?" Sari said it reminded her of *To Kill a Mockingbird,* a book she'd read for school. "It's like Miss Maudie. She says that a Bible in one hand can be as bad as a beer in the other."

Yet young people who do not share Sari's understanding and appreciation for Judaism are guilty of their own disrespect. Omri told me a story about a group of teenagers in the southern resort city of Eilat who held a party in worship of a golden bull. In the Torah, while Moses is on Mount Sinai receiving the Ten Commandments, the People of Israel lose faith in him and begin to worship a bull-shaped idol. When Moses discovers this, he smashes the tablets out of rage. Granted, Eilat is a vacation paradise and hot spot for teenage revelry, but to Omri, the significance of this party was clear. "This bull is a big troublemaker in our religion," he said. "To dance around this bull . . . it's like not being a Jew."

At the same time, many Israeli teenagers see themselves as free thinkers and free agents. To them, Orthodoxy runs in opposition to this independence.

"I need my freedom," Sari told me. "I need to be able to go out with my friends without asking permission or to lock myself up in my room and be by myself."

I saw how indignant Sari became when her parents forced her to follow their religious strictures. Rosh Hashanah, the Jewish New Year, is the first of the High Holy Days. Unlike its solemn partner, Yom Kippur, the day of atonement, Rosh Hashanah is about rejoicing. Traditionally, Jews eat apples dipped in honey to symbolize a sweet new year and round challah bread with raisins to signify completeness of the world. Israelis also eat pomegranate seeds as a symbol of life. Jews who observe the holiday spend the morning in synagogue and then return home to eat lunch with family and friends, so Sari's family invited me to spend the holiday with them.

I walked to shul with Sari and her mom. Aryeh had gone much earlier. The synagogue was nothing like I'd expected. There was no grand building with a balcony for the women and Stars of David carved into the woodwork. Instead, it was a low-ceilinged room with an unswept floor, in a community center filled with folding chairs. The *mechitza,* which cut the room down the center, looked like a rickety fence.

Sari explained that this synagogue was part of a much larger congregation but didn't have the money for its own building. The shul was small enough for the women to see the Torah—traditionally on the men's side of the *mechitza.* I watched with delight as the rabbi unfurled the Torah. The man next to him whisked off both silver handle covers, his eyes sparkling with pride, as though he were presenting a glorious feast to the congregation. These men, as the others, were dressed in suits and wrapped in their talitot, wide prayer shawls with fringes hanging from the corners. They were all wearing yarmulkes, small, disklike prayer hats made of cloth.

The women wore skirts and matching tunic shirts or jackets. But the amazing thing about the women's side of the shul was their hats: these stout, squared objects, looking like dense cakes, on top of each head. Most were subdued colors of black, dark green, or tan, but they all had a gauze trim pinned up with a flower. I pictured myself in one, and decided if I ever wore such a hat, it would resemble one worn by a pregnant woman in the front row: bright crimson.

The young girls wore skirts. Sari explained that it was highly inappropriate for a woman to wear pants to shul. With a wistful expression, Sari whispered to me about the Reform synagogue near her home where anybody could go in jeans. Still, nearly all of the girls at the shul today had on clunky, thick-soled Mary Janes. I wished my mother could be here to witness this. How many fights we'd had over the years about appropriate synagogue footware! And here were all these girls at an Orthodox shul, and not a single pair of dress shoes on anyone under twenty. In fact, Sari's espadrilles were the sole exception to what my parents insisted on calling "clown shoes."

Simply being in this shul seemed to cause Sari discomfort. She continually shifted from foot to foot. Now and then she would whisper something to her mother and Dina would give her a stern look and shake her head. Sari barely followed the service. She didn't like to say the words out loud and found the language of the Torah complicated, but I could tell that her frustration ran deeper than this. As I looked around the room, fascinated by every detail, Sari stared ahead: disinterested, impatient, annoyed. Every now and then she looked at me apologetically, but I was soaking up this new experience, even enjoying the service. To hear Sari talk about her shul I would have expected hours of monotonous, mind-numbing Hebrew. In fact, this service was lively and full of song. The women sang with such vitality. Divided as the room was, the female voices must have carried well into the men's side of the *mechitza*. No one seemed bothered by this, everyone—except Sari—enraptured by the joyous occasion. The sound even made the hats seem lighter, as though they were capable of floating. My arms shivered as the music swept through the room. What finally brought me back into myself was Sari, who I saw make a final appeal to her mother. Suppressing a smile, she motioned that we were leaving.

At first Sari was reluctant to discuss religion with me, especially as it related to her father. She eventually told me that when she thinks of God, she thinks of her father, not because she sees her father as God, but because he is the main emblem of religion in her life. Aryeh is one of Sari's most important mentors. She wanted to share her religious skepticism with him but feared he wouldn't respect her choices. Except Aryeh knew how Sari felt about Judaism.

"Sari is lucky enough to grow up in an environment where she doesn't have to conform to one definition of what it means to be a Jew," he told me in the principal's office. "My belief is that one Jew can be Reform about some aspects, Conservative about others, and Orthodox about others. And usually all the movements and all the plurality are together in one individual. Is there part of me that would like my daughters to be more devout? Probably. But that's more the male omnipotent part of my personality.

Some crazy idea of controlling." In the end, Aryeh recognized that all his daughters are deeply spiritual people. To him, this is much more important than what he called "the details of orthodoxy." Sari may question religion, Aryeh concluded, "but when we're together on Shabbat there's a commonality of language and we can all sing together."

I saw this quite clearly after the Rosh Hashanah service. After lunch Sari and her father sang the Birkat Hamazon, the grace after the meal. I have always liked this prayer—the lively, flowing melody and the community feeling of everyone singing together. In Sari's home, the Birkat is reserved for her and her father. I knew immediately this was what Aryeh meant by the "commonality of language" between himself and his daughters: not because they were singing the same words, but because of the feeling they brought to the song. With the fading of each musical phrase, Sari's stoniness seemed to dissolve. Nothing of her silence in the synagogue hinted at this clear, confident voice—one that moved easily, like a child skipping down a familiar road. Aryeh chanted with closed eyes, his soft, rough sound never overpowering his daughter. At times, Aryeh paused to let Sari finish a phrase on her own. In giving her the song, I saw that he was giving her a gift—something precious she could at once have as her own and share with all of us. Father and daughter never looked at each other as they sang—their voices acknowledging each other was enough.

After the Birkat was over, I excused myself to the bathroom. I returned to find Sari wrapped in her father's enormous embrace, the two of them swaying gently. Aryeh tickled his daughter's ears. "Dad! Stop it!" she shrieked with embarrassment and daughterly love.

It wasn't only Sari's appearance but her politics that first persuaded me of her nonobservance. Most Orthodox Jews have conservative ideological views about the Israeli-Palestinian conflict. As Rabbi Yona Metzger explained to me, "The Jews' connection with the Holy Land comes from the traditions and the Bible. God gave us this Holy Land and it belongs to the Jewish nation from two thousand years ago, from Abraham until today." In geographical terms, Orthodox Jews believe the Holy Land includes modern-day Israel, the West Bank (which most religious Jews refer to by the biblical names of Judea and Samaria), and the Gaza Strip. Thus, to give up any of this land is to relinquish the Jews' God-given birthright. Of course, many non-Orthodox and nonobservant Israeli Jews also share this ideology. Sari told me that even her left-wing friends believe God gave them the Holy Land. When she asked them if they were religious or believed in the Torah, her friends said no. According to Sari, they still used the book to justify their claim on the land. It is comfortable for them to think this way, she told me. Convenient.

Sari refuses to adopt arguments of convenience. "I don't think saying that God gave me this land is a good enough reason to keep on fighting," she made clear. "And I don't like how much religion invades politics, because automatically a very religious person is right wing."

This is not just a stereotype; the majority of religious Jews vote for right-wing parties that support the settlements and oppose giving the Palestinians a state.

Of course, there are always exceptions—like Sari's family. Her father describes himself as politically "left of the left." "There are many people I mix with religiously," he told me. "We pray together, and have meals on Shabbat together. But we don't talk politics. Most of my religious crowd . . . we don't agree politically."

Aryeh supports Meimad, the single left-leaning religious party in the Knesset. Meimad is a Hebrew acronym for "Jewish State, Democratic State." Founded by Orthodox leaders in 1988, the movement was meant to combat groups who used the Torah to justify what Meimad leaders considered religious and political extremism. In 1999, Meimad joined the Knesset as part of Ehud Barak's Labor-led One Israel coalition. They entered the government on a platform of strengthening Jewish values and culture in Israel without trying to legislate religion into society.

Michael Melchior is an Orthodox rabbi and leading member of the Meimad party in the Knesset. He lives next door to Sari's family and is Aryeh's close friend. I went to see him, looking for the answer to one question: How could an Orthodox rabbi like Melchior have such vastly opposing political views to the majority of Israel's religious leaders?

"In Hebrew we have a phrase—we call people a scoundrel," Melchior said slowly, his voice scratchy like sandpaper. "It means you can follow the rules of the Torah, but you're still a bad human being. There is a measure of behavior toward other human beings and societies that is just as important a part of Judaism as following the rules."

According to Melchior, the importance of respecting the stranger— ethnic and religious minorities or even people with handicaps—stems from the Jews' enslavement in Egypt. "The motif of slavery and freedom," Melchior told me, "appears more than any other motif in Jewish tradition. We don't do *anything* that doesn't have to do with that."

I understood what the rabbi meant. The message "we shall overcome" is pervasive throughout the Torah and in Jewish tradition. American Jews' historical identification with slavery was a key motivation for their involvement in the civil rights movement. On the other hand, I had seen how Jews' exaggeration of their historical enslavement led to a dangerous self-victimization. Obsess over your oppression enough and it becomes easy to ignore others' suffering or even worse, becomes a justification for making others suffer. This was a tendency Israelis and Palestinians shared. I thought of all the times I had heard Palestinians say: Israel makes us suffer, so we can't blame Hamas for making them suffer.

"We were slaves and degraded in a land that was not ours," Melchior said of the biblical Jews, "and all this comes to teach us a moral lesson of how to treat the other. You should love the stranger because you've been a stranger in the land of Egypt. You know what it is to be a slave. And when you build your society in your land, this has to be a society that is built on the relationship with the other. . . . Therefore, I think that our [choice is] very clear: either you have a Jewish state [but you don't have] all the land, or you have a binational state that will never happen because it means a Muslim state. You can't have a Jewish state and then sit on a population that doesn't want you. Even if we had the military power to do it, I don't think it would be right."

"So you're saying that there are competing values in the Torah?" I asked.

"Everything is competing." The rabbi smiled wisely. "If there's just one value, if you can only do right and do good, then it's fine. But the problem always comes because in life there are competing values." Melchior gave the example of Hebron, located in the southern West Bank. The city has been a hotbed of Israeli-Palestinian tension for over a century, in large part because the Tomb of the Patriarchs, sacred to Muslims and Jews, is located there. In 1929, Arab rioters killed scores of Jews in the city and in 1994, a fanatical settler named Baruch Goldstein shot down twenty-nine worshipping Palestinians in the mosque near the Tomb. Since then, Palestinians have killed Israelis attempting to pray at the Tomb. "If I want a Jewish state, which I do," Melchior continued, "I have to realize that the Palestinians are living in Hebron and the Jews are not. There are 180,000 Palestinians and 400 Jews."

Melchior was alluding to one of the most serious problems facing Israel's identity as a Jewish, democratic nation: the population shift between Arabs and Jews. Currently, there are about 5.5 million Jews and 4 million Arabs (3 million Palestinians in the territories and just over a million Arab citizens of Israel) living in Israel and the occupied territories.

Some demographers believe that if the Palestinian birthrate continues to outnumber the much slower Jewish birthrate, by 2020 the Palestinian population will surpass the Jewish one. This might very well mean the end of a two-state solution and an equitable peace for Israelis and Palestinians. How will Israel be able to manage an unwilling population, as Melchior refers to the Palestinians in the territories, that is so much larger, and is already squeezed into such a tiny space? The Israeli military would have to use unthinkable means to control the Palestinians, made even more impoverished by such a population increase, as well as their own frustrated and angry Arab citizenry. Even prominent members of Israel's Knesset talked to me about the possibility of a South African scenario—an apartheid state—that would put an end to Israel as a democratic nation.

A binational state in which Arabs and Jews share power is another solution. This is a nonoption to Jewish Israelis, because an enfranchised Palestinian population would inevitably mean the end of a Jewish state. So what possibilities remain? Can Israel be both democratic and Jewish? As Melchior says, Israel must separate from the Palestinians, even if it means compromising on the value of Greater Israel. "I don't know any source in Judaism that puts the value of Greater Israel over the value of life," Melchior told me. "Those who are practicing that value are distorting what Judaism is about."

As I was to learn soon enough, the 250,000 Jews living in the West Bank and Gaza did not entirely agree.

THE
WEST BANK:
MOUNTAINS
OF GOD

Tekoa

Though my father spent twenty-five years at the State Department working in Arab-Israeli and Israeli-Palestinian affairs, he never once visited a settlement. This was no surprise to the residents of Tekoa, a community of three hundred families living just above the Judean desert. By their account, it wasn't only the peaceniks who'd been spurning them, it was also the United States.

Tekoa is part of Gush Etzion, a 43,000-person West Bank settlement bloc. Shani, who works for Gush Etzion's mayor, was quite indignant about this lack of attention.

"Why did Colin Powell agree to see Yossi Beilin?" she wanted to know. "Beilin is not an elected leader. But the leaders of Yesha [the settlers' governing council] are elected. Why not see them?"

Shani told me that the residents of Tekoa were still angry, because according to them, the American ambassador was eager to visit Palestinians who'd lost loved ones in the first intifada (the first Palestinian uprising, which occurred between 1987 and 1989) but not Israelis suffering in the same situation. Her community was tired of being prejudged. "Right away we're the oppressors." Shani shook her head. "The occupiers."

Oppressors and occupiers were my exact thoughts the morning I accompanied my father to Gush Etzion. He'd been out of the government for a year and a half and had accepted an invitation from Shaul Goldstein, Gush Etzion's mayor. I had never been to a settlement, but I held them in the lowest regard. It wasn't that I saw settlers as bearded, talitet-clad men packing Uzis on mountaintops. I knew the majority of them were neither religious fanatics nor violent people, but their ideology of Greater Israel appalled me. This was the idea that God gave the Jews full rights to settle and control the biblical lands of Judea and Samaria (what the settlers call the West Bank) and Gaza. Israel did not "occupy" these lands after the 1967 war, the settlers said, but "liberated" it from Arab hands.

"The Arabs don't have the basic right to this land that we have," Yael, a member of the pro-settlement Women in Green activist group, told me. "They all wandered in here over the last hundred years. So it's all a big lie—Palestine."

It is true that the notion of a distinct and unified Palestinian identity solidified only within the last hundred years, but I did not agree that Arabs lacked the Jews' basic right to the land. Both Arabs and Jews had biblical ties to historic Palestine, and Arabs had been living there throughout four hundred years of Ottoman rule. The majority of these were farmers (called *fellahin*) whose livelihood and identity centered around their villages. During this time, only a tiny percentage of Jews inhabited historic Palestine, but these numbers increased significantly in the mid-twentieth century with the allyot—waves of Jewish immigration.

The United Nations, the United States, and the international community have also upheld Palestinian Arab rights to land in Palestine—at least in theory. In June 1967, Israel's military captured the Golan Heights from Syria, Gaza, and the Sinai Peninsula from Egypt, and the West Bank (including East Jerusalem and the Old City) from Jordan. In May 1967, Soviet and Syrian intelligence erroneously reported that Israel was preparing a large-scale attack on Syria. Egyptian president, Gamal Abdel Nasser, requested that UN peacekeeping forces leave the Sinai Peninsula, where they had served as a buffer between Israel and Egypt since 1956. When the UN troops left, Nasser replaced them with Egyptian troops as a show of force. In the following days, Jordan and Iraq signed defense pacts with Egypt. On June 5, 1967, Israel launched a preemptive attack against Egypt, destroying its air force on the ground. Israel followed with similar attacks on Syria and Jordan. Within six days, Israel had captured the Sinai Peninsula from Egypt, the Golan Heights from Syria, and the West Bank (including the Old City) from Jordan. (Israel returned the Sinai Peninsula to Egypt in 1982 in exchange for peace.)

The war of 1967, known to Israelis as the Six Day War, was an astounding military triumph for the Jewish state. More than this, Israel now contolled all the land of its biblical heritage—all of Greater Israel. But with these lands came the 1.5 million Palestinians who lived there, and for whom Israel was now responsible. The war also created another 300,000 Palestinian refugees, most of whom fled to Jordan.

The UN Security Council responded to the war with Resolution 242. This resolution proclaimed the "inadmissibility of the acquisition of territory by war"; ordered Israel's "withdrawal from territories occupied in the recent conflict"; and called for "a just settlement of the refugee problem." The resolution also requested that a lasting peace in the region be worked out through negotiation. Historically, there has been intense debate over whether this resolution is binding (whether it constitutes international law), and if so, whether it requires Israel to return all the territory occupied in 1967 or simply a portion of it. In a practical sense, Israeli, Arab, and U.S. negotiators have always based their work on the premise that negotiation is the only way to settle issues of borders and land-return. The central issue, however, is that 242 strongly suggests Israel is *not* the *sole* rightful owner of the territories it conquered in 1967. Moreover, the Fourth Geneva Convention, which Israel ratified in 1951, precludes an occupying power from settling its own civilians in an area under its military control. By these standards, the Jewish settlements in the West Bank and Gaza violate international law.

According to Geoffrey Aronson of the Foundation for Middle East Peace, the importance of settling has always been part of Israel's "national enterprise." The ideology of establishing settlements to influence boundary creation stretched back to the first Zionist pioneers. "Without settlement," says Aronson, "there wouldn't have been a state of Israel." In fact, every Israeli government—Labor and Likud—has supported construction and expansion of settlements in the territories. This was true during the Oslo years, which saw three Labor prime ministers (Rabin, Peres, and Barak) and only one from Likud (Netanyahu). Between 1993 and 2000, the number of settlers in the West Bank and Gaza doubled. Still, settlement construction was relatively slow the first ten years after the 1967 war, in part because Israel's government was headed by the Labor party. Labor had controlled the Israeli parliament, the Knesset, since Israel was founded in 1948. They were a socialist-pioneering movement that cared deeply about the land but did not have an intense nationalist motivation for controlling the entirety of historic Palestine. In 1977, however, Labor was overthrown by the right-of-center Likud party. The new Likud prime minister was Menachem Begin, former leader of the Irgun, an organization of armed resistance and terror that fought the Arabs and British during the British Mandate. Like Labor, Likud was considered both secular and mainstream, but it was highly conservative on issues of "Greater Israel."

With his election, Begin launched a massive settlement project. When he assumed office, there were 24 settlements with 3,200 people. At his resignation six years later, the number had increased to 106 settlements with 28,400 people.

While Begin approached the biblical concept of Greater Israel from a secular-nationalist perspective, he was bolstered by the religious settlers' movement Gush Emunim, or Bloc of the Faithful. Founded in 1974, Gush Emunim had emerged from the National Religious party, the Knesset's largest religious party. Gush founded many of the settlements throughout the West Bank and Gaza with direct government aid. In fact, since 1967, Israel has expended at least NIS (New Israeli Shekel) 45 billion (about $11 billion) on settlements. Between 2002 and 2003 the Sharon government spent NIS 2.5 billion on nonmilitary outlays alone.★ In 2004, approximately 250,000 Jews lived in the occupied territories. About 7,500 of these are in Gaza, and the rest are in the West Bank.

Sharon's pledge in 2004 to remove all the settlers from Gaza, as well as small numbers of them from the West Bank, has repeatedly threatened the stability of his government and drawn the ire of the settler community. Some settlers are calling upon Israeli soldiers to resist their orders when they are sent out to evacuate the settlements. Other settlers have threatened to physically resist their own military. There has been great speculation and growing fear throughout Israel about the possible consequences of a settler shooting a soldier. It is unlikely the government will attempt to dismantle Tekoa or any of Gush Etzion's settlements, because of their proximity to Israel proper. Still, Tekoans made clear to me why they believe a Jewish presence in the West Bank and Gaza is so important. "If we weren't here," Yael said, "the Arabs would have taken control of all Judea and Samaria and it would be really threatening to the rest of Israel."

In a sense, the settlers see themselves as men and women on the front lines: brave soldiers prepared to take the first fire. And they are getting hit plenty. As Mayor Goldstein drove us in his armored jeep along the Jerusalem-Beersheba road, he related stories about people Arabs had shot and killed along this very highway. Gush Etzion had lost twenty-two people since this war began, he said. (I noted his usage of the word "war" instead of intifada.) One woman was still fighting for her life, and two high school boys from Tekoa were stoned to death in the wadi behind

★*Ha'aretz*, September 23, 2003.

their homes. Their faces were mangled so badly their parents could hardly recognize them.

These murders are sickening, no matter how legitimate the Palestinian grievance against the settlers may be. Still, as I took my first steps upon the ground of Gush Etzion, I felt uneasy, as though I was trespassing on land laden with booby traps. It wasn't fear; I didn't worry that the Arabs in the neighboring villages would suddenly charge the settlement, but I felt that I was somehow tempting violence. I was overwhelmed by the sense that it was not my right to be here.

Gush Etzion is located along the Highway of the Patriarchs, midway between Jerusalem and Hebron. It is the road upon which Abraham traveled to sacrifice his son, Isaac. Mayor Goldstein drove us along this road, stopping to point out Arab villages in the area and two-thousand-year old *mikvahs* (spiritual baths) built into the hills. He told us that the ancient baths were on Arab land, and that the Jewish territory was only meters away. According to the mayor, the proximity of Arab and Jewish communities proved how peacefully both communities lived together. He had even invited a friend of his, the sheikh of the Wadi Nis village, to meet us.

Goldstein bent down and picked a handful of purple grapes from a roadside bush near one of the two *mikvahs*. These grapes were once used to make wine for the temple in Jerusalem, he told us, and put the grapes in my palm. He explained that travelers may eat the Arabs' fruit, but local custom prevented strangers from taking extra with them. I bit into the sweet fruit, chewed, and spat out the bitter seeds. Before I'd eaten even two grapes, however, Mayor Goldstein turned back toward the jeep. I looked at the remaining grapes in dismay. Either I disobeyed the custom or wasted the food. I ate one more grape and put the rest on the ground. There were no Arabs to judge me, but I felt guilty nonetheless.

Mayor Goldstein drove us to Kfar Etzion, the historical center of the Etzion bloc. According to him, Kfar Etzion had pre-1967 origins. Jews had originally purchased the territory from Arab landowners in 1927, but harsh conditions drove the pioneers away. Two more attempts to establish a community there failed because of Arab opposition, despite the Jews' legal ownership of the land. The movie we watched at the Kfar Etzion historical center illustrated the Jews' final defense against their Arab adversaries in the 1948 war and their eventual massacre—240 people. The film ended with the children of Kfar Etzion (who were evacuated before the massacre) returning to the place of their parents' deaths after Israel captured the West Bank in 1967 and rebuilding the community. Afterward, the screen lifted to reveal the actual basement shelter where the 1948 defenders met their end. The audience was somberly invited to inspect the empty cement grave, now illuminated by glowing stage lights. My father and I walked slowly around the shrine in time to music that seemed plucked right out of *Schindler's List*.

Next we met with the sheikh of Wadi Nis. He and Mayor Goldstein greeted each other warmly, and we sat around a table in the mayor's office. A large window overlooked the West Bank hills. They reminded me of scalps, covered to the horizon in a hair of prickly, cropped plants. Soon the sheikh himself was explaining that Jews and Arabs could live together in peace. The communities were necessary partners, he said. He called the land one house for two brothers.

My father agreed that self-interest, and not a desire to be "friends," would ultimately force Israelis and Palestinians to reconcile. "But what do you mean by two brothers in one house?" he asked the sheikh. "Do you mean a binational state in which Arabs and Jews lived under one government? In that case, Israel would cease to be a Jewish country—something Jewish Israelis would never allow." The sheikh responded vaguely, seemingly unconcerned with this dilemma. We are all brothers, he reiterated. We can live in peace.

After the sheikh of Wadi Nis had left us, Mayor Goldstein asked my father: As a Jew, surely you believe this land is your birthright and morally belongs to you?

Instead of the definitive "no" I would gladly have offered, my father turned on his usual diplomatic charm. Two states for two peoples, etcetera, etcetera. All this watery evasion was getting on my nerves. My father did not believe the Torah was the word of God. He liked to point out how little evidence existed for most of what was written there. So why couldn't he say so? He was no longer obliged to the government.

Mayor Goldstein, however, was as blunt as possible: If he had no moral right to Hebron, then he had no right to Tel Aviv. And as far as he was concerned, the Jews owned both.

Our last stop was the wadi. The mayor eased his jeep down a steep dirt road into the belly of the hills. At the bottom were two picnic tables already set with plastic cutlery and plastic-wrapped salads. The area was a jungle of shrubs and trees, all in dusty shades of brown and green. The wadi walls rose high above us. The mayor had gathered a group of people to join us, among them, Shani and her fifteen-year-old daughter Yonit; a member of Women in Green whose son was killed in an IDF operation in Nablus; and Yonit's friend, a skinny, red-haired boy with a shy half-smile. The boy's older brother had been murdered in the Tekoa wadi.

Despite the informal surroundings, lunch was more like a lecture panel than a picnic. With the exception of Yonit's friend, who never said a word, each person shared his or her views about the situation. The Woman in Green told us of the all-women theater group she runs for friends and families of terror victims. She spoke in particular about the performance of *Joseph and the Amazing Technicolor Dreamcoat* that was about to premiere when the news of 9/11 broke. The women chose to go on anyway, she told us, as a sign of solidarity with the American terror victims.

Shani spoke eagerly of her desire to have kids from Tekoa attend Seeds of Peace.

"You must have their perspective," she told my father. "I keep saying that we all have to learn about each other in order to have peace. It's the only way." She told us how "touched" she was that my father had finally come "to see what the Jewish communities in Judea and Samaria are really about." She turned to me. "Jen, you have to come and spend Shabbat in Tekoa. It's really a wonderful experience. Very special."

I gave a halfhearted smile and turned my attention to lunch. Anything to take my mind off these settlers. As soon as the plastic wrap came off, the flies set in. So much for my appetite.

"The whole experience left a bad taste in my mouth," I told my father when we returned to Jerusalem. "Those people put on such a show. Everything was so contrived, so prefabricated. Just like those illegal homes they park out there."

My dad said how important it was for him to finally hear the settlers' perspective, but I wasn't buying any of it.

"Do you know how much faster this conflict would be resolved if they weren't there?" I said. "And how can they justify raising their children in such a dangerous environment? It's like they're asking to be attacked."

My father looked less than amused with my assessment.

"Shani seemed nice enough," I admitted. "But I could never get close to her or her community on a personal level. Not when I know how much those people's ideology is a part of who they are."

But even as I spoke these words, I suddenly realized what every Seeds of Peace kid feels when he or she decides to attend camp. It's the anxiety of accepting a person whose beliefs you utterly oppose. Eight years with Seeds had not been able to show me this, but apparently one afternoon at a settlement could.

With this newfound revelation, I had no choice but to return to Gush Etzion. Still, it took me nearly six months to seriously consider Shani's Shabbat offer. I kept inventing excuses. First was the realization that I'd be stuck in Tekoa for the entirety of Shabbat, because the community strictly observed the Sabbath (they didn't drive) and public transporation didn't run on Saturday. The second excuse was that getting to Tekoa required a bus. I'd promised my parents never to get within fifty yards of a bus, because they are a primary target for suicide bombers. From August to December, I hadn't taken a single one. The third excuse was that I had already been to Gush Etzion and met a number of settlers. What more could I possibly learn by going back?

In the end, journalistic responsibility got the better of me, and on the third Friday in January, I entered the Jerusalem bus station for the first time. My bags were searched at the entrance—far less thoroughly than I would have liked—and I was scanned. You don't need to worry about the Tekoa bus, Shani had assured me. It's armored. It's safe. I assumed this meant the bus went straight from the station to Tekoa. Once I boarded, I discovered it made stops throughout Jerusalem. I commented on this to Shani's daughter, who was with me.

"I basically know everyone on the bus," she assured me. "It's the same people every week."

Basically? I wanted to question her. Are you sure? I knew the bus would protect us against snipers, but it left us entirely vulnerable to suicide bombers. I had heard that a bomb did twice the damage to a fortified vehicle. The armor contained the explosion, thereby destroying everything and everyone within. Only after the bus left Jerusalem on a straight shot to Gush Etzion was I able to relax.

For three quarters of an hour the bus lumbered southward, the desert rippling past its armored windows, the dirty panes distorting sky and space. I felt the way a farsighted person might, that we were as bleary to the world as it was to us. Perhaps we, too, were no more than a ripple traveling toward an equally elusive destination: a desert Shangri-La.

Tekoa was nothing of the kind. There were no big gates, no fountains or flowers. Some of the communities over the Green Line (what Israelis and

Palestinians call the border between Israel and the West Bank) could be mistaken for Boca Raton, but this one felt campy, like a hikers' retreat or even the Seeds of Peace camp in Maine. The houses, all built of the same tan-gray concrete, reminded me of cabins, and they were connected not by roads but by sidewalk pathways. Other buildings included an elementary school, a pizza parlor, a newly completed swimming pool, and a number of synagogues. Still, walking from Shani's house to a friend's home for lunch felt exactly like a trip from my bunk to the dining hall.

At the same time, Tekoa is no temporary residence. From its physical landscape to the mind-set of its community, the place is deeply rooted. The colors are earthy: tan, fatigue green, brown. Despite attempts at landscaping, the scratchy bushes and flat-faced cacti look thorny and overgrown. I supposed that in such a harsh environment, everything, including the plants, does what is necessary to survive. Shani attempted to beautify the nettle arbor covering her front walk by hanging a variety of colored bottles from its branches, but these trinkets do not mask the arbor's toughness.

Though Shani says her "little house on the prairie" provides a wonderful quality of life that people couldn't get in Jerusalem, thriving here clearly requires a pioneer's will. Tekoa was converted from an army base in 1978. It was initially seven families living in six prefab buildings. Shani and her husband were the eighteenth family. They arrived from New York in 1981.

"I had mud outside," she remembered. "I had to walk to the other side of the community to make a phone call."

Now it was a Friday afternoon in the winter of 2004. Shani was divorced and a mother of five, four daughters and a son. Her house, which already boasts one addition, consists of four squat bedrooms (the sisters doubled up and Shani and her son each had their own), an upstairs study, a narrow kitchen, and a common space that doubles as family and dining room. This is where we now sat, Shani across from me, her New York accent filling the room.

She wore a red-and-black-checked housedress and red slippers. Her curly black hair was unkempt from a day of cooking. A whirlwind of teenage girls, screaming and singing, spun through the tiny house. Multiple radios competed for attention.

"When I moved to Tekoa, none of this was here." Shani waved at the homes outside her window, but she could have simply meant her own.

Today, Tekoa is a community of over three hundred families, a mix of secular and religious Jews from Israel, Great Britain, Australia, the United States, India, Argentina, and Uzbekistan, among others, and the community is modernizing. They recently built a swimming pool, and high-speed Internet became available in November 2003. But the infrastructure isn't good enough to evenly distribute water, and most people use kerosene to heat their ovens. Shani also pointed out that until recently, Tekoa's electricity came from the Arab-controlled plant in East Jerusalem.

"And every Friday night before Shabbat this place would have a weekly blackout," she said, shaking her head. "We had to use seventy-two-hour memorial candles." Shani looked relieved. "Finally we're hooked up to Jewish electricity."

Despite a new road that is supposed to reduce the trip to Jerusalem to eight minutes, I felt a real sense of isolation here, as though Tekoa was a tiny island surrounded by a sea of sand—and Arabs. Hooking up to "Jewish electricity" seemed to bring Tekoans just a little closer to the mainland, or from Tekoa's point of view, brought the mainland a little closer to them. As Mayor Goldstein said, Tekoa is as much a part of Israel as Tel Aviv.

"This is the heart of the Jewish people," Shani said passionately. "It's what we read in the Bible every week. This is where Jacob buried Rachel, where he took Isaac up to the binding. It's part of our heritage, so it's not just a pile of rocks to hand over for peace."

The kids in Tekoa are as protective of their land as their parents. They feel a connection to the environment that few teenagers do. "The people in the city don't really understand," one of Yonit's friends told me. "Every morning I see these beautiful hills and the sunrise."

This is the exact view out of Shani's window: hills that stretch into desert haze, sloping toward the Dead Sea. On a clear day you can even see it, Shani told me. Shani's daughter, Adina, hikes there with her friends. It's a ten-hour walk and they leave at midnight to avoid the heat. I myself remember hiking through this desert, at the age of sixteen, on a summer youth trip. It was thrilling to sleep on the desert floor beneath such vast and starry blackness, exciting to shake out my sneakers for scorpions each morning. One night, as part of a confidence-building exercise, I was blindfolded and left to sleep alone with nothing but a nectarine. I suppose I, too, felt a bit of the pioneering spirit.

That was 1996, also my first summer at Seeds of Peace. Eight years later, when I studied the hills from Shani's home, I immediately recalled the Hemingway story about a pregnant woman whose lover presses her to have an abortion. She sees the barren hills as a prophecy for her own womb, soon to be stripped of life. "We can have the whole world. . . . We can go everywhere," the man in the story says. "No, we can't," the woman tells him. "It isn't ours anymore."

When my parents lived in Israel in the seventies, they traveled freely throughout the country. Now my mother implores me on a daily basis not to go on any hikes. I cannot forget how angry she was when she called my cell phone one afternoon to find me climbing a goat path outside Ramallah. The fate of those Tekoa boys loomed large in her mind. Alternately, she feared a fanatical settler might mistake me for a Palestinian and shoot me.

The desert landscape is as precious to the people of Tekoa as the words of their Bible. To them, both are God's creations. And yet the most striking feature of Shani's view is man-made. It is Herod's hill, the enormous volcano-shaped mountain where the Roman king built his summer palace. Shani told me about an archaeologist who believes Herod himself is buried there. The man has dedicated his life to unearthing the tomb, she said, but after so many years, he's found nothing.

I saw this fruitless pursuit as a metaphor for the Tekoans themselves. As tough as this land is—as tough and settled as Tekoans feel *themselves* to be—there is something restless here. A feeling of uncertainty pervades.

"Every day Sharon changes his mind," Shani says. "Every time you hear the words 'dismantling the communities.' How are you going to do that? How many schools? How many people? How many baby carriages?"

"There's no room here for two countries." Shani's fifteen-year-old daughter speaks urgently, as though something is slipping through her fingers. Yonit wears a nose ring, loves to belt out Celine Dion, and fights with her mother about a bright green miniskirt she wants to wear to a rabbi's home on Shabbat. She *looks* like she'd be right at home in a big American city or even in Tel Aviv, but to her, these places are foreign. She calls New York a frivolous place and though Tel Aviv is only an hour away, Yonit equates it with Europe. Yonit relates to the early Zionist pioneers, not fashion models.

"I'm doing the same thing as [the pioneers] in Tekoa," she said. "I hate when people call me a settler. I feel like I'm being stereotyped. Like I'm an animal. And, I mean, this is my country. Why would I ever think of giving it away?"

Yonit acknowledged that the Arabs—she rarely uses the term "Palestinians"—"are allowed to live here and that they deserve rights." But these rights exclude anything that will jeopardize Israel's sanctity as a Jewish nation, like giving them the vote. If the Arabs aren't happy with this, she said, "they can go to Iraq, or Syria, or Lebanon, or Jordan." Omri had invoked similar terms about Israeli's Arab population.

Yonit knows that none of these countries are eager to receive the Palestinians, but she has little sympathy for them. She'd like to live peacefully with the Arabs, she says, but they've proven again and again that they are incapable of doing so. This belief runs throughout Tekoa, and it's understandable. Even though most settlers opposed the Oslo process and Camp David talks, they still felt a sense of betrayal when the second intifada erupted. Unlike Jews inside Israel proper, those living over the Green Line had frequent and often positive interactions with Palestinians.

"At times our neighbors would work in our gardens, drink our coffee," Shani reminisced. "We'd go to puppet shows together. My neighbor had incredible relations with them. Even as a Jew, Christmas in Bethlehem was beautiful. There was no fear." Then the violence erupted and as Shani said, "it *all* stopped."

Sari was trying to convince her best friend, Kayla, that Israelis and Palestinians could have positive interactions despite the intifada. Kayla also lives in Tekoa, just a few minutes' walk from Shani and Yonit. Both Kayla and Sari attend the Jerusalem school where Sari's father is principal. Sari first told me about Kayla at Seeds when I asked her if any of her close friends held vastly opposing political opinions.

"I have a lot of friends who live in the territories and who are really right wing," Sari said, "and they want all the Arabs to die. And I know where they are coming from. It's much easier to hate your enemy because then, when something [bad] happens, you can go, 'Oh those stupid Arabs.' Instead of hating yourself, you can hate them."

I asked Sari if her friends in the territories knew she was at Seeds.

"Actually there's one friend I talked to before I came—she's so amazing. She's the most gracious person you would ever see. And she's surrounded by Arabs. She hates Arabs. She told me, 'I totally support you going, but I hope you don't get hurt.' Actually, I felt that she would be able to come to Seeds of Peace, because even though she hates Arabs, she knows that it was a wall that she built because she can't deal with the situation any other way. If she came here, she would probably have a huge identity crisis."

I met Kayla for the first time in Jerusalem. She arrived at my apartment in a long black skirt and tattered gray sweatshirt. She was a womanly fifteen-year-old, with fair skin, blond hair, and blue eyes. Her mother was originally from Canada, her father from the States.

Kayla was twice my size, but she looked awfully intimidated standing on my doorstep. Her mother is very skeptical of Seeds of Peace, Sari had warned me. "She thinks you're pro-Palestinian." Originally, I wanted to minimize some of this tension by meeting Kayla on her own turf, but Sari's mother wouldn't let her visit Tekoa. Kayla, however, didn't think the trip was such a big deal.

"You're not afraid?" I asked.

"No," she giggled as though it was an inane question. Then, in a serious tone, she said it was her duty to make that trip between Tekoa and Jerusalem. If she didn't live in the West Bank and travel freely over the Green Line then, according to her, the Arabs would push all the Jews out of Israel.

"Kayla, how can you even start looking on a solution if you're not willing to give something to get something else?" Sari said from one end of my couch.

Kayla looked back across the cushions. "Because I don't think that to give something will change anything. Why can't they give to us? Why do we have to do everything?"

"What can they do?" Sari sounded exasperated. I suspected this wasn't the first time they'd had this argument.

"They can stop bombing us."

"And we can stop destroying their homes."

"If they'll stop," Kayla was matter-of-fact, "we won't go there."

"This was one of my huge conversations with Nida." Sari alluded to her Palestinian friend from camp. "Nida said the bombers were freedom fighters. And I said that they don't protect, they attack. But the Palestinians say that the bombers come in response to what the IDF does. And we say that the IDF is in response to the suicide bombers."

Kayla wasn't swayed. "But when the IDF leaves the cities, the suicide bombers still come again."

"I am pro-IDF and I am going to be in the army one day," Sari said. "I will be a soldier and proud of it. And there's a reason for everything that they do. Maybe they're looking for one person and they destroy a house. But there are other ways."

"But if they do it another way, soldiers will just be killed." Looking out for her own people was obviously Kayla's first priority. When it came to terror, she didn't want to take any chances. She certainly wasn't willing to consider different options for dealing with it.

"Look," Sari continued. "We do need to protect ourselves, but if a suicide bomber comes and does an explosion, then we don't need to invade Ramallah."

"Yes we do!"

"Why?"

" 'Cause—" Kayla started.

"That just creates more hatred and more—" Sari interrupted.

"But what do you want us to do? Just—" Kayla continued.

"But we don't have to go and kill people!"

"Yes we do! Because they'll kill us and we won't do anything?"

As the girls debated, I took photos of them sitting on opposite ends of my couch. It was like being at a tennis match or some other high-speed, high-intensity sport. After a while, my head spinning, I asked Kayla if she thought Israelis and Palestinians would ever reconcile.

"And," Sari insisted, "say the truth, okay?"

"I think maybe they're not listening," Kayla said slowly. "They're just doing what they want to do. Every day I see Arabs and I see the hatred in their eyes. And I see they want to kill me."

"Where do you see them?" Sari looked skeptical.

"On the road to school. Every morning."

"But Kayla," Sari pleaded, "do you see that they're also scared of you?"

"Not of me. Of the soldiers."

"Of course they're scared of you," Sari said. "When I went to Seeds of Peace, so many Arabs said how scared they were of sleeping in the same room as an Israeli. They're scared of us. Just like you're scared of them."

In the desert, in winter, Shabbat comes early. By 4:45 all preparations must be completed: dinner ready and waiting on the hot plate, the necessary lights switched on and all others shut, the office-size electric water heater full. It cannot be refilled, because the act of reheating water is considered work and therefore forbidden on Shabbat. Shani's girls put on their synagogue clothes in the dark. Their bathroom light, which remains on for the next twenty-four hours, made a weak rectangle around the door. They wore skirts, blouses, and thick-soled Mary Janes. One daughter put on platform boots that laced to her knees. We hurried into the dining room to light the candles, then walked to the synagogue.

By the time we arrived at shul, the wind was blowing the desert sand high enough to reach the windows flickering with Sabbath candles. It pushed the desert in, catching not only Tekoa but so many Palestinian homes in its fog. The darker and gloomier the sky grew, the more clearly I saw Israelis' and Palestinians' need for religion. How it must bring them a sense of stability and calm in the face of fear. In biblical times, it was fear of the elements. Today, fear of violence and political instability. And yet it angered me to think that religion—Arabs and Jews clinging to their own versions of God—kept this violence going.

In the synagogue, something caught my eye. We had risen to sing a prayer when I noticed a young woman in the row ahead of me, a few places to my right. Her lips were moving, soundless but desperate, as though she were trying to suck vital moisture from the desert air. Her fingers gripped an open prayer book, though she wasn't reading—her eyes were clenched like fists. Her body rocked furiously, as though she were trying to break through an invisible barrier. Now and then her eyes fluttered open, closing as quickly. For a moment, I wondered if she was having a seizure.

In awe and revulsion, I watched this girl pray. Her conspicuous, unabashed pain made me uncomfortable. Even more startling was the girl's youth—she was certainly not older than fifteen. By that age, I had a full-grown skepticism of religion and prayer and of this current prayer, called the Amida, in particular. You couldn't simply read the Amida; you had to *move* at the same time. I remember being taught to walk three steps forward, then three steps back, then rise up on my toes, and finally bow. Just practicing these motions bothered me. I couldn't bow to a God I didn't believe in, and it seemed awfully disrespectful to "fake it." In the end, I decided to stand still. Now, as I watched this girl bowing furiously before her God, I remembered what it was that eventually compelled me to move in prayer.

My junior year of college I visited my Egyptian friend Tamer, one of the original Seeds from the 1993 delegation. We met at camp in 1996 and had been close ever since. I happened to arrive in Cairo just as Ramadan was drawing to a close. Then it would be al-Eid, the festival following the monthlong fast.

The first morning of al-Eid I woke in the six a.m. darkness, slipped a sheetlike *hijab* over my hair and ears, and put on the only skirt I had with me, bought in a London market on my way to Cairo, and made of bright blue terrycloth. I remember stepping into the quiet street just as the sky was fading to white, and joining the silent procession toward the mosque. I could not recall how these events came to pass. Did Tamer suggest that I accompany him? Was it his parents' idea?

I knew that non-Jews often went to synagogues for bar mitzvah services and weddings, but attending mosque seemed different. I wouldn't be sitting and watching an event; I would be actively involved in the service, laying out the prayer rug and bowing my head to the ground. The physical acts of the Amida were a mere tremble compared to the sweeping motions of Muslim prayer.

"Isn't it sacrilegious for a Jew to pretend to pray to Allah?" I asked Tamer's father.

"No, of course not!" Nagy replied jovially. "They'll be honored."

Tamer agreed. "From their point of view, if you go to the mosque, you're more likely to be convinced in Islam."

But I wasn't going to be convinced. I was going for the experience. I still don't know how I got up the nerve do it. It was like a black kid suddenly deciding to sit at the white kids' lunch table, or vice versa. And I wasn't only crossing racial lines, but national and religious lines as well. I couldn't have put myself in a more uncomfortable situation, not to mention the fact that I'd be alone. Like Orthodox synagogues, mosques separate the women from the men.

Tamer and I arrived at the mosque, removed our shoes, and parted. He promised to wait for me after the service. I was hoping for a space near the wall, preferably close to the door. But the women's prayer room was crowded, and I ended up smack in the middle. I unrolled my prayer mat and snuck a glance around to see what the others were doing. Some were chatting, others putting their mats in place. A few women were sitting quietly, their heads bowed. It reminded me of yoga class, but I was unable to find any sense of calm. I had never felt so white. I had never been so obviously the stranger. I tucked my hands into the folds of the *hijab* and bent my head, hoping to hide. It was a vain effort. The mosque was small enough that everyone knew one another. I would have stuck out even if I was Arab. I tried to ignore the curious looks.

Finally, everyone was assembled and the service began. *"Allahu Akbar!"* the imam chanted. Hands moved to chests, and the Koran's first sura was recited—*in the name of Allah, the most gracious, the most merciful*—and again hands to ears, mine following just a second behind the others.

"Allahu Akbar!" Then, in complete unison, the women bent over, hands on knees. Three times the imam sang: *"Subhaana Rabbiy al-Azheem"*— *Praise my God, the greatest.* A few more motions and suddenly everyone was kneeling, each covered head pressed to her mat. I did the same. I realized I'd been holding my breath.

The mosque was so silent, I half expected to find the worshippers asleep on their tiny carpets. As I turned my head ever so slightly, I saw that the girl next to me was fully awake. Like the young woman in the Tekoa synagogue, she, too, was just a teenager. I watched her, fascinated by her lips mouthing her dedication to God. Though her body was calm, her face revealed an unmistakable intensity.

"Allahu Akbar!" There was a soft shifting of prayer clothes as the women rose to their knees. The girl next to me did the same. Her body was motionless. It seemed she'd gone to another place entirely.

"As-Salaam alayqum wa rahmat ullah. As-Salaam alayqum wa rahmat ullah"—*Peace and God's grace be upon you.* The imam's final words echoed through the mosque, but any peace I'd begun to feel during the service dissipated as the prayers ended and the room came to motion. My surroundings rushed back to me: I was still in the mosque, still a stranger. I folded my mat and hurried to the door, whispering my only prayer of the morning: that I wouldn't have to search too long for Tamer.

Despite the difference in Jewish and Muslim styles of prayer, I saw the same devotion in both the Tekoa synagogue and the Cairo mosque. Both girls expressed their commitment to God as clear as any other emotion. As I thought about myself in relation to these girls, I realized it was neither the language barrier, nor the difference in dress, nor our nationalities that separated us: It was belief. If the two of them were given the opportunity to meet and discuss their faiths, I suspected they would find an unmistakable connection—one that stretched all the way from the congested streets of Cairo to Tekoa's stark hilltops. My own journey to Tekoa led me to a person who shared this view.

Tekoa's head rabbi is a fantastical figure. He wears a long gray-white Gandalf beard and speaks in musically discordant questions like Yoda. But his opinions, perhaps more than his appearance, have convinced the people of Tekoa that Rabbi Menachem Froman is living in a fantasy world.

"I am one of the group who founded the settlers' movement, yes? One of the original ones." Menachem Froman stroked his beard. We were sitting in the dull light of his living room. The space was nearly empty, but the few items it contained—two bookshelves, a table piled with chairs, and tapestry-draped couches—were disheveled and dusty. Though Gush Emunim was officially founded in 1974, Froman exuded ancientness, as though he had been living here since the days of Abraham. His home was more like Yoda's secluded cave than that of a head rabbi.

Froman's long fingers made another trip down his beard. "I am a rabbi—I am not a politician, yes?"

Froman was a student of Rabbi Tzvi Yehuda Kook, Gush Emunim's spiritual leader. Rabbi Kook believed that the lands of Judea, Samaria, and Gaza are the Jews' God-given birthright, and that the Jewish people are obligated to settle this land in order to hasten the coming of the Messiah. Rabbi Froman follows in this tradition. He has been Tekoa's head rabbi for over twenty years, but he differs from his community in a serious way. He has spent years in dialogue with Palestinians, most notably with Hamas's spiritual leader the late Shiekh Ahmed Yassin and the late Yasir Arafat.

I read an interview with Froman after he met with Arafat in 2001. "Religious energy is like nuclear energy," Froman had said. "It can either destroy the world or build it."* And the fallout from Froman's outreach was clear. He was being ostracized from his community. Even Shani, Froman's neighbor and friend, would not actively help me to meet him. He was a good person, she insisted, but how could Tekoa's rabbi speak with Arafat when Arabs were killing Tekoans? Instead, Shani's daughters showed me the way to Froman's home my first afternoon in the settlement. Now I sat alone with the rabbi and his toddler grandson, who sat on the floor slurping spaghetti and tomato sauce, and Froman explained his position.

"I was sure if we want to settle in Judea and Samaria, we have to be the pioneers for peace," he began. "For more than any other Israeli, the settler has an essential interest for peace because we live nearest the Palestinians, yes?"

Froman told me about a dialogue project he once planned for Israeli and Palestinian teachers. The American ambassador was going to assist the project until he discovered Froman was in charge and backed out.

I asked why.

"Why?" The rabbi burst out, flailing his arms emphatically. His grandson looked up like a startled puppy and scrambled onto his grandfather's lap. "Two reasons," Froman said, tickling the boy. "Because Rabbi Froman is a

*Source: http://www.havurahshirhadash.org/issues7.html.

settler and second because Rabbi Froman is a supporter of Hamas. That is the brain of the computer."

In Froman's eyes, Americans are like robots who have been programmed to think and act a certain way. Our code is so simplistic that it cannot compute the contradiction of a settler who wants to have dialogue with Palestinians. All it registers is that settlers stand in the way of peace, and Hamas is a terrorist organization: best to stay away from both.

Froman clarified that he is no Hamas supporter. "They have murdered many of my friends," he said. "But you have to hear them in order to come to any settlement, to any solution." Shimon Peres even gave Froman special permission to speak with Sheikh Yassin during his imprisonment. Which he did, "for hours and hours."

Froman does not believe the core of the Israeli-Palestinian conflict is a political dispute over land. If it is, he says, "The settlements are an obstacle because the presence of the settlements [complicate whether this land] will be an Israeli state or a Palestinian state." If, however, the conflict is one of cultural and religious division—what Froman calls "the Western mind versus the Islamic mind"—then both peoples should be able to live peacefully so long as they understand each other. For Froman, this means being able to see the world as Palestinians do.

"America is trying to bring peace from the point of view of Oslo, of Camp David, and not from the point of view of al-Quds [Arabic for Jerusalem] or Palestinian Tekoa." In other words, says Froman, American and Israeli politicians have not been able to negotiate a solution with the Palestinians because they don't understand the Palestinian culture or mind-set. But the spiritual leaders in these societies might be able to connect in a way the politicians cannot.

"But what about your own community?" I asked. "Few people here seem to be open-minded in the way you are."

"Allahu Akbar!" Froman burst out, causing his grandson to giggle. The rabbi leveled his eyes at me. "Do you know how to translate this?"

I felt like a young Jedi about to fail an important test. "God is great?"

"God is *greater!*" Froman corrected. "Like in school. Great, greater, greatest. Akbar means Allah overcomes. That is the reason for the violence in the way they shout *Allahu Akbar.* He will win victory over all the problems. Of course, peace is a revolution. In order to come to peace, you have to revolt the way you think. So I said before. So the Americans [must] do. So the Israelis have to do. So the Palestinians have to do."

I still didn't understand. "So God is greater?"

"Allah, as you know, has ninety-nine names. The finest one is 'peace.' Also in Hebrew. You are not allowed to say 'Shalom' in a dirty place because it is the very name of God. *Allahu Akbar*"—the rabbi ran his frail fingers down the length of his beard—"means peace will win victory."

Other religious leaders advocate religious dialogue as a method of negotiation. Knesset member Rabbi Michael Melchior is one, as is Israel's chief rabbi Yona Metzger. Metzger believes that the religious leadership should work in conjunction with the diplomats. The day I visited him, the militant Lebanese group Hizbollah was exchanging the bodies of twelve Israeli soldiers for a number of men the Israelis had imprisoned. Months before, Metzger had gone to meet the president of Kazakhstan, who according to him "was the best friend of the leader of Iran." And Iran, Metzger explained, "is the father of Hizbollah." Rabbi Metzger said he was the first chief rabbi to visit a Muslim country.

"My language was to speak with the president of Kazakhstan as a believer to God. And he said to me: 'For the first time in my life I have heard such a conversation with language that went through my heart and not to my head.' "

"My efforts were not the only efforts," Metzger said. "But the push was important."

Many Israelis and Palestinians seem highly skeptical about such connections and their intended consequences. Tekoa's response to its own head rabbi illustrates this well enough. Reem's father called Froman's ideas "ridiculous." How can you ignore the issue of land, he wanted to know. Palestinians want their own state. And what Palestinian will agree to have settlements in that state? I had asked Froman the same question.

"You can be more creative," he said. "I have spent hours talking to Palestinian leaders. Some of them say, 'Why won't the Israelis be citizens of Israel but inside our state?' " Rabbi Froman raised his eyes at me. "Why not?"

Why not? I could imagine lots of reasons, most notably because I didn't think either settlers or the majority of Palestinians would agree to such a solution.

I left Rabbi Froman believing Israel has one option if it wants to remain a Jewish nation: two states for two peoples. And for Palestinians to have a viable, physically contiguous country, the vast majority of the settlers must leave. Going to Tekoa did not disturb my fundamental belief in this, but giving Tekoans a chance to explain themselves and honestly listening to their side of the conflict has begun to alter my view of settlements. I did not want to change—Tekoa's ideology runs in opposition to my strongest beliefs, but that's the risk I ran in entering the world of the "enemy." As Atticus Finch says in *To Kill a Mockingbird,* "You never really understand a person until you . . . climb into his skin and walk around in it."

Sure enough, this happened to me on a drive through the West Bank. A few weeks after my trip to Tekoa, I was going to visit some Palestinian friends. I watched the red settlement roofs rush by as the car rocked me into daydream. And I began to wonder: Which one of those houses would I choose for my own? It would be lovely to raise my children here, outside a crowded city, to give them a real sense of community and a love of the environment—the land.

This last thought snapped me out of my daze. Are you crazy? I reprimanded myself. *Think* about what you're thinking! For you this is blasphemy. But that wasn't all. A week later, I found myself on the road toward Nablus. Unlike the land of Gush Etzion, this part of the West Bank is rich and green. The hills rise steeply toward the skies and dive into the valleys like graceful, plunging birds. A scattered collage of Palestinian villages sit in hill basins below patterned settlement roofs. It reminded me of an illustration in one of the Palestinian textbooks with both an Arab village and a row of settlement houses. The caption makes no mention of the settlement. It is simply there, like a river or a tree.

So it seemed outside my car window. I saw no guns or checkpoints, no angry people. And suddenly, I lost all sense of why these people were fighting each other. It was as though I had spent weeks studying for an exam, and the moment I had it in front of me, my mind blanked. I struggled to recall the ideological disputes and historical grievances, to get back to reality. I could not. For one pristine moment, I felt that land-love that Israelis and Palestinians share and over which they clash. I understood that my initial reaction to Gush Etzion—that Jews had no right to be there—was fueled by my belief that settlers represented a moral injustice and so were not worthy of the same patience and understanding I so willingly gave to Palestinians.

Now, driving through the West Bank, I knew it was more complicated. On a pragmatic level, it isn't smart for negotiators to brush aside such a powerful, committed minority as the settlers. On a humanistic level, it simply isn't just to ignore their religious conviction. I do not mean those settlers who practice terror and violence, but the peaceful majority—

communities like Tekoa. They speak about the West Bank and Gaza the same way Palestinian refugees remember their homes within Israel. To look into their eyes, you wouldn't see a difference between them.

Would reconciliation come more easily if all the settlers suddenly disappeared? I have no doubt. The same is true for the refugees. Indeed, I believe that both peoples deserve sole ownership over historic Palestine. But in an imperfect world, deserving something in the theoretical sense does not grant you automatic license to it. Nowhere is this clearer than in the Israeli-Palestinian conflict; if Israelis and Palestinians hope to receive from each other, they must also learn how to give.

Ramallah

M y first trip to Ramallah after the second intifada began with a driving tour of the city. My guides were Nida, a fifteen-year-old Seeds of Peace graduate, and her father, Osama. Nida arrived with freshly cut bangs and a pair of FOX jeans—a fashionable and affordable Israeli brand that was as popular in this West Bank city as anywhere inside Israel. Osama was a strange hybrid, with a look that was part construction worker, part prep student. He arrived in a weathered work shirt and blue jeans. His burly skin was rough as though from labor and sun, but his shirt was neatly tucked, and he wore soft brown loafers.

Osama owns a restaurant in Ramallah called Angelos. He proudly proclaimed that it had Palestine's only wood-burning oven. More than that, the *Let's Go!* travel guide had given it the prestigious thumbs-up sign. Osama catered for Arafat during the Oslo years and was familiar with my father and his colleague, Dennis Ross. He remembered that Dennis went crazy over soda and that my father never ate anything. "I'm taking you to Angelos later," Osama told me. "I hope you're not like your dad."

Nida and Osama met me just past Qalandia checkpoint—the central crossing point into Ramallah. I had never met Osama before and tried to engage him further about his job and his family, but his attention was elsewhere.

"Look at what *they* have done." Osama pulled up to a pile of bombed-out, overturned cars dumped in a small lot off the road. "They were trying to assassinate people inside." "They" meant the Israelis.

I asked Osama specific questions about the debris, but he only seemed able to point to another pile of rubble, another car shell, in the heap. And then he pointed across the street.

"That's the Muqata," Nida said.

At first, all I could see of Arafat's headquarters was the thick wall surrounding it. Parts were painted white and scribbled over in black spray paint. Rusted barbed wire lined the top. In some places, it looked as though the rubble from buildings inside the compound had been pushed up against the wall, perhaps as a secondary fortification. Trash was scattered across the dirt shoulder between the wall and road. As we circled the perimeter, two flat-topped buildings with small windows became visible. That was all I could see.

"That's Arafat's home," Nida added.

"Where?" I was perplexed. I had been to Arafat's headquarters a year or so before the second intifada started, but none of this looked familiar. I had expected a mass of bombed-out buildings, not these ugly, unimpressive rooftops.

"Do you see the flag?" Nida pointed. It took me a moment to locate the narrow pole and limp flag hanging from it. "He's under there," she said, as though Arafat were perched directly beneath the spot. As though the flagpole stretched like a puppet string through the roof and into the chairman's head.

Indeed, Arafat had been stuck in the Muqata, his West Bank headquarters and home, since the spring of 2002. The intifada had been raging since 2000, with constant fighting between Israeli soldiers and Palestinian militants in the territories and bombings of Israeli restaurants and buses inside Israel proper. Then, on March 28, 2002, a member of the Al-Aqsa Marytrs' Brigades, the terror organization associated with Yasir Arafat's Fatah party, walked into a Passover seder and blew up over twenty people. The seder bombing was the culmination of one of Israel's bloodiest months since the second intifada began. That March, approximately one hundred Israelis lost their lives. The Palestinian death toll for March was twice as high (because fighting between Palestinians and the IDF in the territories was daily and more widespread than inside Israel), but as far as Israel was concerned, the "Passover massacre" was going to be the end of Palestinian terrorism. Within twenty-four hours, Israel had called up twenty thousand reserve soldiers, the largest number since Israel invaded Lebanon in 1982. On March 29, Prime Minister Ariel Sharon addressed the public with the following statement:

The Government has approved principles for extensive operational activity against Palestinian terrorism. As we speak, the IDF is already inside the Mukta'a in Ramallah. Israel will act to crush the Palestinian terrorist infrastructure, in all its parts and components, and will carry out comprehensive activity to achieve this goal. Arafat, who has established a coalition of terror against Israel, is an enemy and at this point, he will be isolated.*

This "extensive operational activity," code-named Operation Defensive Shield, was the largest military action that Israel had conducted in the Palestinian territories since it occupied the West Bank and Gaza in 1967. Though Hamas, by far the largest Palestinian resistance organization, operated out of Gaza, Israel saw Ramallah as the focal point of Palestinian terrorism. The city's proximity to Jerusalem (only twenty minutes north) caused many to believe it was the terrorists' gateway into Israel.

Ramallah is also the Palestinian Authority's West Bank headquarters. Most of the government offices and departments are there. The Muqata was one of Arafat's two compounds. The other was in Gaza. As Sharon's remarks suggested, many in the Israeli government believed Arafat was directly involved in terrorist activities against Israel, most notably with the Al-Aqsa Martyrs' Brigades. They believed he had been directing the second intifada from the start, and during Operation Defensive Shield the Israeli military claimed to have confiscated documents that proved as much. No matter that this man had once shaken hands with Yitzhak Rabin and won the Nobel Peace Prize. Sharon made it clear enough: Arafat was Israel's enemy.

Ramallah, which means Mountain of God in Arabic, was founded in the hills of central Palestine by Christian Arabs. Today it is predominantly Muslim with a sizable Christian community. Ramallah is the most cosmopolitan Palestinian city, due in part to its religious diversity. Women go out to cafés and smoke a water pipe called an *argileh,* and often do so with men—activities that are considered quite inappropriate in other Palestinian cities. There are also liquor stores in the city center, another taboo for most other cities, because Islam prohibits the consumption of alcohol. There are poor areas of the city as well as refugee camps, but Ramallah is

*Source: Israel Ministry of Foreign Affairs Website.

largely middle class. Its neighborhoods wind through the hills, cresting and falling like waves. These streets are quiet, but on weekdays, the city center bursts with life.

Ramallah is a much calmer place to live these days than it was during the first two years of the second intifada. My tour with Nida and Osama took me through the ancient Christian quarter, the more recently constructed neighborhoods, and concluded in the city center. I was shocked at how wide and clean the streets looked compared to what I remembered from my last visit. I hadn't been to the city since the winter of 2002, eight months before the intifada began. It was my first trip to a city considered "third world" and I imagined disorderly streets, with vendors stuffed onto sidewalks like bellies pressed into too-tight pants. This was exactly my first view of Ramallah. In 2003, though, the street stalls were relocated to a covered market across from the central al-Manara square, and the city center assumed a more orderly appearance. It was still crowded and not what I would call clean, but store windows had their items on neat display. In fact, you could buy everything from clothing to cosmetics and the sidewalks looked no different from those of East and even parts of West Jerusalem.

But what surprised me most was how normal—how alive—the city was. Aside from pockets of destruction around the Muqata, I saw neither bullet holes nor bomb debris. The downtown streets were filled with cars and pedestrians. Exhaust fumes mixed with smells of frying meat. Horns blared, kids chattered, and Arabic music blasted from the heavily corroded Mercedes-Benz taxicabs. It was strange to think that two years ago, at the height of Israel's incursion into the West Bank, the only people you'd find in downtown Ramallah were Israeli soldiers. As Osama drove me through the streets, there wasn't a soldier in sight. I knew that the IDF still made arrests in the city, and after one of these incidents I saw the remains of rocks that had shattered against their jeeps. But a few broken stones was nothing. From what I had heard and read about the IDF's Operation Defensive Shield, I expected the city to look like Sarajevo circa 1995. I was stunned to find the city in better shape in August 2003 than it had been during my previous visit. When I noted this to Palestinians, however, they looked at me as though I had spoken some grave offense: "What are you talking about? *Of course* our city is in shambles." At first I found this reaction strange. I wouldn't say that Ramallah was sparkling, but it certainly wasn't devastated. Shouldn't these people be proud of the efficiency and modernity with which they were reconstructing their city? Didn't this display their resolve? Later I came to understand why the Palestinians were so eager to show me their debris; perhaps without their physical scars, they worried the world would ignore their emotional ones.

Of course, the physical signs of resistance and war do remain. Many stores around Ramallah have closed—economic casualties of the intifada. According to the World Bank, sixty percent of the Palestinian population is living below the poverty line, compared with twenty-one percent before the uprising began. Real per capita income is down forty-one percent and domestic investment is ninety percent below what it was before 2000. In the West Bank, unemployment has risen from seventeen percent before the violence to forty percent. Two years after Operation Defensive Shield, some establishments were still undergoing repairs. The fast-food restaurant owned by Reem's aunt and uncle sits on the third floor of a minimall in the city center. It was completely destroyed by Israeli cannon fire.

"The Israelis parked their tanks inside the mall," Reem remembers. "They thought militants were hiding inside and destroyed every store. The soldiers came to Checkers, ate the food, and then destroyed the place."

Ramallah's most explicit sign of unrest are the political posters. You find them on every street, baring the faces of martyrs and militants, plastered in repeating rows like Warhol prints. The most common faces are Marwan Barghouti and Abu Ali Mustafa. The Israelis arrested Barghouti during Operation Defensive Shield for his involvement in the second intifada. He is serving five life sentences. His prisoner status has turned him into a symbol of resistance, as much an icon of Palestinian popular culture as movie stars in America. The poster shows a bearded Barghouti, raising his cuffed hands in the air, smiling triumphantly.

Abu Ali Mustafa was assassinated by the Israelis in 2001, a year after he assumed leadership of the Palestinian Front for the Liberation of Palestine. The PFLP, a Marxist-Leninist party with an anti-Zionist platform, has committed various acts of terrorism over the years, including numerous hijackings of Israeli and Western aircraft. Mustafa's poster shows a drawing of his head with a string of Arabic words spiraling around it like smoke: *"I'm still alive in the mind of the people."* The assassination took place a few blocks from Reem's home, and the site has become something of a landmark. When a friend of mine got lost trying to find the house, Reem told him to "go straight and turn right at the place Abu Ali Mustafa was killed."

Like the words of Abu Ali Mustafa, the ghost of conflict is still alive in the minds of all Ramallah's citizens. Once you become aware of the events that have transpired throughout the city, it is eerie to travel the streets and know that here were bombings, there an assassination, and over there a lynching. It feels the same way to walk by a bombing site in Jerusalem. A blown-up café may be entirely reconstructed, but an uneasy aura hangs about it, as though it remains fixed in the invisible fingers of catastrophe. The first time I walked past the site of the former Ramallah police department, I did not think of the two Israeli soldiers whose muti-lated bodies were thrown from a window into an enraged crowd. In fact, I did not know it was the police department; all that remined was a concrete lot. The first time I drove around al-Manara square I did not visualize the faces of suspected collaborators whose bodies were hung from the monu-ment. Then I learned that Palestinian militants had lynched men they sus-pected of helping the Israeli secret service. No matter how many times I drove around the square after that, I felt a queasiness in my stomach. For-tunately for me, I did not witness these events, so they exist only in my imagination. But many people in Ramallah remember—and when they pass by, relive.

One day after Reem finished school, we walked together through the city center, looking for lunch. It's impossible to walk around Ramallah with an empty stomach. Cafés and sweets' stores are plentiful. There are three ice cream shops within a minute's walk of one another, each selling the same Ramallah special: a vanilla, chocolate, banana, grapefruit, and pistachio combination, with gumlike elasticity. On street corners, kibbe (heavily fried meatballs) and falafel (deep-fried chickpea balls) sizzle in pots of oil. Electric spits roast conical hunks of lamb (called *shawarma*), and mango juice is as plentiful as Coke. This afternoon, Reem took me to her favorite *shawarma* café, a hole in the wall but the city's best.

The man behind the counter shaved the lamb meat into sliced pita bread and covered it with hummus, tahini, and pickles. We bought orange sodas and took our food up a narrow staircase to the café's stifling second floor. The ceiling was low, the lamb-scented air warm, and there were no windows. We squeezed into a table and I thought to myself how claustro-phobia and *shawarma* don't mix. Then it occurred to me that Reem is used to being uncomfortably holed up. Ramallah was under prolonged curfew in 2001 following the "bloody hands" incident at the Palestinian police department and during Operation Defensive Shield in the spring of 2002. During these periods, residents were confined to their homes for weeks, sometimes without working telephones, electricity, and water. When it rained people put out buckets. Because Reem lived so close to Arafat's compound, her family was subjected to an extended curfew even after the rest of the city was allowed out. Reem and her siblings were kept from school for weeks.

As we ate in the tiny enclave, I wondered how it would feel to be shut inside your home. The only similar experience I could think of was being caught in one of those huge northeast snowstorms in which the roads ice over and schools shut down. At first missing school is fun, but the endless hours and isolation quickly become burdensome, especially for a young person. Reem was kept away from her friends and her activities for long periods and ventured outside only infrequently. If a sixteen-year-old in the States stays out too late, she might be grounded. If a sixteen-year-old in Ramallah broke curfew, she could be caught by the Israeli authorities.

Reem and I finished our lunch and reentered the bright, busy streets. It was difficult to imagine this city deserted. I asked Reem to describe the scene when people were finally able to leave their homes.

"After the initial military operations ended," she said, "the curfew was opened for a few hours each week to allow people to go to the store. An announcement aired on local television and soldiers drove through the city shouting, 'We open the curfew!' So we dress, we go out, and we would come here," Reem said of the city center, exactly where we were now standing. "You see *everyone* you know. And everyone is saying, 'Hi. Hello! How are you?' "

"How did you feel when you saw all the buildings bombed and shot up?" I asked as we stood on the sidewalk.

Reem looked around, perhaps imagining herself standing in this spot two years ago. "It's a shock for the first time. I used to see it on TV, but I never imagined it would be like that. I would walk around and think, 'I used to sit here or go there.' Or I bought my clothes at that store and now it's gone. When they killed people in the Checkers' building, they didn't clean it out. We saw blood and bullet shells all over the place."

In fact, we had just walked by the Checkers' building, a small arcade that opened onto the street. The floors were dirty (though blood-free) and the shops nearly empty. Most people wouldn't leave their homes for the express purpose of going to this mall, but the Israeli army wanted to be there so badly, they rushed to get the very best parking space: the lobby.

Even when people were allowed out of their homes, they didn't feel safe on the streets. Soldiers continued to patrol the city. The citizens of Ramallah claim these soldiers were only there to show their force and intimidate an already battered population. The IDF claims they were there to keep the peace and prevent the militants from regrouping. Whatever the reason, Reem remembers the tanks. "They drove around just to scare us," she said with certainty. "They didn't need to be here. And when we passed by, they threw tear gas on me and Dima. And they were just laughing."

"Why did they throw the gas?" It was nearly impossible to imagine Reem and her seven-year-old sister in such a situation.

"We were the only people there," she said. "So there wasn't any reason."

Reem told me another story about her brother, Amir. One afternoon, when he didn't come home from school, the family began to worry. In fact, Amir had been walking home when an IDF jeep pulled up alongside him and two other men walking nearby. According to Amir, the soldiers stopped the jeep, jumped out, bound the men, and hit them with their clubs. They pointed a gun at Amir's head, handcuffed him, and put him in the jeep. A while later, they removed the handcuffs and threw him out of the jeep while it was still moving. He walked home terrified.

As I listened to this story, I wasn't sure I believed it. I didn't think Amir would lie, but I simply couldn't picture Israeli soldiers pointing a gun at an unarmed thirteen-year-old doing nothing more than walking down the street. I certainly could not imagine my Israeli friends in the army doing such a thing—it seemed as impossible, say, as imagining my Palestinian friends picking up a machine gun. I was also so used to hearing propaganda about the intifada from both sides that when a piece of information seemed strange or unbelievable to me, skepticism was my natural response. Before I could accept any story, I had to ask myself a series of questions about it: Could this story be exaggerated or fabricated in any way? Did the teller have a motive for relating his tale? What is the context in which I am hearing it? Though I knew I should believe Amir's account of this incident, I was aware his family knew I might publish the story. They knew I was a vehicle for sharing their suffering with the world.

I was absorbed in these thoughts when I realized that Reem's father was laughing. In fact, by the end of the story the whole family, including Amir, was trying to suppress their grins.

"To arrest a thirteen-year-old!" Muhsin burst out at the absurdity of the event. "Who arrests Amir? Who points a gun at such a boy?" But when he said this, he wasn't laughing anymore.

Reem and I had now passed through the city center. We walked by the Ramallah Friends' school, a private school founded by Quakers, the site of the old police department, and a dirt field with dilapidated goalposts.

"This used to be a soccer field," Reem said, "but it was turned into a parking lot for tanks." She spoke so casually, she might have been pointing out her friend's house or a store she liked.

"How can you say that like it's normal?" It was difficult to believe that Reem could be so detached from the injustice of her daily life. Sometimes I think about what I would do—how I would react—if my freedom and security were suddenly curtailed. If martial law were imposed in Chevy Chase, Maryland, how would I cope with such helplessness and indignity?

"It's not supposed to be normal," Reem said soberly, "but it is. Think of it. If I was always sad about this building or that building—but I can't be sad about it all my life. I can paint and write. I can do things to make it better. Maybe it's because I'm a bit optimistic."

I didn't think I would be even a bit optimistic if I were in Reem's shoes. I would want to lash out against whatever was suppressing me. I could not imagine myself committing suicide for the cause as some Palestinian youth did, but neither would I be eager to sit down and talk with my enemy. I know that Reem used to feel that way. Her older sister went to Seeds of Peace first, and it took quite a bit of convincing for her to get Reem to sign up. Which made me realize for the first time how remarkable Reem's belief in Israeli-Palestinian dialogue was.

Reem took me to one final destination: the Muqata. She thought we could walk around inside the gates, since she'd done so before. When we got there, three or four Palestinian police stood at the entrance, leaning against the walls, looking extremely bored. Their rifles hung limply from their shoulders. *This* was Arafat's security? I scrutinized the men. If an opposition group decided to storm the place, these guys couldn't do a thing about it. Reem spoke quickly to a guard with a flat-looking face and a green beret. A moment later the metal gate slid open before us. And there was the Muqata, an enormous concrete expanse, like a desert of stone. Perhaps fifty yards away were the tan-colored buildings I'd seen from Osama's car. Above one was the same Palestinian flag, looking even less lively than it had appeared before. Next to Arafat's home and office were the crumbling remains of some other concrete structures. Reem told me the space used to be full of buildings but was paved over after Israel's incursion.

The sun was just beginning to set and our shadows stretched long and dark across the asphalt. The guard with the flat face stood by and watched me take photos. I snapped one of him and his gun and one of Reem, smiling in the sunset. The moment was oddly fantastical, with the sun pulsing its colors across the sky, orange and pink filling the atmosphere. I had experienced such a scene before on the massive movie screen on which I saw the rerelease of *Star Wars*. I looked over at Reem, who seemed content, floating in her own distinct orbit. I, on the other hand, felt disquieted in the center of such vastness, as though without something to root me down, I would drift into oblivion.

Because of her home's proximity to the Muqata, Reem heard and felt the IDF assaults on the compond. As she put it, "Everything that happened to the Muqata happened to me." After the curfew on the Muqata neighborhood was lifted in May 2002, Reem and her sister, Raya, decided they wanted to see the results of what they had heard throughout the incursion. They went to the compound with a camcorder to document the experience. Reem and I watched the footage on the video camera's small screen, huddled together on her bed. Next to us was a tray of lemonade and beef jerky that Reem had brought for an afternoon snack. Beef jerky was the last food I expected to find in Ramallah, but I figured it was a useful item to have around during a curfew.

Reem and her sister weren't the only people curious about the Muqata's remains. According to her, teenagers went there to play soccer, and families brought their cameras and their kids. Just like a day at the park, I thought cynically. Most Palestinians had never been inside the presidential compound, but now that they could see it, there wasn't a lot to look at. Reem and Raya somehow convinced the guards that they were journalists and so were given a private tour of the inner rooms. It was lucky they brought the camera. What they filmed no longer exists, because the Israelis renewed their assault on the Muqata the following September, destroying the location of their footage.

"The inside was so disgusting," Reem remembered. "The smell—everything. We filmed this blood on the ground, and this door full of bullets." The picture was shaky as the girls proceeded through the blasted rooms, and the camera swept over a red stain on the carpet. "There was leftover food. The bathrooms were totally ruined." Reem explained that after the bombings, the Israelis moved in to guard the place. "During the curfew, the soldiers get bored. So they eat. They pee on the walls for fun. And do you see what's here?" The screen displayed a giant hole in the wall of an otherwise intact room. "They smash holes in the wall simply to get from room to room." The camera panned away from the hole. On the other walls were drawings of smiley faces and puppy dogs. There was a particularly intricate illustration of a man on a horse. On another wall, the camera zoomed in on two Hebrew words: "Israel Rules."

This looked more like the work of frat kids than a professional army. Then again, who were these soldiers? They were eighteen-, nineteen-, and twenty-year-olds who, instead of going to the beach for summer vacation, were forced to spend two months housesitting—and it was the worst house on the block. I don't want to excuse the behavior of these soldiers, though I know many Israelis the same age who would never act so irresponsibly. Still, the message smeared in piss and paint across the Muqata walls was clear enough. These young men belonged at university, not in uniform. And Reem should be shooting a film of her own invention, not documenting destruction. Reem switched off the camera, and I wondered: How do so many young people end up in places they don't belong?

ARMIES AND
INTIFADAS

Soldiers and Seeds

I remember when I first learned about the Israel Defense Forces. I was sitting in the dark with my fellow nine-year-olds while our Hebrew school teacher projected slides of Israeli soldiers onto the wall. Some of the pictures showed young men standing at attention before their commanders. Others displayed uniformed women and men waiting alongside desert highways hitchhiking. The photos were pale and grainy, the faces a featureless blend.

"That's how many soldiers get to the army base," my teacher said. "It's an honor to pick up a soldier."

I was awed by this fact. According to my mother, hitchhiking was one of the world's foremost dangers, as bad as riding a motorcycle, hanging out at the bus station, or crossing any street with a double yellow line. Even more surprising was learning that every eighteen-year-old Israeli had to join the military after high school graduation.

"What about college? What if you don't *want* to go into the army?" I asked nervously as though I, too, were destined for such a fate.

"But they *do* want to go," my teacher explained. "In Israel, army service is an honor—a right of passage. Israelis are proud to defend their country."

It took me a long time to get accustomed to this idea, not because I was a pacifist, but because I couldn't comprehend such a severe restriction of personal choice. This wasn't a draft for special circumstances; this was general conscription. I later learned that certain segments of Israeli society were, in fact, exempt from military service, including most of Israel's Arab population, the ultra-Orthodox, and people the army classified as "universal" pacifists. Many Israelis looked disdainfully upon these communities for shirking their national responsibilities. My Hebrew school teacher was right. Most Israelis are proud to give up a few years for military service, and they do so enthusiastically.

The Israel Defense Forces was born out of the Haganah, originally a popular military organization designed to protect the Jewish community, the Yishuv, in Palestine during the British Mandate. In the eyes of the British, the Haganah was an illegal and subversive entity. In the eyes of the Yishuv and its leadership, the Haganah was a legitimate armed force. From their perspective, no one else was going to defend the Jewish community against the British, who prohibited Jewish immigration and settlement expansion in the late 1930s, and the Arabs, who were constantly threatening the Jewish settlements.

The Haganah represented more to the Yishuv than a military body. The tenets of the organization stated that "its flag is the national flag—blue and white. Its anthem is the national anthem, Hatikva . . . [and] the function of the Haganah is to defend the Zionist enterprise and the political rights of the Jewish people in the Land of Israel."

To the Jews in Palestine and many around the world, the goal of the "Zionist enterprise" was to form an independent Jewish state in the land God promised them. Thus, the Haganah was a force for Jewish national and political sovereignty. After World War Two, the Haganah began to engage in anti-British operations in order to achieve this goal of national independence. These included liberating interned immigrants within Palestine and conducting massive operations to bring illegal Jewish immigrants from Europe and North Africa into the country. The more militant Zionist factions like Etzel (the National Military Organization) and Lekhi (the Jewish Freedom Fighters) employed tactics of terror and intimidation such as the infamous bombing of British military headquarters in the King David Hotel in 1946. The Haganah, however, practiced *havlaga*, Hebrew for "restraint." They saw themselves as a defensive rather than offensive force, and this policy won them mainstream support in Palestine's Jewish community. After Israel was established, Israel's first prime minister, David Ben-Gurion, was forced to militarily suppress Etzel and Lekhi when they refused to disband.

With the end of the British Mandate on May 14, 1948, the Haganah evolved into the Israel Defense Forces. Its first battle as a national army was against the Syrian, Jordanian, Lebanese, Egyptian, and Iraqi armies that attacked Israel. Even though Israel's army was far smaller than the Arab forces it confronted, it had mobilized combat units, the ability to procure arms, and well-structured intelligence and medical services. The combination of these abilities and the lack of organization of five disparate Arab armies secured the IDF's 1948 military triumph and cemented its existence. Half a century later, Israel boasts one of the strongest, most capable armies in the world. This is due not only to the IDF's military capabilities but to the army's cultural significance and the central role it plays in the life of almost every Jewish Israeli.

During Oslo, attitudes toward the army shifted somewhat. Peace accords with Egypt and Jordan, Israel's nuclear weapons, and its special relationship with the United States make a real threat from the Arab world unlikely. The 1990s came and went without a major Arab-Israeli confrontation—the first decade in the modern history of the conflict to do so—allowing Israeli youth to adopt a greater sense of individualism than their parents and grandparents had as teenagers. Older generations of Israelis have told me about the atmosphere of national unity they experienced growing up, in large part due to an underlying but constant feeling of insecurity and threat. During Oslo, young Israelis across the political spectrum seemed more at ease criticizing the policies of their government and even those of the army. There was and is a growing tolerance for conscientious objectors. But the conflagration that erupted in 2000 has weakened this sense of independence, especially for youth. They now understand what their parents and grandparents always have: Israel's conflict with the Palestinians is existential. Israel cannot afford to lose. For your country to defeat terror, you must be a team player. More than that, you better show up early to practice.

The schools understand this and have a nationwide pre-army education program to prepare students for the transition from civilian to military life. Physical education is mandatory for eleventh- and twelfth-graders; school counselors discuss the challenges, benefits, and significance of national service; and the army's educational branch sends soldiers into schools to speak with students and answer their questions. Eleventh-graders take field trips to army bases, and some classes even stay the week for a taste of basic training.

On the personal side, it's common for high school juniors and seniors who want to join combat units to put themselves on a rigorous training schedule. If a kid can afford it, he might even hire a personal trainer to prepare him for the army's physical exam. There are also nonathletic ways to prepare. My friend Yoyo cut off all contacts with Seeds of Peace over a year before his enlistment to ensure his communications with Arabs would not hinder his chances of entering the prestigious intelligence division. Yoyo knew that intelligence officers are forbidden from traveling to certain Arab and Muslim countries for ten years after they leave the armed forces, so he decided that putting a buffer between himself and his Arab friends *before* his service was also a good idea. He told me it was a difficult but necessary decision; in his eyes, national security came before Seeds of Peace.

The majority of Israelis join the IDF at eighteen, the fall after their high school graduation, though it is possible to postpone enlistment to do a year of national community service such as working in disadvantaged neighborhoods or hospitals. Students begin the conscription process at the start of their senior year when the army calls them to the nearest recruitment centers for aptitude exams, physicals, and personal interviews. The army uses this data to determine which roles best suit each individual. Students receive a list of these positions and rank them in terms of preference, but the army makes it clear: Their needs come first and conscriptees' first choices may not be honored. For example, men who receive a high enough physical score almost always go into combat. Only if a man has outstanding skills with computers or languages, or is not physically fit, will he be exempted from combat.

Conscriptees who are given a noncombat profile usually have greater choice in their placement. Many of the noncombat positions are civilian in nature, including administration, IDF radio, and teaching Hebrew to Israeli immigrants. Only in 1996 did Israel's Supreme Court declare that women had the right to serve in combat units upon request, as long as they met the physical profile and agreed to the same three-year service (most women serve for two) and reserve duties as men.

There are many highly respected noncombat roles in the IDF, but a certain honor is bestowed upon those in combat units; a mystique surrounds them. "Our elites are recruited from the ranks of former generals," says Eyal Ben-Ari, professor of sociology and anthropology at Hebrew University. "The prime ministers, ministers, top civil servants, school principals, and businessmen. If you've been where the action is, withstood pressure, and seen danger, you're more legitimate to society."

Omri, for example, wants nothing more than to be a fighter in the Israel Defense Forces, what he calls a "warrior." His mother isn't so keen on the idea.

"Not every soldier can serve in Ramallah and in Gaza," Sima reminded her son one afternoon in their Bat Yam apartment, "but there are very qualified, very intelligent people who do computers," she continued. "I served my army in Tel Aviv at the base where the big colonel of Israel, where [Shaul] Mofaz [the Israeli Minister of Defense] sits."

Sima and I were sitting on the couch, but Omri was pacing from one wall to the next. In that tiny apartment, he reminded me of a trapped and nervous animal.

"You know why Mofaz sits there?" Omri asked indignantly. "Because he's afraid something will happen to him. It's not very dangerous there." To Omri, military danger was a clear mark of pride.

Sima defended herself. "I used to come every day to my home, but I used to deal every day with very classified things."

"Look, it's okay to work in these places." Omri lingered for a moment in one corner. "Some people can't go to combat physically. Like they're not strong or healthy. That's okay, but—"

"That's not what I'm saying," Sima interrupted.

"But there are those guys who have a profile of ninety-seven!" Omri was on the move again.

He was referring to the score every IDF recruit receives after a series of mental and physical exams. Ninety-seven was the highest physical score given to males, and it meant a ninety-nine percent chance of being placed in a combat unit.

"It's very dangerous to serve in these places," Sima said to me, ignoring her son.

Omri shouted over her. "But someone has to do it!"

Sima pressed her own concerns. "Sending your son! Every . . . day . . . to . . . war. Soldiers are killed there."

"But if we didn't have those soldiers—" Omri was exasperated. "They're the ones who are watching you. Watching my people. It's a really hard job, but it's something I really want to do."

"I'm not saying don't go to the army." She faced him.

"But that's not what I'm talking about. I'm talking about the *real acts.*"

Sima shook her head. "The real acts? That's three years. You know?" Omri understood. Combat meant three years with no exceptions. "You know I need my mother's permission to go into combat." Omri stopped in front of me. " 'Cause I'm her only."

"He's my only son." Sima looked into his eyes. "I have to sign."

Because mandatory service means that the life of every Jewish child in Israel is potentially at risk, mothers with only one child are given the option to keep their sons out of combat.

"Have you made up your mind that you won't sign?" I asked Sima.

"We have another three years to deal with it." Omri flopped down on the couch.

"It's very complicated." Sima was still gazing at her son, who looked quite the teenager sprawled out in front of the television. "I want the army to use Omri's head," Sima said firmly. "Not Omri's body."

"No, mama, you're talking about how you want the army to use me. You didn't talk about how *I* want the army to use me. That's what *I'm* talking about."

"Omri, why is it so important for you to go into combat?" I asked him.

"Someone has to do the job," he said, staring at the blank television as though absorbed in a program only he could see. "Someone has to defend the country in a way that not everyone wants to. I want to do it. I want to go into combat. I want to be a warrior. I want to be something that will live—"

Sima interrupted him again. "You can live doing the computer." Then to me, "He can't be torn from the computer."

"If I had another brother I could go to the army without asking her. It's funny. So, one of your sons got killed in the army, so you have an extra. This is how they treat it."

Of course I understood Sima's concerns. She loved her son more than anything. Though Omri had a father and Sima had a boyfriend, the two were bonded as though they were alone in the world. I knew how difficult it would be for Omri's mother to let him go into combat, though I didn't see how she could deny him his dream of being a warrior. But Omri wasn't a warrior yet, and I couldn't help but think that he'd called her "mama": the word of a small child, not a combat soldier. It was both strange and fitting coming from Omri. Here was the toughest kid you've ever met and a superior athlete. But there was also something delicate about him, inside and out, though he didn't like to show it. I didn't doubt Omri's drive, but could I see in this fifteen-year-old the physical prowess, emotional control, and what Professor Ben-Ari called "the cynical attitude toward life" that historically characterized the Israeli warrior?

More than this, I questioned whether such a man even existed in the real world. Perhaps he was a figure of myth—an Israeli cowboy defending the wilds of Zion. I decided my own peers—those who had actually been through the army—would be better able to answer this question, so I turned to Uri. Uri and I attended Seeds of Peace together but had not been friends. I remember him as a tall, dorky kid with pimples and stringy hair. It was his sarcasm, however, that aggravated me. I assumed he was intimidating me for fun. Fifteen-year-old Uri may not have had the Israeli combat body when I knew him at camp, but he certainly had the attitude. When I unexpectedly ran into him at the Seeds of Peace Center one day in the fall of 2003, there was little trace of the awkward, annoying teen. I had one of those breathless moments when he walked in: Who is *he?* If I'd been wearing sunglasses, I would have lowered them very slowly. He looked familiar, but I couldn't place those pristine blue eyes, impeccable face, and lithe body. He introduced himself and I realized Uri had been transformed in the years since I'd last seen him. The change was in more than his physique. In minutes we had established a connection that we'd never had at camp. We started hanging out in Tel Aviv, where Uri was currently living with his family, and I thought about the strange reversal that had taken place since his teenage days. His humor retained a sarcastic tinge, but he was thoughtful and surprisingly kind. Four years of army service not only gained Uri a body, it seemed to have lost him an attitude, too.

"They put me in army radio," Uri told me one afternoon outside his home, twirling an unlit cigarette between his fingers as he spoke. He had wanted combat, he said, but a medical problem prevented it. He was clearly still angry about this.

"I was thinking, what the hell will happen if, God forbid, one of my friends was injured or killed, and I'll be broadcasting the radio?"

Uri told me that his father had been a combat soldier, as had members of his youth group, and alumni from his high school. Some of them died in battle in Lebanon. That's where he wanted to go when he enlisted in 1998. Israel had invaded Lebanon in 1982 in order to root out Yasir Arafat and the PLO, who were using the country as their operating base. It wasn't exactly a "hot" border in 1998, but there were continued skirmishes in Lebanon between the IDF and Hizbollah, the militant Shiite organization fighting Israel's presence in southern Lebanon and shelling Israeli towns over the border.

Uri never made it to Lebanon, but after petitioning the army, he was granted entry into a combat division. He became a tank gunner, as he describes it: "The one who aims and shoots, pulls the trigger."

"So you were a good shot?"

"Ya." Uri shrugged, smiling, perhaps imagining himself dressed in spurs and pistols. "I guess I was."

After two months of boot camp, the army put him on a simulator to test his gunning skills. He scored so well that the army sent him to commanders' school. I asked Uri what it took to be a commander.

"Being professional, more responsible, with more common sense."

"More common sense?"

"As a soldier who has no one else to take care of, you become very small-headed, as we say in the army. You think about nothing but yourself. For example, as a gunner, you can shoot other tanks in a range of thousands of kilometers, but you can be plain stupid. You don't have to answer questions of your solders if you're not a commander."

"What do they ask you?"

"The soldiers? Oh, they're like little kids. They want to eat, they want to sleep. They're only eighteen-year-olds. They want to go home to their mothers and girlfriends."

"How old were you when you became a commander?"

"Nineteen."

"Your soldiers were only eighteen, but you were only nineteen!" This fact reminded me of a book I had read—a science fiction novel called *Ender's Game* that was disturbingly similar to the experiences Uri was describing. In *Ender's Game,* the army is composed entirely of children. Through his mastery of a gunship simulator (similar to the one on which Uri was tested) the protagonist, Ender, becomes the commander of an elite unit. His "men" are between the ages of eight and ten. Ender himself is six. In the novel, the burden of saving the world quite literally falls upon the shoulders of these kids.

Uri and his fellow soldiers are not considered child-soldiers, but he clearly understood the gravity of having this tremendous responsibility at such a young age.

"My soldiers were only four months younger than me in *army* terms," Uri said soberly. "I mean, some of them were born before I was. And what was I supposed to do? I just went through this course and now I'm supposed to teach them how to act? I didn't have the slightest idea what I was teaching them. I mean, maybe I had great grades in my commander's course, but I lacked experience. Now when I think about it, I lacked some maturity."

I asked for an example.

"For instance, our tank broke down."

"Where were you?"

"Ahh . . ." He sighed like a middle-aged Jewish woman kibitzing with her friends. "In a field somewhere, not so far from the base, but surrounded by sand."

I pictured Uri stranded with his tank, a dust devil rolling by an animal skull long decayed in the dunes, perhaps that forlorn whistle you hear in Westerns. It was a comical image, but I wondered if Uri had felt truly afraid. Did he panic?

"And of course, everyone looks up to you," Uri continued. "To know what's the problem, how to fix it, how to keep going. And you don't necessarily know the answer."

Uri told me that in the beginning, he lacked the maturity to own up to his ignorance. He got defensive when his men asked him difficult questions, and sometimes he took his frustration out on them. But Uri wised up soon enough. He had no choice once the intifada started. "Until October 2000," he admitted, "I never faced a real border, a real enemy."

His had been among the first tanks to enter the West Bank town of Qalqilya after the IDF reoccupied major West Bank cities in 2002. The goal was to secure the entire area surrounding Qalqilya by besieging the city to make sure no Palestinians got out.

"The way you do it," Uri explained, "is to go in there with a lot of forces, which means tanks, carriers of soldiers, and other vehicles. You siege several houses in which you know there are terrorists and locate places that have strategic control. And I stood there with my tank for three days."

"You had to stay inside the tank for three days?"

"It depends. If you have a chance to switch then you switch, but there have been situations where I have been for more than twenty-four hours inside a Palestinian city, which kind of sucks. Which kind of stinks more—"

"Stinks?" I gave Uri a skeptical look.

Uri opened the photo book he had brought outside. "You bring empty Coke bottles," he explained, as he flipped the pages. "You tear the upper part and . . ." he found the picture he'd been looking for. Sure enough, there was a dirt-encrusted soldier, holding up a two-liter bottle of urine. "And if someone has to go for number two," Uri said without a hint of embarrassment, "you don't have any option other than to do it inside the tank. And you find something to put it in and you throw it outside. But we didn't get to that."

"Is this one of your soldiers?" I asked of the young man with the Coke bottle.

"That's me." Uri smiled sheepishly.

"That's you?" I grabbed the book from him. He was so dirty that I couldn't find a single identifying feature.

"Look, it's the same watch." He held his wrist up to the photo as proof. "I loved my hands. I was proud of them." Uri inspected his now spotless fingers, and then: "Look at the soldiers! They are dirty. They are tired. And what for?" There was bitterness in his voice. "God forbid! It's Qalqilya! It's not Hebron. It's not Nablus. It's not Gaza," Uri listed three Palestinian areas that unlike the relatively quiet city of Qalqilya had seen fierce confrontations between Palestinian militants and IDF forces. "There are very few resisters in Qalqilya," he continued, "so what the hell? Is this the most important thing that I can do for my country? Being . . . here . . . in . . . Qalqilya?" Then the clouds lifted from his brow. "But going into Gaza and having specific intelligence. And knowing exactly what you are going to do. You know that *these* are the places that truly risk Israeli lives. These are terrorists who live upstairs. I was excited that I was going on *that* mission, but I was also dead afraid. I was the second vehicle going inside of Gaza. That's amazing. That's terrifying. That's what I've been trained to do because we were stationed at this crossroad and there came the terrorists with the RPG."

"RPG?"

"An antitank missile called a 'rocket propelled grenade' that sits on your shoulder. It was a hard battle. People were injured around me. And it was truly frightening. And I made mistakes. I was shooting . . ."

He stopped, looked down. Around and around spun another unlit cigarette. Something seemed to hover upon his lips. But Uri swallowed and said: "It's not easy."

"Did you ever hit something you weren't supposed to?" I ventured, fearing what the answer might be.

"With what?"

"With your tank—or your gun?"

"With my tank, lots of times. My driver took a turn off the road and hit an electric light and it bounced on my tank. And it looked like the Fourth of July, and then it looked like a blackout."

"For the whole street?"

"For half the town, I think. I guess it was an important line." Uri said that prior to his mission, army personnel talked to his unit about trying not to damage Palestinian infrastructure. "It's not a very big comfort to the Palestinians to know that Israeli tanks are trying to cause as little damage as possible—having tanks down the street is enough. And it's upsetting when you see the Palestinians fixing a water pipe or electric light you hit last night."

He looked me in the eye to make sure I understood. "I've never crushed a car, even though my driver wanted. It's like paper—a car to tanks."

"He wanted to crush a car?" I asked, an image of monster trucks flashing through my head.

Uri adopted his best dumbed-down voice. " 'Um, ya, we can't go through the street. We, a, have to go over this car.' And I said, no you don't. Okay, you have to ruin the sidewalk, but you don't really have to crush that car. That's another reason why that soldier would never be a commander. It's being childish. He has enormous power because he drives a sixteen-ton machine. And he doesn't want to kill anyone, he just wants to play. But he doesn't understand the meaning of force."

"But isn't that what the army is all about?" I asked. "Force?"

"Of course. That's what the army does. Dropping a quarter-ton bomb inside Gaza from an F-sixteen is nothing but force in order to win. If it's justified or not—*that's* what I was talking about. Because if someone shoots me, and I'm inside my tank, and I'm protecting those soldiers who are inside a house, am I not going to shoot back because it's an improper use of force? I didn't think of being in the army in the macro—in the strategic-political way. I wanted to do my job the best I could and not think whether we should be occupying Palestine or not. This is a decision I have nothing to do with. And if I decide to be an officer in the IDF, then there are some decisions that aren't to my judgment."

But as a commander, Uri did have a number of personal decisions, such as whether to drive his tank over the sidewalk or over a line of cars, or whether it was appropriate to use his 105mm cannon. He said he would rather that he handle these dilemmas than someone else.

"But why you?" I asked. I wanted to know how Uri could be so sure of himself. How could he ever know that he was making the best, most justifiable decision in the moment?

"Because I trust my judgment better than I trust most people." Uri had none of my reservations. "Not that I'm perfect, but better me than someone who's so overwhelmed and thrilled just to have a chance to stick a bullet into someone."

Many Israelis told me that abusing one's weapon is the greatest crime a soldier can commit. In fact, all soldiers must swear an oath of responsibility when they pledge allegiance to the military. It's a code called the "purity of arms," or as Uri explained, "the idea that you will never use your weapon when it's not necessary or not proper."

I knew plenty of Palestinians who wouldn't buy this commitment to responsibility. They'd say Uri shouldn't be in the army at all and that if he was really following his conscience he would have objected to serving, even if it meant a jail sentence. The only way to avoid prison was to be exempted from the IDF as a "universal pacifist," meaning you object to national armies and war on principle, including wars of defense. Recruits who petition for such an exemption are interviewed by a committee of military personnel, including a psychologist. It is very difficult for males to convince this committee. From 1995 to 2003, 305 males claimed to be universal pacifists, but only 27 of them received full exemptions. Thirty-two were ordered to serve but allowed to opt out of combat. There are currently a handful of Israelis serving jail time because they were denied exemption and still refused to enlist. Among these are "selective objectors," recruits who object to military service for political reasons, such as Israel's occupation of the territories. Talking to Uri, it seemed he'd been forced to ignore any political objections about serving in the West Bank and Gaza.

"I didn't have any well-thought-out ideas and opinions in the army," he had said. "In the army, too much thinking wasn't good. It made everything too complicated. It would have hurt my ability to react."

Uri also told me that the common sense and education that sent him to volunteer in fighting units was the same logic and common sense that convinced him he could be friends with Arabs at Seeds of Peace.

"You don't see any contradiction," I questioned, "between making Palestinian friends at Seeds of Peace and fighting against them in the army?"

Uri answered with a story about his first trip to Gaza in which his tank stopped at a wall spraypainted with the slogan "Kahane was right." Rabbi Meir Kahane founded the Kach party, whose platform called for Israel's annexation of the territories and the forcible removal of all Palestinians living there. Kahane was elected to the Knesset in 1984, but his party was banned from running a second time because a subsequent amendment to Israel's Basic Law disqualified any candidate whose platform included "incitement to racism." In 1990, Kahane was assassinated in New York by an Egyptian militant, but his legacy remains strong among certain sectors of the Israeli population, especially the more extremist settler communities. Some of these communities claim they will not leave the West Bank and

Gaza, even if the Israeli government orders them to go. After Sharon announced that Israel would pull out of Gaza and certain parts of the West Bank, he ordered the dismantling of some Kahanist outposts to demonstrate his sincerity. These communities are often no more than a few trailers and a makeshift synagogue, but the IDF has been forced into physical confrontations with some of them when they've refused to leave.

Uri continued his story. "And I was sitting, looking at the graffiti and thinking: What exactly am I doing here? Who would have believed a year ago—not even a year ago, half a year ago—that I'd be sitting in a tank in the middle of the Gaza Strip? I mean, because it's the opposite of my political views—and yet here I am."

"If you had known that you'd end up in Gaza, would you still have signed up for combat?"

"I don't know," Uri considered. "I think . . . I think I would have but . . ." he took a long pull from the cigarette and exhaled. "I would have done it, but I'm not sure it would have been for the right reasons. Because today I'm more . . . I'm much more open to criticizing the government's decisions."

"In what way?"

"I thought of the army as something which is above law or above politics. And it's not. It's not supposed to be. I mean, it's a political tool, but this situation in the West Bank and Gaza is much more delicate than the one in Lebanon. Here we've got a creature that's much harder to stop, because it's much more dangerous to Israeli civilian lives. And on the other hand, the fighting itself is much more cruel, because it's a fight that hurts Palestinian civilians, it hurts children, and above all, it draws us back years and years."

After six years of military service, three of which he spent as commander of an intelligence base, my friend Yoyo was having similar feelings. He cut contact with his Arab friends and stopped attending Seeds of Peace activities while he was still in high school in order to increase his chances of getting into the secretive and prestigious army intelligence. During that time we also fell out of touch. Then I learned from a Seeds of Peace staffer that Yoyo was coming to the United States on leave. Before I could contact him, I got a call from my Jordanian friend Shouq. Shouq, Yoyo, and I had been good friends at camp. She was currently getting her B.A. at Georgetown University, and it turned out that she and Yoyo had already made plans to meet in D.C. A week later, I found myself drinking tea in down-

town Washington with a Jordanian college student and an officer in the Israeli army. I asked Yoyo how on earth the army allowed him to be sitting
there with an Arab. He smiled and with a shrug answered, "Well, the army
doesn't have to know everything."

When I reconnected with Yoyo in Israel, a couple of years after our afternoon tea, he had recently completed his job as commander of an army
base. He was tall—a big guy—but much slimmer after so many years in
the army. He now moved and spoke with an air of professionalism, even
in the most casual environment. One evening, I listened to Yoyo reflect on
his experiences in the IDF.

"Ever since Sharon was elected he tried to implement the policy that
the military can win." Yoyo leaned forward in a hard-backed chair in my
apartment—he'd declined my offer of the couch. "But the military—
force—can't win a political discussion or disagreement. It's caused the
corruption of the military. You can just read the papers to see that the military offers something and the prime minister says 'yes.' "

Yoyo wasn't talking about monetary corruption, but corruption of the
military's role in Israeli politics.

"I have no problem with the military," he made clear to me. But according to him, the IDF saw the world through a single lens: the gunsight.
Under no circumstances, he felt, should the military dictate *political* policy.
It was the politicians' responsibility to have the long-term vision to coun-
terbalance the military's short-term security goals. Yoyo said that during
his six years of service he saw very few instances in which the government
refused to endorse the army's recommendations or policies, even if these
actions were immoral, shortsighted, or harmful to diplomatic efforts.

I had a difficult time understanding this phenomenon myself. If the
military's chief goal is to protect Israeli lives, why did it continue a policy
in the territories that fueled more violence? Surely security officials
understand that every time the IDF demolishes the home of a suicide
bomber, a dozen more young people are willing to perform such an act.
Surely they know the kind of frustration, resentment, and anger that
checkpoints, closures, and targeted assassinations incite. Of course, Israel
needs to make security a priority, but the IDF's policies toward the Palestinians seem counterintuitive. I could not understand why the government so easily conceded to a failing strategy. I decided I needed to confront
someone who had years of experience in the system, someone at the top
of the security community.

Ami Ayalon was head of the Shin Bet (Israel's FBI) from 1996 to 2000 and one of the country's most highly respected security officials. He is a small, hard man with cold blue eyes and a razor-sharp stare, the kind I imagined would be less than welcoming in the interrogation room. As expected, he had a definite opinion on this issue.

"If your assumption is that all Palestinians want to throw us into the sea, then you have no alternative than violence, even if you know that creates *more* violence."

"Do you agree with that assumption?"

"No! No. But you are being too logical." Ayalon shook his head at my naivete. "After the explosion of a bus, don't ask questions of what *should* we do. Politicians need to be elected. So they have to take revenge, because otherwise they will lose the election. In a state of war, you elect a warrior to lead you. No matter whether it makes sense."

I was reminded of the shock-and-awe sermons that Jewish and Muslim religious leaders accused each other of delivering to their congregations. But Ayalon wasn't talking about fanatical religious personalities; he was talking about a national military and political leadership whose decisions, if emotionally driven, could lead directly to loss of life.

"Israelis want Palestinians to suffer," Ayalon continued. "And for the Palestinians, it is the same."

This was as sad as it was appalling. I knew that Israel's military leadership was not always a blindly fighting beast. Uri had shown me a small example when he talked of the choice not to crush a car unnecessarily, and Ayalon himself reminded me that the security forces, including the IDF, were an integral part of the negotiation team during the Oslo years.

"I met your father when he came here when I was head of the Shin Bet," Ayalon remembered. "We cooperated with Mohammad Dahlan and Jabril Rajoub. We thought that we were bringing this perception of cooperation to the Middle East."

Indeed, the Palestinian public's support for Hamas dramatically decreased during Oslo, despite flaws in the process. A political horizon and tangible improvements on the ground gave them hope, and hope, according to Ayalon, is the best form of deterrence.

"Deterrence works only when there is something to lose," he told me.

I knew how devastated Palestinians were at that moment. "But now the Palestinians have nothing to lose?"

"Right. So the problem is not a security problem, but politically, what should we do in order to create Palestinian hope. Because they are in a state of despair."

Having completed his army service and having known Palestinians personally through Seeds of Peace, Uri understood Ayalon's sentiments.

"I know the Palestinians suffer, because I create it. If I was Palestinian, I'm sure I'd join Fatah. I don't say I would go and plan bombings, but I'd demonstrate. I'd fight. Even if it's at the university and speaking at podiums. They're struggling and we're not making their lives any easier."

I wondered if Israelis and Palestinians would be in a continually deteriorating situation if their military and political leadership had even a little of this empathy for each other. If they did make more logical, less emotional decisions, could that reverse the "macro" picture as Uri called it? The Israeli army would still exist as a force to fight Palestinian violence. Nothing would change that. Though Uri had a greater perspective on his military service now that he was out of the army, he still felt uncomfortable taking an active stand against the policies of the IDF. He said he felt robbed of his right to oppose Israel's occupation of the territories, because he remained part of that occupying force. He knew that for thirty more years, he'd have to serve in the army reserves. His first call to reserve duty could be less than a year away. There was a good chance, he said, of being sent right back to Gaza and the West Bank.

Uri paused and once more examined his spotless fingers. He looked at his palms as though he were a fortune-teller trying to divine his own future. "I will have to go back." Uri pronounced his fate. "That's my country."

An experience of my own put Uri's statement in perspective. In Jerusalem at the corner of Etzel and Lekhi Streets—named for the two Jewish militant-terror groups—is a hill covered with rubble and dirt. At the top of this hill is a large building of Jerusalem stone. With its flower-draped balconies and vibrant green-and-white flag, it resembles an embassy or ambassadorial residence; indeed, some have sarcastically dubbed it "the palace on the hill." If the building seems strangely out of place, the events that take place inside are stranger still. It is the Seeds of Peace Center for Coexistence in Jerusalem, the organization's regional headquarters that runs follow-up programming for Seeds of Peace graduates.

Not long ago I attended one such event. Instead of going home after school, fifty young Israelis and Palestinians walked up the dusty hill to meet one another. For Palestinians, the checkpoints turned a fifteen-minute trip into an hour. For Israelis, extra or unnecessary travel meant the unpredictability of suicide bombings. Still, against the backdrop of nonstop terror and violence, these teenagers threw down their school bags and gathered around plates piled with pita and hummus.

An hour into the gathering, a twenty-year-old Israeli named Yaron dropped by the center. This wasn't unusual except for the fact that Yaron appeared in full IDF uniform—with an automatic rifle. Yaron had come from his army base to see me and didn't realize a large-scale event had been scheduled. He seemed as surprised to see the center overflowing with Israeli and Palestinian Seeds as they were to see him. Sami, a highly respected Palestinian staff member, put his arm around Yaron's shoulder. Sami had spent nearly a decade in Israeli jails for his resistance activities in the 1980s. He learned to speak Hebrew there and began reading Gandhi and Martin Luther King. He'd been dedicated to Seeds of Peace and Israeli-Palestinian coexistence for years. Sami assured the Palestinian kids that Yaron was a loyal Seed with a good heart. He encouraged them to judge Yaron by his personality, not by his outward appearance. Yaron apologized, saying he would not have worn his uniform had he known about the meeting. He knew the Seeds' kids—Palestinians and even some Israelis—would find a soldier in the Seeds of Peace center offensive.

In a city where Israeli-Palestinian tension is often explosive, most would have expected an angry or violent reaction to Yaron. But there was no overt response. If Palestinians felt discomfort, they masked it well. They were determined not to let a soldier's uniform bring politics into an otherwise personal gathering.

Yet this event raised troubling questions for me, especially in light of Uri's feelings about the reserves. For all his reservations about the army and Israel's military presence in the territories, Uri would go back to Gaza if called to do so. "That's my country," he'd said. That statement, made by Israelis and Palestinians alike, means that even if Seeds of Peace gives its graduates a greater sense of individuality, and even if these young adults come to feel part of a broader Seeds of Peace community, their national identities can still trump their personal allegiances to one another.

So what were the Palestinian kids at the center really thinking when Yaron entered in his uniform? How could they reconcile Yaron as a Seed with what he could easily do to them in the field as a soldier? And how could the Israeli Seeds reconcile their own military service with their view of Palestinians as friends and human beings? Clearly, Israel's mandatory army service as well as the occupation creates an intense physical and emotional separation between Israeli and Palestinian Seeds. But is it an in-surmountable barrier to coexistence? I wanted to know whether the gradu-ates saw a contradiction between the role of soldier and that of Seeds.

Yarden, an Israeli with gold earrings, a rat's-tail braid, and yellow glasses with red fire streaks painted up the sides, was fifteen years old when he came to Seeds in 2002. He lives in a middle-class neighborhood twenty minutes outside Tel Aviv. His room is decorated with weapons. Rusted knives and tarnished bullet belts hang on the walls among posters of his favorite bands. He has arranged a collection of inactive grenades on his dresser. Yarden flopped down on his bed—a mattress without a box spring—and said, "You can sit there." He pointed to a zebra-striped bean-bag chair. I looked around the room. Apparently, my other option was the floor.

In light of his unusual decorating tastes, I almost didn't have to ask Yarden how he felt about joining the IDF. "Do you think the army will change you?" I wanted to know.

"Of course you change," Yarden said. "In the army, you don't go by your parents' laws anymore. . . . You don't have the same way of life. You change your opinions, beliefs, and your tolerance. But I won't turn into an evil person when I join the army."

Yarden appears to treat the change he'll experience in the army like any other in his life. "I'm not the same person now that I was in elementary school," he said. "I'm not the same person now that I was before I went to Seeds of Peace."

"And what about Seeds of Peace?" I asked. "If you change your opinions and beliefs once you're in the army, will that change your relationship with your Palestinian friends? Can you be a soldier and a Seed?"

Yarden saw no contradictions. "I'll be a more humane soldier after Seeds," he said. "Just because I'm a soldier doesn't mean I'll think, 'Okay, I can kill Palestinians now that I'm in the army.'"

"What will you do if you confront Palestinians in battle?" I asked.

"If they are throwing stones," he explained, "I'm going to take my rub-ber gun and shoot them in the legs. Maybe use some tear gas or small grenades. We try to make our weapons as least dangerous as we can."

Rubber bullets and grenades seemed dangerous enough to me. "What if one of them was a Seed?" I asked.

"Then I would talk to my commander and say that this Palestinian was a friend. But I can't refuse a command. It's the law. So if I have to shoot someone," he told me, "I'd shoot at a different Palestinian."

Listening to Yarden, I could understand how easy it was for a fifteen-year-old, who had years before he entered the army, to conceive of such an option—and how naive it was. Yoyo, who had been through the army, saw no room for the type of compromise Yarden was describing.

"As long as the majority of Palestinians do nothing to stop the violent minority, we have no other choice than to stop every civilian, impose closures, and search homes in the middle of the night," he said. "These actions are not just a question of one officer who hates Arabs. They're a necessary part of Israel's defense. If the Palestinians would take responsibility for their actions, I would be the first person to call off the army."

"And how do you respond to the claims that Israel uses excessive force?" I asked him. "Do you really think the army takes every precaution not to harm civilians? The Palestinians in the territories didn't seem to think so, and neither do a number of human rights organizations, including Jewish ones."

"No act is planned against innocent Palestinians," Yoyo said definitively. "But if a taxi driver from Jenin helps a suicide bomber get into Israel, we have to go looking for this man. We have to search the whole city to find him. The city is crowded. It's not so easy as to go to his house and get him. To get him, we have to interfere with the lives of innocents." Yoyo paused to let this sink in. Then he said, "Jen, it's all about the fight to survive."

Ruba attended Seeds of Peace in 1994, 1996, and 1997. As campers, we became good friends. When I sat down with her in September 2002, two years into the second intifada, I didn't know how our meeting would unfold. She has always had a fiery edge, especially when arguing politics, and I often left our discussions feeling guilty for being from a powerful, free, and safe country. In other words, for being American. Ruba made sure that I never forgot my national identity. U.S. foreign policy caused Ruba great annoyance, namely because she believed we were hypocrites. "How can you claim to uphold human rights and the rights of individuals," she would question me, "when the United States has killed hundreds of thousands of innocent Iraqi civilians?" "How can you be an impartial third party in Israeli-Palestinian negotiations when you've given Israel the very Apache helicopters used to assassinate Palestinians?" *How can you?* When she said "you," I knew that Ruba meant the U.S. government, but her attacks often felt personal. The reason was clear enough. For months, Ruba's anger boiled under the surface. Then her American friend showed up—a person she loved, but as a U.S. citizen, also a convenient punching bag. I know Ruba has never meant me any harm, but when it comes to political discussions, I am constantly searching for the balance between acknowledging her feelings of victimization and standing up for myself and my country.

Thankfully, in September of 2002, she seemed happy to talk about herself and leave the United States out of the equation.

"I'm so tired—I need a vacation" was the first thing she said. She explained that the intifada was weighing on her. It was tough living in Jericho and working in Ramallah, because the frequent closures prevented her from getting to work.

"And whenever I do go to a checkpoint," she told me, "I always look to see if any of the soldiers are Seeds."

I asked her what she would do if she encountered any of her Israeli friends.

"I don't know," she said bitterly. "I hope I never see one."

Ruba said she would be interested in talking with her Israeli friends in the army, but only if the conversation was focused on politics. "I would talk with those soldiers who are part of the occupation if we could get to a solution," she said, "but I couldn't be friends with them. And for those people who weren't in combat, like Koby [an Israeli Seed who served in the IDF's foreign relations division], I don't have a problem being friends."

During that same visit to Jericho, I was present for a conversation between Dalal Erekat and her father, Sa'eb. Dalal attended Seeds of Peace twice, including two Seeds of Peace youth summits—one of which was the mock-negotiations in Villars, Switzerland. Sa'eb Erekat was an adviser to Arafat and head of the Palestinian negotiating team.

We were sitting in the Erekats' living room talking about the intifada. Sa'eb asked his daughter how she felt about her Israeli friends joining the army.

"I cannot be friends with them," Dalal answered tersely. "I will not even talk with them."

"But just last fall," Sa'eb pointed out, "you went to the Seeds of Peace youth conference in New York City. You spent a week talking with your friends there. So will you refuse to talk to these same people a year or two from now? Aren't they the same people?"

"Who knows the kinds of things they will have done!" Dalal exclaimed. "They might have killed Palestinians and I wouldn't even know it." She was determined to be obdurate on this point and she gave her father a mean look.

"But Dalal, I sit down with Israelis every day. I have had coffee with the Israeli minister of defense. Every single Israeli with whom I have negotiated has been through the army. Do you think," he asked with the slightest smile, "that I should refuse to meet with members of the Israeli government because they were once in the armed forces? Should I quit my job?"

"No." She gave her father a look that in plain daughter-speak read, "Quit trying to embarrass me in front of our guests!"

"And one more thing." He gave his daughter a stern expression. "One day the Palestinians are going to have an army. And you will be called upon to serve—and also your children. Would you not take up arms to protect your country?"

Father and daughter looked at each other. Dalal could not protest, so she said nothing.

In my mind, Dalal's ambiguity sums up the paradoxes that Israel's mandatory army service raises for all the Seeds of Peace graduates and for all Israeli youth who are interested in finding a peaceful solution to the Israeli-Palestinian conflict through coexistence. If Dalal and Yarden were friends, I knew his decision to shoot a Palestinian stranger as opposed to a Palestinian Seed would not win her sympathies. She would argue that no matter how kindly an Israeli soldier treats a Palestinian civilian, the fundamental relationship between them is occupier and victim.

I spoke with one twenty-year-old Israeli soldier who was in the IDF's most elite antiterror unit. Many of his field missions were designed to "secure" houses in order to gain a strategic vantage point against Palestinian militants. This required him to storm into Palestinian homes without warning the families and quarantine them. As the young soldier told me, during these operations, the entire Palestinian family must sit in one corner of the house, sometimes for two days, and cannot eat or even use the bathroom without getting permission from the Israeli soldier guarding them. "It's a horrible thing to have to do," this soldier told me. "It's incredibly degrading, especially for the fathers. In Palestinian culture the father is the head of the family and to see him ordered around by young men is humiliating." But the soldier added that such actions were necessary to fight terror. "I'm a good person," he told me. "I want to respect people, to treat them with dignity. And in these situations, in order to protect Israeli lives, I have to do things that are disrespectful and undignified."

This IDF warrior caused me to wonder: Perhaps Seeds of Peace is too idealistic for what the real world requires. What's the point of learning peaceful values if you can't or won't exercise them?

When I expressed this to Yoyo, however, he was quick to set me straight. "Seeds teaches you important things," he said sternly. "They don't necessarily apply at the moment, because of the situation. But it's wrong to say that Seeds shouldn't teach those values even if they're difficult to uphold right now."

I could imagine Sa'eb Erekat saying the same thing to his daughter. "Before the intifada, things were easier. Now that they're not, should we give up? Would you drop out of Seeds? Would you have me quit my job?"

Yoyo continued. "In Seeds of Peace, you see one side. In the military, you see the other side. Both are biased viewpoints. But because I've been to Seeds of Peace, I've been able to see the whole picture. Reality is somewhere between Seeds and the army."

I suppose the reality for Palestinian Seeds would be somewhere between their Seeds of Peace experience and their experiences living under occupation. As Ruba said, she resists the occupation in her every action. For her, resistance is a mind-set, a worldview. But somehow, she can relax this seemingly implacable position for the Israeli Seeds: if not for their friendship, then for their political opinions.

All the graduates are struggling with the contradictions of being a Seed of Peace in a time of war. You may see a Palestinian Seed wearing a *kiffiyeh* and an Israeli Seed dressed in IDF khakis, and to most people, these individuals are as opposed to each other as black and white. In reality, however, they are awash with shades of gray. There are as many contradictions inherent in the Seeds of Peace experience as there are in the Israeli-Palestinian conflict. Even the location of the Center for Coexistence, one of the city's most neutral spaces, is controversial. Because it sits on the dividing line between East and West Jerusalem, it is an emblem of coexistence. Because it sits at the intersection of Etzel and Lekhi Streets it is an emblem of conflict; as the Seeds know too well, one country's independence is another's catastrophe.

Through the Gates of Gaza

I t felt like a trip to an amusement park. My friend Jen and I were speed-ing down a long, sunny highway, a balmy wind blowing through the open windows, anticipation stirring in my stomach. Then, just when it seemed we'd never get there . . .

WELCOME TO EREZ CROSSING. The sign swung into view, as bold as any theme park billboard. Behind it the parking lot—that necessary feature of all large attractions—stretched into the distance. But there was something unusual about the Erez Crossing parking complex, the first sign that this was no fun park: space after space was empty.

It reminded me of a scene in one of my favorite movies, *National Lampoon's Vacation*. In the film Chevy Chase, a.k.a Clark Griswold, drags his family across America in search of the Wally World Theme Park. After a trek of countless blunders and mishaps, the Griswold family arrives at Wally World only to find it closed. Like *Monty Python and the Holy Grail, Vacation* is a quest movie in its own right; Wally World is as much of an ideal for Griswold as the Grail is for Arthur. And like the great king, Clark Griswold finds his dream dashed just short of its fulfillment.

Unlike Clark Griswold, who doesn't worry that his car is the only one in a virtually endless parking lot, I knew exactly why Erez was empty, and I found it troubling. Erez Crossing was built in order to allow Gaza's res-idents access to Israel for work. After the second intifada started, the Israeli military allowed only a fraction of these Palestinians to enter. Frequent closures due to terrorist threats make it impossible for workers to leave Gaza. When Israel imposes a full closure, usually after a terror attack, not even internationals have access; if you are outside, you can't get in, and if you're inside, you're stuck.

Gaza is one of most densely populated areas in the world and a veritable prison for the 1.5 million Palestinians who live within its borders. A third of these inhabit overcrowded, intensely deprived refugee camps created after the 1948 and 1967 wars. The Gaza Strip is about twenty-five miles long and in some places, only four miles wide. Israel controls all of its borders including the western one, which straddles the Mediterranean Sea; the southern one, which bumps up against Egypt; and the northern and eastern borders, which are separated from Israel by a security wall built in 1994.

Getting out of the car in the Erez parking lot, I saw neither the wall nor any other part of Gaza. Only the low-slung structures of Erez were visible, with green Israeli fields in the distance. This was no contrived amusement park, and for me it was the edge of the unknown. From photographs and documentaries I had seen, Gaza was a wasteland of scorched buildings and parched ground. It seemed impossible that the skies *wouldn't* turn dark and swallow me the minute I crossed the threshold. That's how far away Gaza felt—and how dangerous. But Jen Marlowe, Seeds of Peace program director and my companion for the day, was already walking toward the first passport check. It's not as though you're standing at the gates of Mordor, I reminded myself. People live in Gaza. They raise families, attend university, and go to work. Not so different from you. What are you so afraid of? I set off after Jen.

We were going through as VIPs. That's how diplomats, journalists, UN workers, and members of registered NGOs (nongovernment organizations) enter Gaza. Workers pass through an area that Palestinians call "the workers' pen." It is just that: a long, stall-like structure with a corrugated roof through which thousands of Palestinians were meant to pass each day, checked by the IDF before they entered Israel. It was a rough place, I'd been told, with frequent fighting between the workers and the soldiers.

In comparison, Jen and I were traveling in style. The first passport check stood at the end of the car lot like a parking attendants' booth. There were two soldiers inside, each with rifles and walkie-talkies. Jen put on her most congenial face and wished them good morning in Hebrew. We handed over our passports and waited for them to contact the Erez registration center. Nowadays, tourists aren't allowed to enter Gaza, so Jen had registered me with Seeds of Peace. We had called and faxed the Erez offices all week to verify that they'd received my information. If not, we'd be stuck outside Gaza for hours. After about ten minutes, the soldiers waved us through.

VIP registration resembled a ranch house: a long, single-floored structure with glass windows and a porch. As we approached the building, a shaggy-haired soldier skipped down the steps to greet us.

"Hello!" He waved excitedly. He reminded me of a little kid whose first birthday guests have arrived. "Welcome to Erez! Hey, you're new."

"I'm Jen," I said.

The soldier's face lit up. "Jen—" he looked at me—"and Jen"—he looked at Jen Marlowe. "Jen and Jen! Well, isn't that something!" And there on the pavement, he did a little jig. I looked at Jen Marlowe in disbelief. "You'll have to excuse me," the soldier apologized. "I'm tired. Very tired. Nope, haven't slept in a while. Come on in!" He skipped back up the steps. Was this really a soldier, I wondered? He seemed more like the Mad Hatter in fatigues. "After you, ladies." He held the glass doors open.

The inside of VIP registration looked like an airline ticket office. The floors were shiny and white, with a waiting area near the windows and felt ropes designating each line. An insipid watercolor of pink and green flowers hung on the wall. Jen and I approached the counter where a female soldier smiled at us and took our passports.

"Didn't I speak with you on the phone?" she asked Jen. "You're with Seeds of Peace, right? I haven't seen you here in a while."

She pulled some papers from beneath the counter and began writing on them.

"It's been tough to get permissions," Jen explained.

The soldier nodded with an empathetic smile.

"How are things going at Erez?" Jen asked.

"Oh, we're doing all right. You know, we're doing what we can. Okay." She stuck paper slips into both our passports and handed them back. "You're all set. Have a good trip in Gaza." She waved us into the next room to have our bags scanned.

"You know the way?" the soldier in charge of the scanner asked us.

"We do," Jen said.

"All right, then have a good day." The soldier waved good-bye.

As Jen and I walked to the next army check, I wondered at the cheerfulness of the VIP office. I had never seen soldiers so helpful, so positive. Was it all a big show? Treat the foreigners like passengers in first class so we'll ignore what Gazans tell us about IDF brutality? But the good-naturedness seemed genuine, as though the soldiers' humor was a defense against the depressing reality just beyond their doors. A defense for them and for us: a few last encouraging words before sending us into chaos.

It occurred to me that some of the soldiers here might never have been *inside* Gaza. It seemed strange to think that, by evening, I would return to this registration center with knowledge that the people, working day and night at Erez, did not have. I would be better qualified to prepare visitors than they. But I did not have this knowledge yet, and it was time to get going.

After leaving VIP, we walked onto a wide road once used for car passage. Now cement blocks and large coils of barbed wire restricted automobile movement. Jen and I walked down one of the empty lanes. To our left was the workers' pen. It looked like a prison, a place meant to contain wild animals rather than fathers, brothers, and sons trying to get to work. Still, if it was full of people, I knew I would feel afraid, as though all that penned up anger and frustration might suddenly burst upon me. This is exactly how Israelis felt about Gaza. The security wall around the Strip had created a sealed container; in ten years, not a single Palestinian suicide bomber had penetrated that wall. (Only in March 2004 did two Palestinian suicide bombers sneak out inside packing crates.) This only increased Israel's feeling that Gaza was a pressure cooker on the verge of explosion. The images of Gaza most frequent in the Israeli media were of massive Hamas protests and funerals. But this winter day Erez Crossing was eerily quiet. Our feet scraped the white pavement. The sun glared. I had never felt so small or exposed.

Jen and I arrived at the next army check, where another soldier checked our passports. Another army station lay a few yards beyond that. We passed through a metal detector to get there, but it was turned off. This checkpoint was a cement hut covered in netting and army camouflage. We slipped our passports through a narrow rectangular window just above head level. Above the window an English sign read: *Identificaction Check*.

"You've got to be kidding me," I said as we waited for our passports. "Identificaction?" The mistake had been there for years, Jen said, and no one had bothered to change it. A friend of hers almost had his camera confiscated for trying to take a photo of the sign.

We received our passports and turned away from the hut to find ourselves facing another long stretch of road, this one without barbed wire. At the end of this street was the Palestinian checkpoint, and after that, we would enter Gaza. A taxi honked at us. It wasn't the driver we had arranged for, but a man hoping to make a few extra shekels by taking us one hundred feet. Most likely we were his only passengers that day, so we got in and in less than thirty seconds arrived at the Palestinian check. We handed our passports to a Palestinian policeman who wrote our names and ID numbers in a book. Five checkpoints and forty-five minutes after we arrived at Erez, we were ready to enter Gaza. Jen's driver, Raed, was waiting with his taxi.

The road into Gaza is a continuation of the one that began at Erez. As we sped down it, all I could think was "I'm in Gaza. I'm in Gaza." The road has an island down its center with squat palm trees and traces of grass. Overall, though, the environment was brittle and dull, stripped of color. On the right we passed the bombed-out buildings and streets leading into Beit Hanoun, the farming village that once had 8,000 dunams (1 dunam is 1,000 square meters) of orange trees. The IDF damaged 5,500 of these, Raed said, in its assault on the village—an operation intended to stop militants from firing al-Qassam rockets into Israel, only two and half miles away.

The fields on our left sloped down into Jabaliya refugee camp, where 100,000 people live in 1.4 square kilometers, and where the first intifada erupted in 1987. The intifada (in Arabic, "to shake off") was a spontaneous uprising of Palestinians against the Israeli occupation. It initially consisted of strikes and other acts of civil disobedience. Young Palestinian males protested, threw stones at Israeli soldiers and burned tires. An underground leadership with links to the PLO in exile arose and directed activities. Footage of Israeli soldiers with guns confronting unarmed Palestinians was broadcast throughout Israel and the world and began to incur criticism of the occupation. At the same time, the intifada grew more violent. Palestinians wielded Molotov cocktails, knives, and guns. It was at this point that Hamas began to garner support among the masses for its aggressive approach to fighting the Israelis. Notably, there was no suicide terror employed during the first intifada.

From the road, Jabaliya camp looks like a gigantic pile of rubble—the effect of so many cement buildings crammed together. Up ahead, Raed pointed out, is the place where, several months before, an American convoy had been destroyed by a charge detonated in the road. It was the first Palestinian targeting of U.S. citizens since the second intifada began.

We entered Gaza City, the hub of the Gaza Strip, and drove down its main boulevard, which was wide, dusty, and strewn with trash. Cars mixed with old men and boys on donkey-led carts. Uniform-clad school-children filled the streets. It was only eleven a.m., but the schools ran two shifts in order to accommodate the mass of students. The sidewalks were lined with stores, some displaying pristine signs, painted or lit with neon, others dark and hollow as caves. We drove past tall apartments and sordid lots, past long stretches of garage-door storefronts, faceless and closed. It wasn't hot, but everything shone beneath a white glare. It made the city feel thin, even more washed-out than the countryside. It was, I thought, a city of bones. A skeleton that had yet to develop its life forces, its flesh. I did not know how Gaza had looked before Israel occupied it in 1967, or what it had been like after the Palestinian Authority gained control after the Oslo Accords. Had it always been underdeveloped, so stricken?

But one aspect of Gaza City burst with life: the graffiti. It filled the streets, thick and bright as blood. There was intricate Arabic calligraphy, Koranic verses, and militants' fiery mottos: *I want to die for God.* There were images of Al-Asqa intertwined with *Adhan,* the call to prayer, the invocation curling skyward, its letters twisting in every conceivable color. There were hands gripping the sacred mosque and squeezing the shape like a lemon, forcing out droplets of blood. On the walls surrounding Islamic University, the defiant faces of martyrs were drawn in perfect likeness. I saw one image of a foot stomping on a Jewish star, with the acronym of the Islamic Resistance Movement tattooed across the ankle. *Hamas.*

The word once sent shivers down my spine, but it had become commonplace to me during my time in the Middle East. My origninal fear of the name was a product of my ignorance and an overactive imagination. I had seen and heard plenty about terrorism growing up: a combination of movies, the news media, and the stories of my father's Middle East travels. Not that Hamas isn't frightening. It certainly is to many people, including some Palestinians. But in order to understand the organization's role in Palestinian society, I realized I had to understand Hamas as Palestinians did.

"Hamas" means zeal in Arabic, and in Gaza, it's a household name. The organization was born in the Gaza Strip during the first intifada. It grew out of the Muslim Brotherhood, a fundamentalist Islamic movement with Egyptian roots. The Brotherhood was committed to the gradual, universal spread of Islam through social, religious, and political action. Beginning in 1967 (at the same time that Israel occupied the West Bank and Gaza), the Brotherhood began to take an active role in building Islamic charitable organizations in the Palestinian territories. It was especially active in Gaza, which had been administered by Egypt until Israel captured it. Its broad-based social services were usually connected to mosques and provided support for thousands of impoverished Palestinians. Because the Israeli authorities saw the Islamic movement as less of a threat, and perhaps easier to control, than Yasir Arafat's militant Palestinian Liberation Organization, the Muslim Brotherhood established itself relatively unhindered.

As resistance to the occupation intensified, some members of the Muslim Brotherhood grew impatient with the organization's social orientation. In 1980 a group of Palestinian activists separated themselves from the Brotherhood and formed Palestinian Islamic Jihad. Seven years later, Ahmed Yassin, who had been highly active in the Muslim Brotherhood (and whom the IDF assassinated in April 2004), founded Hamas, a much larger offshoot of the Brotherhood.

According to the Hamas charter of 1988, Palestine is an "Islamic Waqf [trust] consecrated for future Moslem generations until Judgment Day." The charter attacks both the Zionists and the Jews for their invasion of Palestine and strictly prohibits its division through "initiatives and so-called peaceful solutions." Hamas's charter proclaims: "The Koran is its constitution. . . . Jihad is its path, and death for the sake of Allah is the loftiest of its wishes." In other words, the charter implies that Hamas will employ violent methods of Jihad (literally "striving" or "struggle") to create an Islamic state in all of historic Palestine.

But the charter does not tell the whole story about Hamas.

"There was only a very brief period in terms of the overblown rhetoric of Hamas's charter," Alastair Crooke told me. Crooke, the former European Union security adviser and British intelligence official, had been involved in dialogue with Hamas for years. "The struggle was almost immediately redefined as one not against Jews but against aggressive Zionism," Crooke added. Yet to those people who believe God promised Israel to the Jews, an attack against Jews and Zionism are one and the same. Moreover, it is difficult for any Jewish person to see the image of a foot stomping on a Star of David and not feel threatened, even if Hamas is officially treating the star as a national rather than religious symbol.

Ghazi Hamad, longtime Hamas member and editor-in-chief of the Hamas-affiliated newspaper, *al-Risalah,* assured me that Hamas was not anti-Semitic. "We don't fight against Israel because they are Jews, but because we are living under occupation," Hamad told me from his unornamented office in Gaza City. Hamad went on to say that "if Sharon stops the occupation and expanding settlements, I would be ready to stop the suicide," but until this happens, Israel will "pay the price of bloodshed."

In fact, Hamad believes that Hamas has long since given up its claim to historic Palestine. "For a long time we accept a state in sixty-seven," he said. "But in our literature and in our education we say forty-eight."

If Hamas has truly accepted a state within the 1967 borders, I asked Hamad, then why do they preach a solution based on historic Palestine, the lands of 1948? This means the negation of Israel's existence—there's no other interpretation.

"I agree for the 1967 state," Hamad answered, "but in my heart and my mind I believe Israel will not give it to us. When Sharon says he will not give the West Bank, then I say that I will not give up my homes inside Israel."

In other words, Hamad was saying that Hamas would settle for 1967 borders if the people felt Israel was serious about such a deal. As long as Israel wasn't serious, Hamad warned that Hamas's only option was to fight the occupation.

I had seen and read plenty of interviews with Hamas leaders who claimed they would stop attacking Israeli civilians if Israel ceased targeted assassinations against their leadership. There was the *hudna* (in Arabic, "truce") in the summer of 2003 in which the Palestinian Authority negotiated a temporary cease-fire with Hamas based on this very premise. But the Israelis did not believe the *hudna* was genuine. They pointed to the word's Islamic origin: In 628 C.E., when Mohammad marched with his followers from Medina toward Mecca, a superior anti-Muslim army came out to oppose him. Instead of fighting, the armies established a nine-year *hudna*. Within two years, Mohammad had strengthened his forces enough to march again on Mecca, thereby breaking the truce. Israelis believed that like Mohammad, Hamas was merely biding its time, using the period of calm to rebuild it capacities.

All of this made me wonder about Ghazi Hamad's claim that under the right circumstances Hamas was willing to give up its claim to historic Palestine. I asked Alastair Crooke his opinion. He said that Hamas had a two-step territorial solution: an interim solution of accepting the lands of 1967 and a historic solution of ultimately conquering historic Palestine.

He felt the interim solution could become a "political reality" if Hamas believed the solution was "representative of Palestinian society." But Hamas would never recognize a deal negotiated between Israel and the Palestinian Authority, and in any case, Crooke believed, Hamas "would never exclude the possibility that one day Islam would cover the globe."

After arriving in Gaza City, Jen and I picked up Hamdan, a twenty-year-old Seeds of Peace graduate. Though he was from one of the roughest parts of the Gaza Strip, Hamdan didn't seem to have a single jagged edge. His face was dark and round, with an accommodating smile. He carried a pink cell phone covered in fake diamond studs. But Hamdan was taking us to his home in Rafah, where we soon discovered nothing sparkled.

As we drove out of the city, I asked Hamdan what he thought about Hamas. Hamdan supported Arafat's Fatah party and attended al-Azhar University, whose student union was run by Fatah-affiliated students. Islamic University, whose student council had close Hamas connections, was directly across the street. Hamdan said he was friendly with some Islamic University students, including the student union vice president.

Hamdan was convinced that Hamas was changing. "They used to be closed, but now they are becoming open-minded," he said. "And I'm hearing many spokesmen like Rantissi and Zahar saying that we are asking for the sixty-seven territories with a truce, which is different from before. They used to say they wouldn't give up the struggle once we got the sixty-seven territories."

"So you think they'll be satisfied with sixty-seven?"

"I'm sure. One hundred percent. I'm sure."

I remained skeptical. "And what about their desire for an Islamic state?"

"Hamas adopts the Islamic concepts," Hamdan said. "They say that they are the best because they have the right thinking, and many people were upset about that. They said, 'Hamas is so much proud of itself and they're not accepting anyone else's views.' But that was before the second intifada. Now Hamas has so wide a majority and people believe they are right, because we have no other option."

I heard this everywhere. After seven years in the Oslo process, the Palestinian Authority had failed to deliver an end to the occupation, and people were desperately seeking other options, especially from groups that opposed Israel with violence.

Khalil Shikaki, a prominent Palestinian pollster who heads The Palestinian Center for Policy and Survey Research explained it this way: "People who say they support the Islamists do so not because they strongly believe in Hamas's ideological positions. It may be reflecting emotional factors. More desire to see revenge being exacted from the Israelis because of what the Israelis are doing, which gives people a measure of satisfaction."

I asked Hamdan why he, unlike so many others, wasn't switching his support to Hamas. He had a long list of reasons. "If you get into Hamas, you have to be obliged to them. You have to be so much pious, and religious, and you have to learn the Koran by heart, and you have to go daily to the mosque, and learn every prayer. According to my religion I do have to pray, and go to the mosque, and learn the Koran. But I don't like the strict laws. I can do it by myself. So you don't need to force me."

Hamas is very strict in terms of its religious requirements: adhering to ritual prayer, modesty for women, refraining from alcohol and other activities forbidden by Islamic law. It is not surprising that Gaza, Hamas's stronghold, is religiously conservative. Few women walk outside without the *hijab* (in Southern Gaza I saw many wearing the *niqab,* the face veil, as well), you cannot purchase alcohol, and social behavior (such as interactions between men and women) is strictly guided by Islamic norms. For these reasons, Hamas also has a substantial presence in many of Gaza's mosques, among both worshippers and religious leaders.

Some have suggested that Hamas is not as religiously fundamentalist as its charter suggests. "The priority for Hamas, as a Palestinian organization, is to end the occupation [and] not an Iranian-style revolution to bring out a theocracy," explained Beverly Milton-Edwards, assistant director of the Center for Ethnic Conflict at Queen's University in Belfast, Ireland. Milton-Edwards told me that if Hamas ever gained control of Palestine they would form an "Islamic governance," or Islamic society. Alastair Crooke, who works with Milton-Edwards on these issues, said such a society would look socially and religiously similar to present-day Gaza. The fact that Hamas's slogan calls the Koran their constitution and Jihad their path does not mean they strictly observe Islamic law, Sharia. For one thing, the Koran strictly prohibits suicide. Even Hamas member Ghazi Hamad told me that "it is written in our Koran that someone who kills himself will go to Hell forever because the life is a present from Allah. The principle is to keep the life."

The Koran also has strict rules against killing civilians. Sheikh Abel

Majid, former imam at the Al-Aqsa mosque, explained to me that the Koran outlines five different types of Jihad, most of which have nothing to do with Holy War against non-Muslims. "Jihad is to protect the idea, and the people, and the land of Islam and the holy places," Sheikh Majid told me. "Fight in the name of God, those who fight you. But do not transgress limits."

I asked the sheikh about these "limits."

"You can't attack civilians unless your enemy does it first," he said, "and you can only do so to make equality between you and your enemy. But if you can solve any problem without fighting, you don't have the right to fight. The Koran says that it's best to be patient."

These seemed to be logical reasons why Islam forbade the targeting of civilians. First, as for whether Israelis or Palestinians "started" the conflict, neither side could agree. Second, how could you ever determine what "equality" meant in this context? Was it simply trying to balance out the death toll or did you have to take other kinds of casualties into account? Third, who was to say that a military solution was the only feasible one? Especially when people on both sides, religious leaders as well as politicians, are working toward peaceful solutions.

In the end, the sheikh agreed: Even if Hamas did claim to work in the name of Allah, and assured its prospective martyrs that Paradise awaited them, the Koran did not prescribe such actions. "Their operations are not related to religious teaching," the sheikh told me. "They are related to Israeli actions."

This is exactly why Hamas has gained so much popular support. Palestinians view Hamas-perpetrated bombings as part of the nationalist struggle and not so much the struggle for Islam. Hamas knows this. From its inception, Milton-Edwards explained, Hamas had to compete against the PLO for the people's support. "They had to have an alternative message," she said. "They've never been purely Islamists. They've always had a nationalist dimension."

The truth is, Palestinian resistance groups often conflate Islam and Palestinian nationalism. Today the secular Al-Aqsa Martyrs' Brigades, the militant group that associates with Arafat's Fatah party, has initiated many of the suicide bombings against Israeli soldiers and civilians. It's not surprising that a nonreligious group would name itself after the Al-Asqa mosque, the third holiest site in Islam, because Al-Aqsa is as culturally symbolic to Palestinians as Yasir Arafat himself. Jerusalem, Al-Aqsa's home, is the holy grail of their national struggle.

A Christian Fatah activist told me that if his government tried to arrest Hamas members, he would oppose the Palestinian Authority with all his might. I asked him why a Christian would support a group that desires an Islamic society. The Fatah activist replied: "Because Israel is surrounding us, killing us. You have to help your brother."

It took me a while to understand his point. Why would a Christian who was ideologically opposed to Hamas want to accept Hamas as a legitimate part of his family? From the Palestinian perspective, the occupation makes these contrasting viewpoints compatible. The occupation is the most unifying force in Palestinian society. It allows a nation—divided between Muslims and Christians, West Bankers and Gazans, refugees and nonrefugees—to see itself as one.

This is most apparent in the way Palestinians interpret the act of suicide. To them, suicide is synonymous with resistance. This is not just a question of calling the act by a different name; to them, it's a different act altogether.

"I hate it when people call it a suicide bombing," Reem told me. "I say martyr. But if I want to be a journalist, I must say freedom fighter. To say martyr is pro-Palestinian, and suicide bomber is pro-Israel. But freedom fighter is in the middle."

To me, "freedom fighter" sounded incredibly biased. No Jewish Israeli, I told her, would agree that Hamas members are blowing up buses in the name of freedom.

"I know that if an Israeli heard me say 'freedom fighter,' he'd think I was biased," she said. "But he's wrong."

"So why do you think that using the term 'suicide bomber' is pro-Israeli? Couldn't you argue that that is simply a literal description of the act? A person blows himself up—commits suicide—with a bomb?"

"Suicide means to kill yourself, but not for something. When people kill themselves, it's because they feel useless. But the martyr dies for a reason. The word 'suicide' doesn't explain the reasons why he sacrificed himself."

This statement explained how in the Palestinian mind-set, killing yourself for the national cause was not synonymous with suicide but with resistance. Of course, anyone who commits suicide has a reason—usually depression and despair—but to Reem, the suicide bombers aren't acting selfishly. As she sees it, the bomber's act has a distinct place in the history of Islam and the Palestinian national struggle. This is why she prefers the term "freedom fighter."

"Freedom fighters are fighters for freedom," she continued. "They fight, and die, and suffer for freedom. When you call a person a suicide bomber, do you bomb for suicide?"

"No but—" I tried to interject.

"The Israelis are occupying us. We are fighting for our land and defending our land. The Israelis call us terrorists and I don't agree with that word. They call us suicide bombers—and suicide is bad in religion. Because if you kill yourself you go to Hell. By calling us suicide bombers it means we're not honored but disgraced. And the one who kills himself is precious; he does something very great."

I knew that Reem supported the targeting of Israeli soldiers inside the territories (i.e., those people who physically enforced the occupation) but not civilians. Still, her views on suicide bombing and freedom fighting demonstrate the degree to which martyrdom has infiltrated Palestinian culture. Aside from the Gaza graffiti, color posters of deceased men hang in every city. The game of "martyr" is popular among little kids; I once watched a Palestinian girl play dead as her sisters carried her by her arms and legs in a funeral procession around the house before finally depositing her into her "grave," the family room sofa. In fact, anyone who dies by Israeli hands, whether he blows himself up or is hit by a stray bullet, is considered a martyr. But as Reem said, to actively give up your life in fighting the occupation is the greatest honor of all.

Palestinians also appreciate Hamas, because the organization helps people. Hamas is closely affiliated with the social service network built by the Muslim Brotherhood, and its members are active in most Islamic charities and foundations throughout the West Bank and Gaza. These charities provide social services to an estimated one in six Palestinians. Aside from this, Hamas gives direct assistance to those in need. Khalil Shikaki surmised that "Hamas probably spends millions of dollars each month to pay for social services that the poorest of the poor needs." This includes paying university tuition and housing costs, and subsidizing the families of martyrs and those in jail. In a sense, Hamas provides a measure of security to people who feel their lives are hanging on a wire.

Hamdan explained this well: "Once you see all of the militants around you, they've got so much spirit in themselves and you never feel afraid at all. You feel the support of them, because they say, 'We have nothing to lose. Why should we be afraid? The whole infrastructure is destroyed, so what do we have to lose?' " Hamdan's home, Rafah, has seen some of the worst destruction by IDF forces. It's a dangerous place; a stray Israeli bullet hit Hamdan's cousin in the head on Hamdan's doorstep. Hamdan believes that over fifty percent of Rafah's population call themselves Hamas sympathizers, and Rafah isn't even a Hamas stronghold.

The 2005 municipal elections, in which Hamas won a majority of the local councils in Gaza, verified its popularity there. The fact that Hamas participated in these elections, however, and decided to run for the Palestinian Legislative Council, signaled a change of course within the organization. To Hamas, Arafat's Palestinian Authority was a corrupt entity, obsequious in the face of Israel. They believed any solution negotiated by the PA couldn't possibly represent the true desires of Palestinians. Therefore, to maintain its integrity, Hamas refused to give up terror and shunned political participation. Yet after Arafat's death in 2004, Hamas, like many Palestinians, saw the potential for a rejuvenated political system. IDF-targeted assassinations had crippled their military leadership (though they were loath to admit it), and rumors circulated that the group was hungry for international legitimacy—something terror would never achieve.

Hamas's involvement in Palestinian politics does not automatically mean it has relinquished violent tactics. It is possible Palestine could see a situation similar to that in Northern Ireland where Sinn Fein and the IRA operated simultaneously. It is equally possible that political participation could be a mitigating force for Hamas. Khalil Shikaki believes so. He acknowledges that hard-liners exist in Gaza but says Hamas's West Bank military leadership is defunct. "Hasan Yusuf is the most senior Hamas official in the West Bank," Shikaki told me, "and you'll find it hard to distinguish between him and Fatah."

Driving south along the coast on a sunny day, Gaza didn't seem so bad. It felt good to be with Jen Marlowe and Hamdan, speeding past the beautiful blue of the Mediterranean. We were going fast enough so that the trash scattered across the beach blended into the sand; you hardly noticed it. This was prime beachfront, and yet it was completely undeveloped. Imagine what this coast would be like under other circumstances! As overdeveloped as Eilat, with grand hotels, restaurants, and Europeans chartering planes for weekend getaways. It was on this coastal road, however, that I finally saw my amusement park. The rusting structures—Ferris wheel and food stands—stood alongside the highway, overlooking the ocean. Palestinians had once visited this place on their vacations but had deserted it, Hamdan claimed, under threat of settlers' gunfire. Another Palestinian friend told me it simply shut down after the second intifada erupted. Now its attractions lay derelict, drooping into the sand.

On our way south, we picked up Hamdan's friend, Khalid, who worked at the Yabbos community center in Khan Yunis refugee camp, next to Rafah. I asked him about the children who participated at the center: What impact did the refugee camp environment have on their behavior?

"Our children are different from the world's children." Khalid turned to face me in the backseat. "The world's children have all the things they want. Let's talk about the clothes of the children, transportation, how they can express their opinions. All these are available in the world but not here," he said of Gaza, as though it were another planet entirely. "Our work is to make the children able to ask for their needs. And pacifying their resentful feelings against the whole situation. And encouraging their talents and skills. If nobody actually takes care of these skills they will lose them."

I told Khalid I'd heard of youth institutions—summer camps throughout the West Bank and Gaza—whose activities did exactly the opposite: inflamed the anger of young people. When I asked Ghazi Hamad about Hamas-run camps, he called them "a fabrication." I countered that an IDF consultant on terrorism and incitement had given me a pile of pamphlets about Palestinian youth camps.

"They exist," Khalid said. "You can't just put the children away from the political situation."

"So what happens at these camps?" I leaned forward eagerly.

"They teach them about patriotism. And their legacy. Is this what the Israelis call incitement?" Khalid asked.

"Well, the Israelis would say that having the kids sing songs or recite poems praising martyrs is incitement."

"If we sing a song for Muhammad Dura is it incitement?" Hamdan wanted to know. He was referring to the young Palestinian boy who was shot just days into the second intifada while cowering next to a wall with his father. The footage was broadcast worldwide, the thirty-second clip playing like a fast-flip book; one minute you saw the boy gripping his father's jacket and the next he was slumped over dead.

"But what about the show on Palestinian Authority TV (the government-sponsored television station) called 'The Children's Club'?" I asked. "The footage I've seen shows little kids holding guns and singing that they will spill their blood for Palestine."

"First of all, we don't watch PA TV," Hamdan said. "We all have Arab satellite. And second, this show is just formal. It has nothing to do with reality. Because it is impossible. You've never heard that a kid has actually done something like that."

To me, the implausibility of a six-year-old suicide bomber was beside the point. Why, I asked Hamdan and Khalid, would an adult dress a little kid in a *kiffiyeh* and place a machine gun in his arms?

"Our kids never had toys," Khalid said, as though this somehow explained giving a child a real gun.

"A child sees all of that on a daily basis," Hamdan tried to explain. "The guns, the bullets, the sounds of the bombings and shellings. So he has no more fear of that. Seeing a Kalashnikov is normal. I can have bullets and I can trade them."

"Like American kids trade baseball cards," I scoffed.

"Exactly. People have actually asked me to buy bullets and sell them."

I continued to brood over Khalid and Hamdan's bizarre moral indifference toward children and weapons. Shortly, we arrived at Yabbos. It was a one-story building with a corrugated roof and life-size cartoons painted on the concrete walls. A skinny but jovial Mickey Mouse with a Palestinian flag oversaw the small playground and sandbox out front. A few kids were playing there and stopped to inspect us as we climbed from the taxi. Encouraged by Khalid, they followed us inside. We were greeted by Yabbos's director, and I asked him what kind of psychological effect he thought the intifada was having on the kids in Khan Yunis. He responded by pulling out a collection of pencil and crayon drawings.

"They are so much interacting with their situation," Hamdan said. "When we ask them to draw something, they all draw pictures of the tanks, the guns, the battles." In other words, I thought, proof of our conversation in the car.

I had heard about these kinds of drawings from pro-Palestinian organizations, but had never seen them up close. Most of the pictures were crude, but the scenes were unmistakable: bombs rained down from the sky; an Israeli flag dripped blood upon a figure lying prostrate, his hands tied beneath him; a tank stood opposite a militant who aimed his gun over a pile of rocks. One picture depicted a militant, with an Iraqi flag over him, pointing his gun at a soldier with an American flag. The Arabic above it read: *The American Occupation.*

I was surprised that only one of the drawings referenced the United States, but one was more than enough for me. The picture left no doubt about the young illustrator's view of U.S. involvment in Iraq: The American soldier was being likened to an Israeli soldier, the U.S. occupation in Iraq equated with the Israeli occupation of Palestine. Apparently, this child did not care that Saddam Hussein had been captured. When it came to good guys and bad guys, the Iraqi militants were the honorable ones, the U.S. soldiers the scoundrels.

Just before we left Yabbos, I had a few words with the kids who had followed us from the playground. There were three boys and one girl. The boys were wearing slacks and button-down shirts. They were all skinny, their hair unkempt. The girl wore a bulky winter jacket with an enormous hood lined with fake fur. She was the only one of the four who dared to look me in the eye. The director told us that the girl's home had been demolished a few weeks ago, but he would not say why. When I asked the children what they wanted to be when they grew up, the girl burst out in Arabic, "A doctor!" Her eyes gleamed.

"Why a doctor?" I asked.

Hamdan translated the question. For a moment, the girl squirmed in her heavy jacket, its fake fur collar scratching her chin. Then she decided, "I want to take the patients and help them."

I asked the boys what they wanted to do.

"A teacher," one of them replied. The other two followed his lead.

"A teacher," they echoed.

"Why a teacher?" I asked the first boy.

He looked embarrassed to be singled out, but Hamdan coaxed a response. "He says he loves learning."

When I asked the kids whether they wanted to live and work in Gaza when they grew up, I was shocked by their unanimous *"Yes!"*

Back in the car we headed toward Tal Es-Sultan, the housing project built to absorb the overflow of refugees from Rafah. Hamdan said the name meant "Sultan's Hill," but the name I initially heard was "Sultan's *Hell.*" I found the pairing of sultan and Hell strange, but the place only confirmed my mistake; Tal Es-Sultan was Hell-like. We pulled up to the edge of the project alongside the beach to see a group of boys playing soccer barefoot in a vacant lot. By the time we got out of the taxi, they had already collected around us: a sea of dusty, expectant faces. A sewage stink wafted through the chilly air.

"Of course they don't have access to the beach," Hamdan said to make sure I knew. "There's an army base over there." Sure enough, an Israeli flag waved nearby. "I wanted to show you this." Hamdan turned toward the row of concrete apartments, but with all the rubble, it was difficult to distinguish one from the next. "Do you see how this wall was punched?"

For a split second the holes seemed the work of a thousand tiny fists, not bullets.

Lower down it looked like a large portion of the wall had been knocked through and then patched up.

"That was the living room," Hamdan said. "A tank went through it."

I took a photo of Hamdan, Khalid, and two of the children in front of the bullet-battered wall. They stood upon the rubble, in a row, by height. The last in line was a little boy, who peeked out from behind his taller friend. They flashed bright, happy smiles—in fact they could have been tourists standing not in front of a shot-up building but before some of the ancient ruins of Italy or Greece.

Then, quick as a camera snap, we were back in the car, trying to shut the doors against the children who had flocked around the taxi. Their hands slapped against the windows like wings. One boy pulled the door open and Hamdan shooed him away. A boy outside my window made a monkey face, giggling as he stretched his cheeks. The car began to move slowly, shaking off the kids. As it sped up, they ran after us, jumping and calling in the dust. I thought about the boy who had tried to climb into the taxi. Did he think we could rescue him? We were no rescue mission, but the plane that flies close to the deserted island, missing the stranded sailors, despite their flares.

Rafah refugee camp sits in southernmost Gaza at the Egyptian border. Ninety thousand people live there. Hamdan's family is native to Rafah town, which existed before the camp. Though Hamdan is not a refugee, the town and the camp are indistinguishable. Both have severely felt the effects of the second intifada. IDF raids and house demolitions are common in this area, because the army is looking for weapons-smuggling tunnels between Rafah and Egypt.

I asked Hamdan what he knew about this.

"Actually, a close friend of mine was arrested two weeks ago," he said as we drove into the heart of Rafah. "He was a weapons smuggler. Just for the militants, not for his personal interests. And he was so much decent, you know? Once I heard the story of arresting him, I feel so much touched. Because they tortured him so much."

"How do you know the Israelis tortured him?"

"Well, my neighbor told me about it. They got him from the crossing point with Egypt. And with the hummer jeeps all around his house."

"How old is your friend?"

"He's older than me. He's twenty-six, I guess. He was so much good and pious and decent. And the way they arrested him was so much painful. They tied him with shackles and they punched him on the head with their sharp tools. He had a friend who was waiting to do bombings."

"The friend was about to do a suicide bombing?"

"In Gaza, not in the West Bank. You know it's so hard to get past Erez."

The IDF had captured Hamdan's friend and ordered him to call the bomber, tell him he was safe, and ask to meet. The soldiers gave him a mobile phone to make the call. But when the bomber was on the line, Hamdan's friend told him not to come. "And once the Israelis heard this word," Hamdan said, "they started to beat him up."

"How can he be a pious and a decent man if he was helping to smuggle weapons?" I asked Hamdan.

"To smuggle weapons not for himself, for the militants."

This answer proved how little I truly understood Hamdan and others living in his situation. Hamdan thought I was questioning his friend's motives. That I believed his act to be selfish instead of selfless. He never thought for a second that I was raising the contradiction between being decent and pious and helping to smuggle instruments of violence.

"Aren't the militants using the smuggled weapons to *hurt* people?" I asked.

"Ah, to hurt people. Well, that's the cornerstone," Hamdan said with a Shakespearean flourish and added, "I don't think the smuggling has something to do with the intifada." I raised an eyebrow at this, but Hamdan explained that there weren't many Israelis in Rafah to fight. The settlers were fortified in their "strongholds" and only a few soldiers manned the crossing points and outposts. "Since the intifada, there were not a huge number of soldiers killed in Rafah," Hamdan said with certainty. "Maybe ten." According to him, the violence that took place in Rafah was mostly inflicted *by* Israelis, not against them.

"It's so horrible," he said. "Once you see the Israelis coming to take someone and destroy their home for nothing. Destroying 150 homes for a tunnel? Does that sound reasonable to you?"

But after a recent operation in Rafah, senior IDF officials reported that the weapons smuggled through the Egypt-Rafah tunnels could have a "strategic impact" on the intifada. The weapons may have included "stinger shoulder-mounted anti-aircraft missiles that could shoot down the attack helicopters Israel often uses in operations in Gaza [as well as] threaten Israel Air Force warplanes or civilian aircraft flying close to the Gaza Strip." Also, the sources said, "The Palestinians were trying to smuggle Katyusha rockets, which have the range to hit Israeli cities near the Strip." Finally, "IDF officers expressed surprise at the extent of the militants' firepower, including the hundreds of bombs, grenades and anti-tank missiles Palestinians threw at the troops."*

We arrived in Rafah two months after this operation had taken place. It was late in the afternoon, and the sun was hitting its final peak. Hamdan pointed out an Egyptian flag across the border, and we had to squint to see it. But this was not Gaza City; there was no glare, no washed-out whiteness. The only color was cement. When light hit these buildings, it fell dead.

Rafah is a world caved in on itself. There was so much rubble, it was impossible to tell how far the Egyptian border was from where we stood. Some buildings seemed fully intact, though lacking any signs of life. Other buildings crumbled, their windows gaping hungrily at us. Then there was the *stuff* over which we climbed. What was all this detritus? Had these been homes? If I removed the debris, stone by stone, would I excavate someone's bedroom? And if I dug deeper, would I indeed find a tunnel? Through which I could crawl and pop up on the other side? Stand next to that Egyptian flag and wave back at Hamdan?

I turned to find my group heading back down the street on which we'd come. It was a dirt road, potholed, and wider than I would have expected for a refugee camp. There were a few kids scattered around, but unlike those at Tal Es-Sultan, they paid us little attention. I supposed this was a typical street. It had rows of concrete houses crammed in together in a strange mismatch of levels and heights. There was plenty of destruction here, too, although these toppled structures had obviously been homes.

*Source: http://www.labournet.net/world/0310/rafah4.html; *Ha'aretz,* 10/13/03.

They seemed to have collapsed as though they'd been held up by a single supporting structure that someone suddenly yanked out.

I wondered how the IDF actually went about this kind of operation. Why was one home destroyed and the one next to it left intact? And how did the army even know which house they wanted? The buildings and streets lacked numbers and names—and I didn't think a family would publicize the existence of a tunnel beneath their home.

As I stood contemplating this, I heard a rapid series of pops in the distance.

"I think we should go." Hamdan sounded nervous.

Suddenly I realized that I wasn't safe. Whom I should fear, Palestinians or Israelis, I didn't know. It had taken quite a bit of courage for me to come to Rafah in the first place, and now that I was here, I was taking my security for granted. Just because it seemed quiet, I reminded myself, didn't mean it was. As I started toward the car, I saw Jen Marlowe with a group of refugee children climbing around the corner of a house, on a small pile of debris. I went to the base of the house to inspect. I couldn't see anything, so I began to climb after them, my sneakers wobbling on the sharp-edged stones. After I'd gained a little height I saw what they did: a bulldozer, sitting in the middle of a sandy lot, its shovel frozen at mid-height. The kids were pointing at the thing as though it were some dangerous animal they'd spotted in the wild. Jen climbed higher to get a better look and a photo.

"We really should go," Hamdan said.

Immediately I turned around and scooted back to the road.

"Jen," Hamdan was calling to Jen Marlowe. "Jen, we should go now. This isn't a good place to be."

I didn't hear whether Jen responded, because I was already sitting in the car, anxiously tapping my feet. I saw Hamdan disappear up the slope after Jen. I knew that I should give Jen some credit for coming here with me; she was the only person at Seeds of Peace willing to go to Rafah. When I told my friend Jared I was going there, he said I was nuts. But Jen was walking around as though this were as much her home as it was Hamdan's. I remembered the morning, which now seemed light-years away, when she'd picked me up in the Transit, that elephantine van, and I'd climbed in to find her wearing a long-sleeved dark green shirt, formless and huge beneath an even larger jacket, and pants of some other camouflage color. Her shoes looked about to unravel. I glanced at my own sneakers, blue jeans, and black sweater. All this time I thought I'd chosen a "Gaza appropriate" outfit, but next to Jen I felt like a beauty queen. The truth is, Jen looked more like a refugee than most of the refugees I'd seen. But she wasn't. She didn't know Rafah any better than I did. And it was dangerous enough being here, let alone tempting bulldozers.

When Hamdan finally coaxed Jen back to the car, we drove to another typical Rafah site. These were the Red Crescent tents in which recently displaced Rafah families were living. The three we saw were made from heavy green plastic and pitched on a dirt mound directly below the bombed-out apartments from which their inhabitants had fled. Jen and I climbed up the small hill and surveyed the camp. Most of the other buildings around appeared sound, but devoid of life. Kids ran through the streets; all over Rafah, the absence of adults was astonishing.

Outside the tents a fire burned in an empty oil barrel. We peeked inside one tent to find a floor covered with sleeping bags. Clear-glass teacups sat upon a cardboard box, and an old man slept in the corner. Another man came out of his tent to speak with us. He wasn't living there anymore, he said, because the United Nations Relief and Works Agency (UNRWA) was helping subsidize an apartment for him and his family through the winter. I wondered what he was doing at the tent if he had an apartment, but before I could ask, the man was describing the cause of his homelessness.

"We saw the tanks approaching and heard the planes," he said of the raid. "I took my family from my home. There was no warning."

"Why do you think this happened?" I asked him.

"It is obvious. It is an organized policy of the Israelis to force all Palestinians from their homes."

A bubble of protest rose in my throat and I forced myself to swallow it. If some army had just sent me fleeing in fear of my life, had just destroyed my home, wouldn't I believe the same thing? And yet my overwhelming reaction was to tell this man that he was absolutely wrong, that there was no policy of organized expulsion. My heart pounded with the realization that hundreds, perhaps thousands, of Palestinians carried this horrible idea with them everywhere they went. They believed it as much as they knew they were alive—and it wasn't true. It simply wasn't true! I wanted to shout at the man, to shake him out of this terrible misunderstanding. To convince him before it was too late. But too late for what? I had no idea, but I felt something horrible in the pit of my stomach.

"Jen, are you cold?" I must have been shivering. Hamdan was offering his jacket. "Please, take this. I don't need it." I told him that I was fine, mine was in the car.

"If you're sure." He looked concerned. "So we are going now. This man from the tent has invited us to his apartment for tea."

I stumbled down the dirt mound and into the car.

The UNRWA-subsidized apartment was four flights up a crumbling and muddied stairway. There were no lights to guide us. It was nearly dark outside, and we had to walk slowly so as not to trip. I resisted using the concrete wall as a guide, because I didn't know how soon I'd be able to wash my hands. I thought about my college dorms and how no one went into the shower without the protection of shower shoes. Could I even imagine what a shower in this refugee camp looked like? Or what the already sewage-sprayed streets of this place would be like in the rain? A person living in West Jerusalem, or Tel Aviv, or Chevy Chase, Maryland, simply had no idea. Whatsoever.

We entered the apartment. Straight ahead was a narrow kitchen where a grandmotherly figure sat cutting vegetables and a younger woman held her child. We were introduced to the old woman, the matriarch of the family, and then led into the sitting room. It was large and square with a reddish carpet and shabby couches around the perimeter. The grandmother joined us as did a number of young men—brothers, perhaps friends. The young woman handed the baby to the grandmother and returned to the kitchen.

"So what do you do?" The man from the tent turned to me and Jen Marlowe.

Jen said she worked for a youth organization. I told him that I was writing a book about young Israelis and Palestinians. I waited for his response to this, but he didn't seem concerned with the specifics.

"And you are from the United States?" he asked.

We told him where we were from.

"Oh, Washington, D.C.," he said with mock appreciation. "The U.S. government knows the truth but they don't want to do anything. Do you know that the U.S. Congress takes a salary from the Israeli Zionist gangs?"

We shook our heads.

"A paper in Egypt reported this. It is clear as the sun. Some of these congressmen even confessed!" He looked at us as if to say, "You can't possibly deny this if they confessed." "They receive more money than *twice* the salary they get from the U.S. government." He looked at us wisely. We said nothing.

He tried another route of persuasion. "You know the Zionists control the mass media all over the world? One of the largest mass media networks in Great Britain was founded by the Zionists."

"Did you read that in the paper as well?" Jen asked without an ounce of sarcasm. "*Al Hayat* newspaper," the man said and took a tea from his wife's tray.

"So what kind of work do you do?" Jen asked, after taking her tea. My heart was pounding. I was awed by her composure.

"I studied in Egypt," he told us. "Shakespeare. *King Lear* is my favorite." He looked at us knowingly: "He who doesn't read English literature loses many things in his life. One of the people's rights is to be acquainted with different cultures."

Are you sure you mean all cultures? I wanted to ask him. *Even Israeli and American?* I doubted it and didn't want to listen anymore. I was starting to feel nervous, but this was more than butterflies before an important exam or interview. My feeling bordered on chaos; if I had felt slightly out of orbit that previous evening outside the Muqata, at this moment I was on the verge of being sucked into a black hole.

Even so, I wasn't at all prepared for the conversation that came two hours later. We'd left Rafah and returned to Gaza City to visit Ola, a Seeds graduate from 2000. Ola was only nineteen but she was already in her third year as an engineering student. Her body was delicate, her outward manner demure. Her tongue, however, was capable of astounding sharpness when she had something on her mind.

She looked so pristine sitting in her parents' living room, offering us miniature pizzas and sweets, and pouring us tea. Her words were not so pretty. I asked Ola how Palestinians in Gaza City responded to the events of September 11, 2001. I told her about the footage I had seen of Palestinians dancing in the streets and how the Arab-American community responded with outrage, saying the images were out of context and that the U.S. media was deliberately trying to demonize Islam.

"Yes, people's first reaction was to celebrate," Ola said slowly, her hands folded in her lap. "Nine-eleven was a slap in the face of the American government." It may have been a great tragedy, she said, but the Palestinians didn't care about American deaths. "Innocent Palestinians die every day," she said. "It's a part of life, not something you take extra time to dwell on. I don't agree with the hijackers, but I understand their motivation—why the Arab world hates America. The United States is the world's super-power," she continued. "Look how your government gives weapons to the Israeli government, invades Iraq, does so many things against the people. I don't agree, but this [was] why most people in Gaza City didn't think 9/11 was enough."

I hardly had time to let this sink in, because I suddenly realized it was eight-thirty, and Erez closed at nine. How far were we from the check-point, I wondered? I went to the window to check that our driver was there; he wasn't. Jen called him and told him to come. I sat back down to wait for Raed, tapping my foot against the carpet. If we got to the check-point after nine would they turn us away? Would we have to spend the night in Gaza? And where would we go? Back to Ola's house or to another Seed's? Perhaps we could find a hotel. But were hotels still operating here? Where was the driver?

Raed arrived at eight-forty. Our good-byes to Ola seemed to last for-ever: first in the living room, then down the stairwell, then in the door-way. Jen seemed entirely cool, but I was panicked. The ride from Ola's house to Erez was one of most nerve-racking twenty minutes of my life. I'd never had this kind of visceral fright-flight reaction before; I had to get out of Gaza! I just wanted my own bed; to be tucked warm and tight into my Chevy Chase cocoon, or even that of my apartment in West Jerusalem. I tried to convince myself that I'd be back there in no time, but all I could see was the car pulling up to Erez just as the gates slammed shut.

Jen and I spent the ride home singing along to musical sound tracks. We'd gotten to Erez with plenty of time to spare, passed the two bag checks that confirmed we weren't bringing anything suspicious or illegal into Israel, and waited as they reprocessed our passports. My tourist visa now had a green circle stamped on the back: Erez. It was a mark of pride; I'd done it—I'd gone to Gaza. Even better, I was going home. Every second brought me closer to my bed.

Jen pulled up outside my apartment, and we sat in silence, the motor running.

"Are you doing all right?" she asked after a moment. "It was a hard day."

I searched myself as best I could. "I'm fine," I said, and I meant it. I am good at distancing myself from painful experiences. I can see or hear something horrible and keep it at arm's length. "I'm sure it'll catch up with me soon enough," I added, "but now I'm just ready for bed."

"Okay, if you're sure."

"I'm sure." We hugged good night and I got out of the car.

But the second I turned from the car, I erupted into tears. I knew it was best to shove back down whatever I was feeling, have my shower, and go to sleep, but once I felt the water over me, no amount of scrubbing seemed good enough. The grime of Gaza had sunk through my skin.

I felt utterly disgusted. I was disgusted by those disgusting refugee camps, the disgusting ideas I heard there, and the disgusting circumstances that fed them. I was disgusted with myself for thinking all day long how lucky I was to not have been born in such a cesspool: among sewage and soldiers, Kalashnikovs and Qassam rockets, bulldozers and graffiti proclaiming death. Even though these people were stuck in Gaza against their will, I was disgusted that any Palestinian would dare conceive a child in such a cage. It was a horrible, unfair thought, but I didn't care. I was as disgusted with the Gazans as I was with the Israelis.

But my disgust came from more than what I saw. It came from a newly discovered emotion within myself: fear. Listening to Ola and the man in Rafah, I suddenly understood the congruence between circumstance and ideology. How easily a well-educated man, a man who spoke fluent English and had studied Shakespeare, could believe that the Zionists controlled the mass media the world over and that they paid secret salaries to U.S. congressmen. His environment confirmed everything his newspapers claimed. How else could he explain his seemingly inexplicable circumstances? Hamdan had said it himself: "One hundred and fifty homes for a single tunnel—is that logical?" And Hamdan had said something else: "It's all about revenge. The rule I have in my mind is that if someone punishes me, I have to punish him equally." This was many Palestinians' way of restoring logic and order to their world. But I now saw that there were ideological as well as physical ways of evening out the score. Only belief of a mega-conspiracy between Israel and the United States could "rationally" explain to Palestinians why they'd become so powerless and depraved.

It didn't make me feel better to hear Ola say that Palestinians hate American policy and not its people. Or to have the editor of the Hamas-affiliated newspaper assure me that Hamas has no intention of targeting Americans, as he had when I met with him. There were a lot of people, I knew, who despite being good, peace-loving human beings, were thinking that September 11 "wasn't enough." Not because they hated freedom, but because they wanted it. Desperately wanted it. And they saw the United

States and Israel as two powers that existed only to strip them of this right. In light of this, it seemed implausible that buses *weren't* already blowing up in Washington and New York.

"They can't get a visa," Jen Marlowe joked when I worried about militants entering the United States. The truth in her statement lent me little security.

WHO
INHERITS THE
HOLY LAND?

All About Abu

Eight-year-old Hadeel is afraid to sleep alone. This is clearly a testament to her environment. All children living in Gaza have fallen asleep to the sound of missiles and gunfire at one point, but Hadeel is no ordinary Gazan. The perimeters of her home are patrolled by armed guards; not sleepy overnight security, but black-clad hard men packing automatic pistols. The fact is, you'd be a fool to come near Hadeel's house uninvited. Her father is Mohammad Dahlan, one of the most powerful men in Palestine.

Dahlan, known to his close associates as Abu Fady, has Bill Clinton–esque charisma and the easy self-confidence of a man with the world (or at least the Gaza Strip) in his pocket. I walked into his Gaza City office to find him reclining behind a mountainous wooden desk, talking fast and low into the phone. When he saw me standing there, he looked startled, like a thief caught in the act. Then he smiled, a grin at least the width of the desk. His eyes exploded with light.

"Jenny! Welcome. How are you? How's Aaron?" He reached across the wooden expanse and enclosed my small hand within his own solid grip. "It is wonderful to have you here!" He relaxed back into his chair, his eyes admiring my face as though I was a long-lost friend. "Let's call Aaron!" With magicianlike dexterity, a silver cell phone appeared between his fingers. "Aaron? Mohammad Dahlan here." Dahlan's smile expanded to colossal proportions. "I have your daughter here . . . yes Aaron . . . yes." Dahlan looked at me and winked. "Yes, I promise to take very good care of her . . . okay, bye."

At that moment, an aide rushed in and whispered into Dahlan's ear.

Dahlan cleared his throat and his face grew serious. But a split second later he was grinning again—a smile that seemed to me at once winning and wolfish.

My first view of Dahlan, with his flashy cell phone and fancy suit, hid a lot. Beneath his glossy exterior are the rough and squalid streets where he got his start. He was born in 1961 in a Gaza refugee camp and built his reputation in Yasir Arafat's Fatah movement in "the places that were the poorest": in the camps and among students. Throughout the 1980s, his direction came from the Palestinian leadership in exile, men like Arafat and Abu Jihad, whom the Israelis assassinated in 1988. Despite Abu Jihad's alleged terrorist activities, Dahlan assured me that the focus of his own activities with Fatah were political, not military.

"We didn't have special armed wings at that time," he said. "We educated people for Fatah. We took part in elections for student unions every year."

Dahlan was drawn to Fatah ("conquest" in Arabic) because its aim was to unite Palestinians under a single slogan: ending the occupation. "Everyone can agree on this," he explained. "But if we say to get rid of the occupation you have to follow the Koran and the Islamic belief, that would be a problem. And the same if we adopt Marxism." In the old days, he said wistfully, all sectors of society took part in demonstrations. Dahlan credits his work and influence as a major cause for the first intifada. His activism got him jailed nearly a dozen times between 1981 and 1986. In 1987, just as the intifada was breaking out, the Israelis deported him to Jordan.

Dahlan was allowed back into the country when the Oslo process began. From 1994 until 2002, he served as Arafat's chief of preventative security in Gaza. From 2002 to 2003 he was minister of the interior under Mahmoud Abbas (Abu Mazen), Palestine's first prime minister and Arafat's eventual successor. Dahlan listed his job responsibilities as "confiscating illegal weapons, closing the tunnels, implementing laws, stopping the violence, and maintaining the cease-fire." In short: hunting down Hamas and arresting them. After only a few months as prime minister, however, Abu Mazen resigned out of frustration. He lacked support from Arafat, the Israelis, and the Americans. Dahlan went with him.

Clearly, Dahlan's Fatah activities before Oslo were never purely political. At heart, he is a man of the street. He has power there, allegiances. He can make things happen or stop them from happening. And if he asks you to do something, I suspect, it's best to comply. I visited Gaza twice under Dahlan's care. Both times I had to simply mention the name of someone

I'd like to meet and within an hour that person would appear for an interview. Dahlan even arranged for Palestinians living within Israel to drive me from Jerusalem to Erez Crossing—a two-hour trip that would ordinarily have cost me at least $100 each way in a taxi. I don't know how or if these drivers were paid.

In fact, the only person Dahlan was not able to produce on the spot was Abdel Aziz Rantissi, former Hamas spokesman and leader. Rantissi was in hiding most of my time in the region because the IDF had been assassinating Palestinian militants in Gaza. Finally, however, Dahlan promised me an interview. "I'm going to see Rantissi next week," Dahlan told me. "I will ask him for a meeting next time you are in Gaza." Before I was able to meet Rantissi, the Israelis assassinated him.

I found it strange that Dahlan would be casually meeting Hamas leaders, considering he was supposed to be hunting down these men and arresting them. In fact, as loyal to Fatah as Dahlan is, he has a long-standing relationship with many members of the Islamic movement. He attended Islamic University, today a stronghold of Hamas support, and befriended Rantissi even before Hamas recruited him. Still, I asked Dahlan, if you know these men, shouldn't you be arresting them rather than inviting them to tea? And why are they willing to meet with you if you're their adversary?

"Hamas knows that the main concern for me is the interest of the people, not the interests of the Palestinian Authority," Dahlan told me over coffee at his kitchen table. "That's why I consider my relationship with Hamas people as an exception. Sometimes they like me, sometimes they don't like me, but I'm clear with them and with the people."

"But if you have this kind of double relationship with Hamas, how can you actually make them stop their activities?"

"Sometimes you have to convince them by force," Dahlan said matter-of-factly. "But I have never humiliated a prisoner in my jail. I don't consider this prisoner a criminal. He has his own political position and I have mine."

A Palestinian academic told me a rumor that Dahlan's men once pulled Rantissi into his car; when they threw Rantissi back out, the hair on his head, including his beard, was gone. Dahlan's personal assistant called the accusation ridiculous.

But if Dahlan was capable of stopping Hamas, why didn't he? He clearly favors Israeli-Palestinian partnership and a negotiated settlement to the conflict. As Gaza's preventative security chief during Oslo, he worked closely with the Israelis and Americans. That was how he knew my father as well as Ami Ayalon, then head of the Israeli secret service, and Gilad Sher, Israel's head negotiator. When it came to the peace process, these men held the most senior positions in their governments. They spent hours together, talking and arguing. They shared midnight meals and smoked *argileh* into the morning. The current situation has not damaged the respect between them. Gilad Sher summarized the group's feeling: "I personally had during Oslo and I still have throughout the crisis, and terror, and bloody tragedy a very friendly and trustworthy relationship with the Palestinian negotiators. Sa'eb Erekat, who is my friend, Mohammad Dahlan, Mohammad Rashid."

Still, Dahlan was frank in saying that during the Olso years he did not make a consistent effort to stop terror. When he felt the Israelis were making good on their agreements, he came through. But "in many cases," Dahlan said, "the Israelis asked for unreasonable things, and I refused."

According to him, it was unreasonable for Israel to expect him and Abu Mazen to clamp down on Hamas in the middle of the second intifada. "Sharon doesn't want us to succeed," he told me. "He wants to create a political vacuum on our side to show that there is no partner. Secondly, after three years of attacks by Israelis, they've destroyed the majority of the security apparatus here. The third reason is that the Palestinian public doesn't see a political horizon."

Dahlan explained the relationship between these points. Without a political horizon—a process through which Palestinians see tangible improvements in their daily lives and ultimately a sovereign state—the Palestinian Authority will not have the popular legitimacy to fight terror. Any help they give to Israel will be viewed as collaboration, the equivalent of treason. If Israel truly wants the Palestinian Authority to take action against Hamas, then the IDF must pull out of the West Bank and Gaza. There is no way, Dahlan said, that his men are going to assist the Apache gunships that are killing innocent Palestinians. The public won't stand for it. Moreover, Israel has destroyed so much of the PA's security apparatus that a real crackdown is impossible. Dahlan said the Israelis didn't leave a single Palestinian Authority jail intact.

I didn't understand why Dahlan needed popular approval in order to destroy Hamas's infrastructure. Even if a huge percentage of the population now claimed to support Hamas, did Fatah really risk starting a civil war if they went after the Islamists?

"Of course not," Dahlan dismissed the suggestion. "I have been in my job for twenty-five years. It won't happen."

"So then why are you so worried about how the people will react to arresting the militants?"

"First of all," he said, "we don't have the capacity to do it. Second, why should we do it? This is my question now. Why should I do it? For the benefit of the Israelis? Or is there a common language, a common interest between us? This is the difference. If I will know in advance that there is something I can gain for our people, then of course, we will do it. But first, we have to be sure of that. Now, in this situation, no way."

"The Palestinians won't stop terror" is exactly what Ehud Barak has been trying to convince the world since Camp David in July of 2000.

"Many Israelis and others, including your father, are feeling guilty, saying, 'Why couldn't we just make peace?' The reality is that the other side didn't want to."

Barak was speaking from his new offices high above Tel Aviv from where he now works as a business consultant. The suite is the epitome of professionalism, but what stands out is the photo display across from the reception desk. Picture after picture shows Barak, smiling, shaking hands with every walk of world leader. Yet these men, obviously lesser lights, are dimmed next to the real idol. It could pass for the bedroom wall of a star-struck teenager, only instead of a dozen Britneys, there are a dozen Baraks. Barak reminds me most of Tolkien's Gimli in *The Lord of the Rings*. He is sturdy and compact, a man who made his name in the military and approaches politics with the same stolidness. Whether the assault is physical or polemical, Barak does not budge; his attitude is his ax.

"Ultimately, Chairman Arafat didn't want to do what Egyptian president Sadat or Jordan's King Hussein had done." Barak folded his hands on the desk as though that closed the issue. I knew that Israelis respected both these Arab leaders for their courage and initiative. Israel and Jordan had signed a peace accord in 1994. Sadat was particularly idolized by Israelis, because following the 1973 war in which Egypt and Syria launched a surprise attack on Israel, he flew to Jerusalem to extend the olive branch to the Israeli Knesset. In 1978, with the efforts of Jimmy Carter, Sadat and Israeli prime minister Menachem Begin signed a peace accord at Camp David.

After ten days with Arafat at the second Camp David summit, Barak had no such respect for Arafat. "He didn't want to correct sixty-seven, but forty-seven," Barak continued. "There are many legends that people try to say. They say, 'Oh, Barak tried to make it a take it or leave it.' But that's not true. It's not true!" He slammed his fist on the desk. I jumped.

Barak said one of these legends was that Camp David II was intended to produce a final agreement. He went to the summit, he told me, believing they were going to establish a framework, what had happened at the previous Camp David. He said it took Begin and Sadat a year after their summit to negotiate a real peace.

"And what do you think about the Palestinian argument that they were not prepared for a summit?" I asked, bracing myself.

Barak frowned with disbelief and began to answer, his voice growing progessively louder. "When I came to power, there were literally metric tons of documents, covering meetings over thirteen years, all around the globe, in all continents, EXCEPT FOR ANTARCTICA!"

Barak made clear that he felt the negotiations didn't collapse over a lack of preparation or a misunderstanding over the purpose of Camp David. "You need two to tango," he said. "You can impose war on the other side; you can't impose peace."

This is absolutely true. At the same time, I believe critics overlook some crucial aspects of what happened at Camp David in July of 2000. First are the openings into issues of security, territory transfer, and Jerusalem that Israeli and Palestinian negotiators (if not their leaders) made at the summit. These would not have been possible had there been no Israeli-Palestinian partnership—or "two to tango" as Barak put it. There were members of all three negotiating teams—Israeli, Palestinian, and American—who truly understood each others' needs and concerns. It was not simply a question of Israelis versus Palestinians. Good versus evil. A take-it-or-leave-it deal. The unofficial talks in Taba, Egypt, that took place after Camp David and greatly expanded upon the progress there proved as much.

Barak's head negotiator, Gilad Sher, agreed. He said he was proud of the new doors they'd opened. Unfortunately, neither team had the authority to implement a final decision. "And the only one," Sher said, "who held the authority in the Palestinian camp, didn't present even one counterproposal except 'no.' So what the Palestinians consider a trap was the fact that they were asked to negotiate."

This is the second important consideration. It is absolutely true that Arafat never suggested a counteroffer. Sher is probably right in suggesting

that Arafat never intended to strike a deal. For future peace talks to succeed we must understand the root of Arafat's inaction. Before the summit,
Arafat told U.S. negotiators, "You will not walk behind my coffin." Anwar
Sadat was assassinated, in part for signing an Egyptian-Israeli peace accord,
and Arafat refused to accept the same fate. This meant that he, the leader
of the Palestinian nation, never intended to compromise on Jerusalem: a
place that might be the Palestinian capital but was also the third holiest site
for a billion Muslims. Perhaps if prominent Muslim leaders had been involved in these talks and had backed Arafat, he would have been more
flexible. Of course, there were plenty of other issues on which Arafat
could have offered counterproposals, but his mind seemed to be made up.
If he was going it alone, he wasn't taking any risks.

I believe Arafat was alone for another reason. It wasn't just because he
lacked an "okay" from the larger Muslim world. He arrived at Camp
David without the support of his own people. It had been seven years
since Oslo began, and where were the Palestinians? It seems to me Arafat
had forgotten about them. When I asked the chairman what he had done
to prepare his population for a final agreement and a two-state solution, he
gave only a three-word answer: "I am proud." No matter what question I
asked him, it was the same response. "I am proud." But proud of what, I
never discovered.

Barak told me that a great leader doesn't need popular support to make
historic decisions. He said that three weeks before the first Camp David in
1979, seventy percent of the Israeli public was against Menachem Begin
signing a peace deal with Egypt. Three weeks later, seventy percent were
in favor of the agreement. Barak was certain that "if there is a leadership
which is ready to take decisions and change the reality, the public, at least
in democracies, will follow."

I believe neither Arafat nor Barak adequately prepared their publics for
the painful concessions that a final agreement would require. Even Gilad
Sher admitted that the Israeli government "did not prepare the Israeli
public opinion for the notion of ending the conflict through historical
compromise. We were dealing with give-ups," Sher said, "and not what
we would gain. So the Israeli public was exposed to concessions without
the balance of the fruits of peace."

This is also true on the Palestinian side, only there the problem runs
deeper. Every Palestinian I talked to felt they'd been "dealing with give-
ups" throughout the Oslo years. Most say Israel was the one taking, but

according to Palestinian analysts and younger government officials, the Palestinian Authority was also stealing from its people—their money, their resources, and their dreams of a democratic nation. U.S. and Israeli pressure on the PA to reform compelled Arafat to appoint Salam Fayad minister of finance, a man who was well-respected by Palestinians and considered honest in the international community. Though Fayad worked hard to make the Authority's financial dealings more transparent, his powers were limited. He gave me the impression that there was a lot of money unaccounted for—money that should be going into education, health care, and the development of infrastructure but wasn't.

From the outside, Mohammad Dahlan's home resembles a government compound. Approaching it, you see high white walls and bodyguards cradling their guns. The only entrance is through the garage. Stepping from the garage into the courtyard is like entering a color illustration from the *Arabian Nights*. Stepping-stones wind past lush flowers and trees and a glass-walled gazebo. The stones taper off at a door that opens into what I can only describe as a modern-day Persian palace. Though not palatial in size, Dahlan's home is enormous for Gaza City, as it is for most of Israel's modest apartments. The house is luxurious down to the tiniest detail. Mirrors, faucets, pillow covers, and doorknobs are gilded. There are waist-high flower boxes, blooming with white roses. Hadeel's room, where I slept, is large and pink and swimming in frills. It connects to a private bathroom of which any little girl would be envious.

But Hadeel neither sleeps in her pink bed nor uses her large bathtub. She is afraid an intruder will climb up the courtyard wall and break in. She prefers to sleep with her thirteen-year-old brother Fady for protection.

"Are you afraid, too?" her heart-shaped face looked lovingly at me when she learned that I would be sleeping there. "Because if you are, you can sleep with Fady, too."

At first, I didn't understand Hadeel's fear. It is highly unlikely that either the Islamists or the Israelis would physically harm her father or burgle her house. But driving around with Dahlan in his armored sedan, I began to understand why his daughter might be afraid. The fact is, if you need protection, there must be some threat to your safety. According to Dahlan, everyone knows his car and house, so if you did want to find him, you'd know where to go. He keeps the curtains in the sedan closed as he drives around the city. I peeked out between them, trying to gauge the reaction of the people we drove past. Mostly, we saw boys and young men, skinny and wide-eyed, staring with a kind of blank astonishment. What were they thinking as we rolled by in such fortified luxury? Were they wondering how one man could have so much while they were so vulnerable? When I asked Dahlan about his wealth, he swore he wasn't corrupt.

"I never took more than my due salary," he said as we cruised down the street.

I was silent.

"Really, Jenny. I am telling you the truth."

A 1997 *Ha'aretz* report exposed Dahlan's partnership in a fuel monopoly that helped to fund his security apparatus as well as his own pocket. The report also stated that Dahlan's control of the loading forklifts at Erez Crossing allowed him to extort money from merchants and trucks passing through.★ Or perhaps his brother really was a wealthy businessman, as others claimed. A Palestinian academic (the same one who told me about Rantissi's beard) said it was well known that the CIA pays Dahlan a salary of gargantuan proportions in order to help him maintain his status and position him to be the next Arafat. After Arafat's death, Dahlan did not run for the office. Abu Mazen became the new president and appointed Dahlan minister of civil affairs, a significant change from his previous security positions. I asked my father his opinion about the rumor and got the same answer Dahlan's personal assistant had given me: ridiculous.

Dahlan insisted he was a man of the people. He had grown up among them and fought among them. Ever since he resigned from his position as preventative security chief, he said he was devoting all of his time to giving the people a voice.

"The whole system of government, the whole structure, is built on corruption," he told me a year before Arafat's death. "We're fed up with this way, with Arafat and his leadership. But now the majority of the people are looking for new elections in the Palestinian Legislative Council and the Fatah movement."

Dahlan said that after he resigned from the Palestinian Authority, he used his influence to spread the idea and importance of elections. Until Arafat's death and the subsequent election of Abu Mazen in January 2005, there had been no presidential elections in Palestine since 1996, when the people first elected Arafat and the members of their legislative council.

What would the outcome of new elections be, I asked?

★ Source: http://www.mfa.gov.il/MFA/Archive/Articles/1997.

If elections occurred before Arafat's demise, Dahlan was certain the people would reelect him because of his symbolic importance. He also believed that eighty percent of the Fatah Central Committee would be kicked out. The Central Committee members had been Arafat's closest aides for decades. It is their body, and not the Palestinian Legislative Council, where the real money and power lies. Unlike the PLC, the Central Committee members were chosen by the Fatah leadership in exile. That was in 1989. It was largely their corruption and incompetence that caused Arafat's party to lose the hearts and minds of Palestinians to the Islamists.

"They only think about themselves," PLC member Qaddura Faris told me. "They are not active enough to convince the people to be with us. . . . They do nothing. They . . . do . . . nothing!"

Dahlan reiterated this point. "The leadership of the Palestinian people doesn't want elections, because some of them will lose their positions. I am adopting a new generation that didn't have a role in the PA and didn't have a chance."

"But if you're really adopting the young leaders," I said, "then when I ask them who they admire, why don't they all jump up and say Mohammad Dahlan? Why do they accuse you of corruption like all the others?"

"Because they see me as part of the government."

"But you're not."

"But I was. Maybe the people don't know that I am not there anymore. It takes time."

"Okay. So now that you're out of the government, how do you and the Palestinian people pressure the government to have elections?"

"We have created an atmosphere in which all the people are talking about elections, in the media, in the camps, everywhere. The second point is that any orders sent by the government to the grass roots won't be carried out."

"And how do you make the people ignore the government?"

Dahlan flashed a sly smile and winked.

"Oh," I said. "I see."

One way to look at Palestinian politics is from the perspective of insiders and outsiders. The insiders, or young guard, are those Palestinians who lived in Palestine throughout the years of Israeli occupation and struggled in the first intifada. Most of them spent time in Israeli prisons. Today, many are members of the Palestinian Legislative Council. The outsiders, or the old guard, are the historic leaders of Fatah and the Palestinian national movement. They lived most of their adult lives in exile, directing resistance inside the territories from Lebanon, Jordan, and Tunis. When Oslo began, they were shipped back into the country. Like prefab buildings: Arafat's ready-made executive branch.

To my mind, Mohammad Dahlan doesn't easily fit into either group. He spent his formative years working with the people, getting his hands dirty, doing jail time. But he also lived in exile, forging alliances in the PLO, learning the values of wealth, power, and self-interest. He is a strange hybrid, an inside-outsider, and he embodies the uneasy transition through which Palestinian politics is struggling. Palestinian society is the most democratic in the Arab world, but it is still mired in corruption and authoritarianism.

I discussed this transition with Ruba, who in 2003 was working for U.S. Aid and International Development (USAID) in Ramallah, helping to improve the quality of Palestinian products. She was a recent graduate of Birzeit University with a B.A. in business administration. Ruba is outspoken and has the kind of severe beauty and pointed personality that intimidated me for many years. It wasn't until I lived in the region that I began to see the gentleness that glowed within her.

Our conversation took place in Birzeit, the city next to Ramallah. We arrived at her apartment, in the wake of a heavy winter downpour, to find the entire city in a blackout. According to Ruba, the outage was typical. We needed more propane to run the open-flame heaters that warmed her home, but every store we went to was sold out. Also typical. We scoured the dark apartment for candles, slid beneath the blankets on her bed, and began talking over a candlelit dinner of pita, canned tuna, and *labneh*—cream cheese with a kick.

I asked Ruba if she thought Palestine was a democracy. I had heard about Arafat shutting down the *al-Jazeera* offices when the paper criticized him. She said the media never directly contradicted Abu Amr (Arafat's nom de guerre), but in the streets people said what they liked. "But," she added, "it doesn't matter if the people speak out. The government lets people talk in order to pacify them. In the end, the PA does what it wants. They were under the Arabic dictator system and I don't blame them. They were taught this way. It's different for us, because we lived under Israeli occupation. We saw how democracy works. But they didn't. They think that when you're in the government, you must get everything."

I looked up, startled. "When you say you learned democracy, you mean from the Israelis?"

"They have the Knesset, they vote—all these things. We learned from it. Our leadership didn't live in it. They didn't learn.

"They see that Jordan and Syria have their own states, so they want to make Palestine this way. And it's wrong. It's totally wrong."

Ruba said that to have a democratic government in Palestine, the country needs new leadership. "I think the young people of Palestine are really willing to do something. I feel there's an energy in the people, but we are not getting advantage of this energy. It's not fifty years ago. And Arafat is not getting the point, obviously."

"So you think it's just a matter of time before the leadership changes—basically dies?"

"I don't know. This is the problem. Why do they have to die?"

I wondered the same thing and remembered a brief interaction I'd had with Ahmed Qurei (Abu Ala), the current Palestinian prime minister. "The leaders are the obstacles," he'd said in his brand-new office just weeks after he'd replaced Abu Mazen as the Palestinian prime minister. "Therefore, if you remove all the leaders . . ." Abu Ala paused as though on the brink of something serious, but then broke into a deep-bellied laugh. It seemed he found the proposition truly ridiculous.

Ruba went on to lament how the Hamas-affiliated students won the Birzeit Student Union elections by a significant margin. "It was a shock for everyone," she said, dismayed. The Fatah-affiliated group lost because their entire campaign focused on Arafat. "I'm not against him," she said. "But the government is corrupted. The intifada didn't end. If we're not thinking in a political way, what are we doing? We don't even know how to negotiate. We have to put in a new system. We have to take advantage of every Palestinian. We're not doing that." She sounded desperate.

Ruba told me about a girl she knew who voted for Hamas. "I was shocked," she told me. "This girl wears these tight pants and tight blouses and a lot of makeup. And she only voted for Hamas because she doesn't like Fatah."

I asked Ruba who in the Authority she admired.

"From the Authority? No one."

"So what makes a political leader legitimate to the Palestinian public? To you?"

"Being elected by them. But you have to find the right person. Why do you only think about Abu Mazen or Qurei? There are other people in Palestine. I can't get it."

Before the collapse of Oslo, I asked my father who he thought would replace Arafat when the chairman died. My dad said it would have to be someone close to Arafat, to his money and his guns: most likely Abu Ala or Abu Mazen. The January 2005 elections turned out just as Ruba predicted. Abu Mazen won—no need to look further. In 2003, before Arafat's death, I asked Ruba whom she would choose as the next president. The gist of her answer was clear: nobody named Abu.

On one trip to Ramallah, I had the experience of meeting the ultimate Abu. Abu Amr, known to most of us as Yasir Arafat, had led the Palestinian national movement since the late sixties when he was elected head of the Palestine Liberation Organization. (The PLO is an umbrella organization of Palestinian political factions, including Arafat's nationalist Fatah party.) Over the years, Arafat headed the Palestinian national movement in exile—first from Jordan, then Lebanon, and finally Tunis. He was finally kicked out of Lebanon in 1982, when the Israelis, led by Defense Minister Ariel Sharon, invaded the country. In part, the incursion was an attempt to dismantle the PLO infrastructure there and undermine its leadership. Growing up, I knew none of this history. I knew of Arafat only from my father's stories. He was a shady international figure, a sometime terrorist, and a man who, according to my dad, "never slept in the same bed twice." I suspect many people in the world saw the PLO leader this way, hence our surprise when he ended up winning the Nobel Peace Prize for signing the 1993 Oslo Declaration of Principles with Israeli prime minister Yitzhak Rabin.

After the Oslo process began, Arafat returned to Palestine and established two headquarters, one in Gaza City and one in Ramallah. It was the Ramallah compound, known as the Muqata, where I awaited my meeting with the chairman in August 2003. I had been asked to wait in a small room in the section of the Muqata that had not been destroyed during the 2002 IDF incursion, Operation Defensive Shield. The room was a combination infirmary–coffee lounge. There was a doctor's table pushed up against a wall, three chairs, and a medical machine I couldn't identify. Next to my chair was a low set of shelves piled with dirty glasses, jars of coffee grounds, sugar, and tea. The carpet was brown, and there was one dirty window. Two men sat in the room with me, blowing cloud after cloud of smoke between them. Not the best atmosphere for a sick person, I thought, though given the way many men in the Arab world smoked, the patient would probably have a cigarette too.

I had been driven into the compound that morning, through the gates where Reem and I had walked, and right up to the entrance of the ugly tan building. The door was set at an awkward angle to the pavement and half covered by a fence-scaffolding-curtainlike structure that reminded me of the kind of fort I used to build with sheets and blocks in my basement. If you were looking for this entrance in a hurry or in the dark, you'd probably miss it. I assumed that was the intention.

Little did I know that the world would come to know this entrance well in the coming weeks. Shortly after my visit to the Muqata, the Israeli cabinet announced its decision to expel Arafat. For the first time in months, the Palestinian leader stepped outside his headquarters to greet the thousands who gathered to support him. Media footage of the cheering crowd made Arafat look like a beauty queen. He smiled his quintessential big-lipped grin and waved to his adoring admirers, blowing them kisses, as though riding by on a float.

Only Arafat wasn't riding anywhere, not if he had anything to say about it. He had raged at the Israelis for forbidding him to attend his sister's funeral in Gaza, but when they finally acquiesced, he refused to leave. As one PA official explained, "If he went, the world would perceive him as free. For his own status and credibility as a leader, he chose to maintain his captivity, even at the price of missing his sister's funeral."

I recalled the image of the Palestinian flag attached to Arafat's head that I had imagined when driving by the Muqata with Nida and her father. Like a puppet string, I realized. Only in this case, Arafat was both the puppetmaster and the puppet. He was the most powerful symbol in all of Palestine. He *was* their flag: their reason, their justification, their excuse. As such, he had the power to move the people as he liked. But the flag also controlled Arafat. He was nothing without it, and so was forced to do its bidding.

Today Arafat's only admirers were a small group of reporters guarding their equipment. They seemed perturbed when I got out of the car and was escorted inside, as if they had been expecting someone much more important. I imagined myself being particularly snooty and saying to them, "I have a lunch date and I can't be late!" Instead I was grappling with the butterflies in my stomach. The smoke-filled medicine cabinet in which I waited didn't make me feel any better. Ten minutes passed, then fifteen, then twenty. I wondered if I'd been forgotten. I wanted to peek into the hallway and see if anyone was there, but I didn't dare move. I wasn't about to wander through the Muqata unescorted.

I wondered why I hadn't been taken to a proper waiting room and then considered the possibility that the waiting room had been destroyed. But where did the truly important people wait? I couldn't imagine the head of Egyptian intelligence or the United Nations representative to the Palestinian territories crammed in *here*.

Finally, I was summoned and led down the hall, up a short flight of stairs, and told to wait in the hallway outside the conference room. A door across from me was open and I caught sight of two cots. Did Arafat sleep on one of those? Someone saw me looking and shut the door. Suddenly, Sa'eb Erekat was standing in front of me; solid, tanned, with his head shaved. He wore thick spectacles that made his eyes look like fish swimming in twin bowls. His suit and sharp cologne gave an air of professionalism and importance, and it brought to mind those special weekday visits I used to make to my father at the State Department. Sa'eb had known me for many years and he had arranged the meeting with Arafat.

We kissed hello. "The chairman would like to invite you for lunch," Sa'eb announced. "You can speak with him for half an hour and then we will eat. It will be just a few more minutes."

Sa'eb had been senior negotiator for the Palestinian Authority since 1993. He had worked with my father throughout the Oslo years and appeared frequently in Arab and Western media. Sa'eb's son and one of his daughters had attended Seeds of Peace. His girls were twins around my age—and it was with them that I first met Arafat before the intifada. On that occasion, I remember Dalal and Salam being fairly at ease; they had met Arafat a few times before. My friend Christine and I were in a veritable state of shock the moment we found ourselves standing not five feet from one of the world's most infamous men. One day he was a wanted terrorist who kept an automatic rifle under his pillow, and the next day he was winning the Nobel Peace Prize and sipping coffee with Bill Clinton. In fact, Arafat visited the Oval Office more times than any other world leader in the year 2000. People called him one of the richest men on the planet, others called him the ugliest. More than once I had heard someone comment, "Have you ever seen him without his *kiffiyeh*? Do you think he ever *washes* it?"

That day, Christine and I had watched with amazement and trepidation as Arafat took Dalal's head between his trembling hands, pulled her toward his lips and slowly, slowly, kissed both her cheeks and forehead in blessing. He shuffled over to Salam and performed the same ablution on her. Then, as per the inevitable course of things, he moved over to me and Christine. Our hearts were pounding; Christine looked terrified—not because of *who* Arafat was but because of *what* he was about to do to her. I looked over at Salam and saw the glistening spots on her face. I didn't know if Christine had been baptized, but she was about to get a good dose of the chairman's saliva. Before I knew it, Arafat was bestowing his blessings upon her reluctant forehead. I quickly decided that it would be best to submit; so I shut my eyes and came out the other side an anointed woman.

Afterward, Arafat presented us handmade Palestinian jackets. They were black with red, green, and blue embroidery, and according to the Erekat girls, the most expensive gifts you could buy in Palestine. Then the chairman presented us with small, round pins with "Bethlehem 2000" inscribed in gold. New Year's was a week away at that time, and the PA had the pins made for their millennium celebration. Arafat seemed particularly proud of them and he presented them to us one at a time, with the manner of a king bestowing decorations upon his most noble knights. "Bet-le-hem too-tousand," his small voice chirped as he laid the shining object in Dalal's palm. "Bet-le-hem too-tousand," he repeated, moving on to Salam. And twice more to Christine and myself. This was followed by a dozen photographs of us with Arafat. Our friends at home hardly believe the pictures when they see them. They look artificial, as though Christine and I are standing on either side of a cardboard cutout or wax model.

On our way back to the States, Israeli security asked whether Christine and I had been given any gifts. Despite my appalling mathematical abilities, my head quickly calculated that Palestinian jackets and pins plus Arafat plus Israeli security equaled a one hundred percent chance of missing our plane. I looked at Christine and we lied through our teeth.

Sa'eb was standing in the doorway of the conference room. A group of Palestinian officials and aides filed out, and I was ushered in. Then Arafat was before me, looking exactly as he had looked three years ago: stiff general's uniform, checkered *kiffiyeh,* prickly beard.

"You remember Jenny Miller—Aaron's daughter," Sa'eb said.

Arafat's big lips grinned.

"It's wonderful to see you again," I said and extended my hand. We shook and leaned in for a two-cheeked kiss. Phew, I thought. No blessings this time.

"Please sit down," the chairman said in his usual stutter.

"Jenny, you sit next to Abu Amr." Sa'eb directed me to the chair next to

Arafat, who sat at the head of the conference table. "Not too many questions, Jenny. It's almost time for lunch."

"No problem," I told Sa'eb. "Mr. Chairman," I began. "I would like you to tell me what practical steps your government is taking to—" I didn't even finish the question before Arafat interrupted me.

"Do you see!" he said excitedly and stabbed at his lapel. "I became a member of Seeds of Peace—from the very beginning." Sure enough, pinned among the flags of a dozen other countries, was the Seeds of Peace logo. Arafat looked up at me with an expression that suggested the interview might as well end right there. What else could I possibly need to know? I put on my most encouraging smile and repeated my question: "What practical steps is your government taking to educate its young people toward values of tolerance and democracy?"

"We are holding meetings with our kids," Arafat replied quite seriously. "Meetings with our children and Israelis."

This sounded curious, so I pressed for more information. "Since the intifada started?"

"There are camps in Gaza—some of these camps are joint."

"Joint meaning Israelis and Palestinians?"

"In Gaza."

"Is the PA sponsoring these joint camps in Gaza?"

"In Gaza and in Europe," he repeated.

Even if I could believe that the Palestinians were running summer camps for Israeli and Palestinian kids in Gaza—which, frankly, I couldn't—I wondered what Israelis would come to such a camp. I tried to imagine some settler sending his kids out the door in the morning: *Have fun with little Mohammad today, and remember to stay away from the bulldozers.* It didn't make any sense, but I asked anyway: "And who sends the Israelis?"

"Their own organizations."

"And what are the kids taught in these camps?"

"You can imagine, how to live together as friends."

"And do you think that Palestinian youth will accept living with Israelis as friends?" I knew that most Palestinian youth considered friendly relations with Israeli youth highly inappropriate during the intifada. In their eyes, programs such as Seeds of Peace fostered *tatbiyeh,* "normalization." Such normalized activities were a form of selling out the Palestinian cause for independence.

"We have Jews in Palestine."

"Jews?" The only Jews I knew of in the West Bank and Gaza were settlers, and I was sure Arafat was not referring to them.

"The Samaritan Jews are Palestinians and they are living with us completely equal in all ways. Even in the parliament they have a representative. And also we have a strong relation with Neturei Karta. And they are famous in America. New York especially."

These were, in fact, two examples of Jewish-Palestinian coexistence. The Samaritans are a community of about 350 people who live in the hills alongside Nablus. Their presence there dates back to biblical times (i.e., "The Good Samaritan") and their religious practices are similar to Jewish ones. They are one of the few communities in the world to read, write, and speak Aramaic, though they are conversant in both Hebrew and Arabic. The West Bank Samaritan community has remained relatively neutral in the intifada (though another 350 Samaritans live inside Israel and serve in the army). In 1996, Arafat offered the sect a seat in the 88-person Palestinian Legislative Council.

The Neturei Karta is a tiny group of ultra-Orthodox Jews who are ideologically opposed to the Israeli state because they believe only the Messiah can give the Jews a homeland. For this reason, they have aligned themselves with the Palestinian cause. As Arafat mentioned, members of this group are largely concentrated in New York. While Arafat had technically answered my question, neither group was representative of the majority of Jews in the region.

I decided to switch gears. Did Arafat think the PA could play a role in teaching young Palestinians to be independent thinkers?

"We are proud of it," he said matter-of-factly.

"So you are doing this already?"

"Yes, we are proud of it. This is one of the main platforms of our policies with our kids."

"And how are they taught? If it's the main platform, how is it communicated to them?"

"We have programs."

"Could you elaborate on what these programs do?"

"But we are proud of it, as I told you. And it is very famous in the whole area. Among the Arabs, and the Israelis, and even Europe."

"And what does it mean, Mr. Chairman, for a young Palestinian to be an independent thinker in Palestine? What can he or she accomplish?"

"They have a strong Palestinian personality. . . . For your information, we are proud, we have the highest percentage of education."

"So the majority of Palestinians are well educated and have access to education?"

"Not the majority, the *biggest* majority. All the schools are open to them."

"Including the universities?"

"There is an Israeli institution that did a very important report that mentioned that among each one thousand Palestinians that graduate from their B.A., there are 18 percent who get a master's certificate. The Israelis only 14 percent. And it's not 18 percent," Arafat reconsidered. "It is 19.2 percent."

I knew the Palestinian population strove to be educated, but I wondered about the cost of university during the intifada and the feasibility of students going to school when they needed to help support their families.

"What about in the younger grades? Primary schools? How are these kids being educated?"

"We are proud of it."

"You said before that young people are being educated to have a strong Palestinian personality. What does that mean to you?"

"We are proud of it."

"But to be educated to have a specifically strong Palestinian personality, what distinguishes that from—"

"The platform of the Palestinian state is depending on them."

"So what qualities must they have?"

"The rule of law. Salam, peace. Also religion."

Before I had the chance to say anything, Sa'eb cut in: "He means respecting all religions. Judaism, Christianity, and Islam."

"This is the Holy Land," Arafat echoed, as though on cue.

"Let me ask you about Seeds of Peace. What can the PA do to help the efforts of Seeds?"

"From the beginning we are—" Arafat began, but again Sa'eb interrupted.

"He is behind Seeds of Peace more than any other Palestinian, more than me. Because he is the one who is in touch with the teachers, with the schools. He meets the kids before they leave. He meets them after they come home."

"I know." I was getting annoyed with Sa'eb. I wanted Arafat to speak for himself.

"Now in my siege, part of the Seeds come to see me," Arafat continued.

"I know, I met them this summer. But I have to be honest with you, Mr.

Chairman. I have spoken with Palestinian youth who say they will not sit with Israelis. There's a stigma attached to this."

"Listen, of course we will have to reach our participation. But this occupation against our people day by night and this damage is difficult for *all* our people."

"But this is why Seeds of Peace should do more," Sa'eb cut in accusingly, as though I were responsible for the organization's policies.

Arafat continued, "And for this, we are waiting for the Seeds of Peace to work . . . for the peace. For our people and for the Israeli people and for the whole peace in the Middle East."

"I agree that this is very important." I nodded at Sa'eb and then toward Arafat. "What can the Palestinian Authority do to help Seeds of Peace reach a broader group of Palestinians—"

Now it was Arafat's turn to cut me off. "From the beginning we were helping!"

"Jenny, maybe one last question?" Sa'eb said quickly, sensing that the chairman was getting anxious.

"Okay. No government is perfect, Mr. Chairman. And when you look back over the years of Oslo, what do you think the PA could have done better to educate young Palestinians toward peace and tolerance and a two-state solution?"

Arafat looked at me intently. "I have—and this is a point—I have nothing to regret. Because in accordance to the capabilities that I had at that time, I can tell you—I can swear—I have done my best."

"Jenny, I think it is time for lunch," Sa'eb proclaimed the definitive end to the interview. A number of people filed back into the conference room. An aide brought Arafat documents to sign and waiters carried in the food. My interview was over. My one shot with the father of the Palestinian national movement, and what had I come up with? What had I learned? The chairman had lied about Palestinian-run coexistence camps in Gaza; he was "very proud" of himself and everything the Palestinian Authority did for its young people; and he was waiting for Seeds of Peace to fix his problems with Israel. A high-ranking Fatah official sitting across the table seemed as skeptical as I was and said, "You know, every day there are hundreds more Palestinian youth who are eager to strap on a belt of explosives."

"It's time for eating, not talking!" Sa'eb cut in before I could open my mouth.

I couldn't help but feel as though, for the last twenty mintues, absolutely nothing had happened. The interview seemed so vacuous, I wouldn't have been surprised if the tape was blank when I went to listen to it. But as Sa'eb had said, it was lunchtime. Sure enough, the men around the table (I was the only female there, not to mention the only person under fifty-five) were eating heartily. The Muqata's food was about the same caliber as its decor. The rice was dry and cold, the vegetables were of the frozen carrot and pea variety, and the lamb had a slightly blue glow. Each person received one container of yogurt. There were also trays of kibbe and falafel spread around the table. Sa'eb began to serve me with a vigor nearly as great as his wife, Na'ama, who never put less than a pound of food on my plate, and cooed at me throughout the meal, "*Coolly,* Jenny, *coolly.*" Eat, Jenny, eat.

Sa'eb put my plate down, and I looked at it, despairing. There weren't any trash cans handy, nor any Muqata pets to feed under the table. Well, I reminded myself, at least Arafat hasn't asked me to eat off his plate, as I knew he sometimes requested of my father. Then I noticed something out of the corner of my eye: pale, quivering, and moving closer to me by the second. It was Arafat's hand. Sitting in the center of the hand was an over-boiled tuft of broccoli. With a big smile, Arafat dropped the broccoli from his palm into mine. I thanked the chairman, did my best to bury the limp vegetable beneath the mountain of rice in front of me. But that wasn't all. Soon, I had become the first person in a vegetable conveyor belt. Arafat would pick up something from his plate, hand it to me, and motion for me to pass it down: broccoli, corn, carrots, all in a sorrowful state of over-saturation.

Arafat was the only person in the room with fresh vegetables. And why? Because even Yasir Arafat had caught on to the latest health craze. From the looks of the food spread around him (boiled veggies, skinless chicken, and a bowl of kashi), he was on Atkins or perhaps South Beach. Regardless, he seemed eager to share his health consciousness with everyone at the table. Finally, Sa'eb pushed back his plate. "Okay, Jenny, it's time to go."

Relieved, I pushed my still-heavy plate away and began to stand when a voice rang out, freezing me in mid-squat.

"She did not eat enough!" Arafat eyeballed me. "You must eat this." He picked up a kibbe from the plate of appetizers and handed it over.

"Thank you, Mr. Chairman," I said, "but I'm very full."

"Eat," he repeated.

Now I was in a predicament. I really didn't want to eat this kibbe, not simply because it was sitting in Arafat's hand but because I didn't like the idea of a deep-fried Muqata meatball in my stomach. I took a nibble, gave my best "mmm, delish" smile, and put the kibbe down. But the chairman wasn't satisfied.

"Finish," he instructed.

I looked around the room. Everyone else had finished. They weren't talking. They weren't heading off to their after-lunch meetings. They were sitting around the conference table waiting for me to finish Arafat's kibbe. I turned to Arafat, and against all better judgment, protested, "Who do you think you are? My mother?"

For a moment, Arafat looked mildly confused. Then his face lit up as with a flash of inspiration. "Your mother is my sister!" He threw his hands up as though tossing confetti into the air.

Great, I thought. *Now we're related,* and I popped the entire kibbe into my mouth.

At that moment, Sa'eb pulled me out of my chair, and without time to say good-bye, pushed me out the door. *Just a few more steps,* I thought, and *I'll be free of kibbe and all other epicurean overtures.* But as we were nearing the stairs, I felt a tap on my shoulder. Behind me, dressed in full uniform, was a Palestinian guard holding a tray of baklavah.

"You must eat one," he said. "From the president."

I chose a small one, but the moment I bit down, the guard broke into an enormous grin: "That one," he exclaimed "has one thousand calories!"

My experience with Arafat was funny, but only at face value. The silliness signaled a reluctance on the part of the Old Guard—Arafat and many of those close to him—to assume responsibility for the depressed state of the Palestinian people. These men use the occupation as a shield to deflect calls for governmental reform and to hide rampant political and monetary corruption. Palestinian prime minister Abu Ala joked to me about the Old Guard dying off, but I found little humor in the statement, because of how true it was. In 2003, it seemed the upper echelon of the PA would never relinquish power of their own accord. As long as they grasped the money and weapons, they would maintain authority, if not legitimacy. By sitting back and doing nothing, as Qaddura Faris said, they were leading the country down a dangerous path. More and more, young people are turning to those they feel are legitimate: Hamas. These militants are credible because people do not perceive them as corrupt, and because they are seen as fighters. During the height of the second intifada it was fighting the occupation and not calling for governmental reform, democracy, and elections that increased one's legitimacy on the street.

Legitimacy gained through resistance, often violence, is how much of the young guard made their mark. This includes those who are now calling for reform. Qaddura Faris is a perfect example. Like many of his generation, he began resisting the occupation as a teenager. At sixteen he was in the streets throwing stones and refurbishing weapons for Fatah. Like Dahlan, Faris was also under the command of Abu Jihad. In 1980, the Israelis arrested him. The fourteen years he spent in prison reshaped his life. He began to study Palestinian history as well as the history of the Zionist movement. He became fluent in Hebrew. The Israeli guards said he spoke it better than they did. And he became a leader within his cell. As Ruba indicated, the Palestinians really did learn democracy from Israel. According to Faris, Palestinian prisoners have their own mini-governmental system.

"We prepare the elections secretly," Faris told me. "The prisoners choose the day, make the papers, have an independent committee to run the elections."

Faris explained that party affiliates ran for leadership positions within their cell blocks. The elected cell-leaders were then in the running to join the prisoners' central committee. Faris became a member of this central committee inside his jail and later the prisoners' spokesman. He says that in 1992 he led the largest hunger strike in an Israeli prison, with eleven thousand prisoners involved. He was the man who negotiated with the police.

More than this, Faris was the Fatah official responsible for overseeing the relationship between Fatah members in and out of jail. When I asked him how such communication was possible, he produced two pieces of nearly transparent paper filled with minute Arabic script. "We wrap this into a capsule," Faris explained, "and cover it in plastic. If the soldiers get suspicious—" He popped the imaginary pill into his mouth.

Faris was released from jail in 1994, after the Oslo process began. Though the Palestinian people supported him, Arafat did not. In the end, Faris was elected to the Palestinian Legislative Council but without the chairman's support.

Faris acknowledges that today popular opposition against him has increased. He says his support of the Geneva Initiative (a comprehensive solution for the Israeli-Palestinian conflict drafted by former minister of justice Yossi Beilin and former Palestinian minister of culture and information Yasser Abed Rabbo) has given him a "bad name."

"It's not easy," he told me. "Maybe Yasir Arafat until now did not take this big step. It makes a shock in minds of the Palestinian people." Yet Faris is not deterred. "We are trying to have a partner. We have to have dialogue. Not only to fight but to speak."

This was the main point Faris wanted me to understand: Being in jail and actively resisting the occupation is important, but it is not the be-all and end-all of leadership. You must know the other side, their language and history, in order to deal with them. You must know how to deal diplomatically with the world.

Faris was clear. "We have the legitimacy and the right to have an armed struggle against the occupation, but I told Fatah that we must always think about our target: to have an independent state. We have legitimacy to fight Israel, but in the end, negotiation will end the conflict. Not fighting. We must have compromises with Israelis."

Reem has given a lot of thought to the divide between resistance and diplomacy. She holds deep respect for those who go to jail. "But that doesn't mean we don't need someone from Seeds of Peace," she said. "There are a lot of people who didn't go to jail or who weren't active in fighting the Israelis and soldiers, but they really believe in the Palestinian cause. . . . It's what he has inside; this is what we call *Wataniyya*." The word means nationhood or peoplehood.

I acknowledged that Reem had a great deal of *Wataniyya,* but I reminded her that she comes from a fairly privileged background compared to most people in her society. Both her parents have steady jobs; she wasn't raised on the streets.

"I was talking with my best friend about this issue yesterday," she said. "And I told her that we suffered, but I don't think we suffered as much as the people in the refugee camps. Ya, I know a lot of things and I'm a patriot also, but maybe it's different. I can't compare. People sympathize with her and maybe not me. Because I have money and I go to school."

"So if you really wanted to be active?"

"The refugee could be active in her ways, and I'm active in my ways. She's active by going and fighting the Israeli soldiers. I don't go and fight them, but I go to Seeds of Peace. I write, I draw—all these things that I do,

I put my beliefs into them. Maybe some people see me and that girl differently, but that's normal, because people have a lot of different opinions."

"So you feel confident that if you want to rise to a prominent position, you could do so by the virtue of your patriotism?"

"Sometimes I think I need to suffer more so I can create more. Or not suffer but see more. But at the same time, I thought, no, I suffer and it's the same thing."

Sa'eb Erekat has always chosen the diplomatic route. "I never put a gun in my hand," he told me from his home in Jericho. "I never was jailed for a long period. I never advocated violence. In fact, I condemned it."

At heart, Erekat is an academic. He says he was the first person to teach political science at Najah University in Nablus. He also calls himself "the first person to call for dialogue with the Israelis." In 1980 he invited Israeli students to Najah, an unthinkable move at the time. People at home accused him of treason. "But I led the movement," Sa'eb remembers. "I was alone. Very lonely."

Sa'eb says the PLO in exile—Arafat, Abu Mazen, Abu Ala—were supporting him all along, even through the 1991 Madrid talks when a joint Palestinian-Jordanian delegation attended the conference. After Oslo began and Israel accepted the PLO's legitimacy, Arafat appointed Sa'eb his head negotiator. His most important job was helping to prepare elections.

"The Israelis insisted that we have one [executive] body over everything, because we're not an independent state." Sa'eb shook his head at the incompatibility of democracy without separation of powers. "I said to Yitzhak Rabin one night in Cairo: We have problems. And he asked me, 'Does your chairman really want elections?' And I said yes. Not because he's the father of democracy, but because he wants to legitimize himself. And Rabin said, 'If your chairman is true in this, we'll give you what you want. Because a democratic state is the best security for Israel.' He was a man of vision . . ." Sa'eb trailed off into the bubbling of his hookah pipe. "And this was my biggest achievement," he said exhaling a cloud of smoke. "I will never top this."

Sa'eb says the polls reflect his legitimacy among Palestinians. He won a seat in the PLC with sixty-two percent of the Jericho vote. He beat out seven candidates. National polls in 2003 gave him fourteen percent of the popular vote for potential Arafat replacements.

"Only fourteen percent?" I questioned.

"Come on!" Sa'eb burst out. "For one who is not campaigning? Who does not have a party? Who is condemning suicide bombings? And still in the darkest times, fourteen percent?"

I asked Sa'eb what I had asked Mohammad Dahlan: If you have so much support, why don't the young Palestinians I talk to jump up and say we respect Sa'eb Erekat?

"They won't," he said, "because we don't represent the changes in the structure they want to be part of. We don't offer them elections. And they don't know that Sa'eb Erekat sat with Colin Powell and begged him to have elections and that it did not help."

Sa'eb took another pull from the *argileh*. Behind that hookah cloud, dressed in a gray sweat suit, he looked worn-out. At least tired enough to reveal that he'd begged the American secretary of state. I knew Sa'eb wanted to get out of politics. Every time I saw him, he spoke about how he was losing touch with his family.

"In public life, you are almost denied a personal life and sitting with your family," he now said. "Every daughter wants a father and a friend, and I hardly have any relations with my son Ali." There was pain on Sa'eb's face, the look of a man who carries a great burden.

"Peacemaking is not a job for me," Sa'eb said as the *argileh* smoke cleared. "It's a life commitment. And every time I hear Israelis and Palestinians are killed, I look in the mirror and feel responsible."

Clinton's Applause

T he banner lorded over Rabin Square. From its center glared a pair of reproving eyes, a look that sought each individual—in the square, in the country—with sharpshooter precision. Beside the eyes a splash of red ripped through the blackness: *Shmone Shanim Meaz Haretzach—Eight years since the murder.*

Uri and I stood on the balcony over the square in central Tel Aviv, listening to the speeches of politicians and the songs of middle-aged rock stars. It was the anniversary of Yitzhak Rabin's assassination. We looked up at the banner of Rabin and down at the crowd that had come to remember him: young people dressed in youth movement regalia, peace activists, Laborites. An estimated 100,000 people. It was the largest memorial rally in years. Gigantic banners waved languidly in the air. "Get Out of the Territories for the Sake of Israel." "Yes to Tolerance, No to Violence." "Peace Now." "Support Geneva." It wasn't just a memorial, *Ha'aretz* reported the next morning. It was a peace march.

Yitzhak Rabin, twice prime minister, minister of defense, chief of staff, and distinguished war veteran, was assassinated November 4, 1995, by Yigal Amir, a fanatical religious Jew. I remember coming home that afternoon to find my mother teary-eyed in front of the television. My parents knew both the Rabins, Yitzhak and his wife, Leah. My father had worked closely with the prime minister during the early Oslo years, and he had been backstage with Rabin in the moments before his historic handshake with Yasir Arafat. Afterward, Rabin posed for a photo along with Arafat, Bill Clinton, and Shimon Peres. The four men stood in a row, each holding a Seeds of Peace T-shirt. Behind them were the forty-five original Seeds. Each man eventually signed his name beneath his picture. "I bet it's worth ten thousand dollars," I said, ogling the photo when my father obtained the last signature. But I knew the photo was priceless.

Not long after Rabin's murder I went to look at the picture, only to make a horrible discovery. The signatures had disappeared, as though the men had signed with invisible ink. It reminded me of the Polaroid Marty McFly carries with him in *Back to the Future*. As his father's past begins to change, Marty sees his own image—his future—disappear. Only later did I realize that the disappearing names symbolized not only the death of Rabin, but the demise of a peaceful future for Israelis and Palestinians. I couldn't help but wonder how the region might look had Rabin survived. Would Camp David have failed? Would the second intifada have begun?

"I cannot swear to you that peace would have been done if my father wasn't assassinated," Dalia Rabin-Pelossof, Rabin's daughter, former member of Knesset, and deputy defense minister, told me. Today, Rabin-Pelossof heads the Rabin Center for Israel Studies. She explained how, the summer before her father's murder, there had been a wave of suicide bombings. No one in the Israeli government was sure Arafat truly wanted peace. "Maybe if my father wasn't assassinated," Rabin-Pelossof said, "he would have stopped the peace process himself." But she told me something else: after the assassination, "Arafat was saying all along, 'I lost my only partner.' Because there was something unique between them. And it wasn't love and it wasn't friendship. It was the first stages of trust. Because Arafat respected my father and he knew that yes is yes and no is no. And he can't play games."

I asked Dalia how her father was able to have such a unique relationship with Arafat.

"Because that's the kind of person my father was," she said. "He was looking into your eyes and what you saw was what you got. And when he decided to go along with Arafat, it came from his own convictions that right now, this is the only way."

Even as the head of Labor, Rabin was known to be hawkish. "He was very attached to the land," his daughter admitted. "He *hated* giving up land." Settlement expansion continued freely during Rabin's tenure as prime minister, though not in densely populated Palestinian areas. So perhaps Rabin's decision to begin negotiations with the enemy was a little like Nixon going to China. Just like Arafat, Israelis knew he wasn't a pushover.

Even so, there were and still are plenty of Israelis who don't like him—and not only the fanatics. Sari's friend, Kayla, from the Tekoa settlement was six years old when the Oslo process began and only eight when Rabin was assassinated. Her high school has a special day to commemorate the murder, but Kayla doesn't go.

"They're worshipping him like he's the Virgin Mary," she told me. "It's not right."

Omri felt the same way. "You know about the *Altalena?*" he asked me. "Rabin killed Jews—his own people."

The *Altalena* was the ship Jewish militants used to bring weapons into Israel shortly after the 1948 war. At that time, Rabin was deputy military commander to David Ben-Gurion, Israel's first prime minister. Ben-Gurion recognized that if Israel was to survive as a democratic state, it must have a single unified army; the militant National Army Group, the Irgun, had to go. When the Irgun refused to disband, Ben-Gurion gave Rabin orders to fire on the ship. Sixteen militants were killed. In the end, the Irgun disbanded, their fighters absorbed into the newly created Israel Defense Forces. In 1977, Menachem Begin, one of the Irgun's most ambitious leaders, would be elected Israeli prime minister and would also sign a peace accord with Egypt.

Still, many people view Rabin as one of Israel's last great politicians.

"Rabin was an initiator," Uri told me. "He had what Sadat and Begin had. Every other prime minister reacted to what Rabin started."

As an Arab living in Israel, Yara's mother said there wasn't a single Israeli prime minister who made her community a priority. Still, Rabin made a significant impression on her. "I can't say that he liked the Palestinians," she said, "but he was a *real* man. He knew that peace was the only way to make Israel stable."

"My father was the last leader who was considered with integrity and real dedication to the future of the people," Dalia Rabin-Pelossof told me. "Whoever came after him was considered more or less cynical."

It's not only the political leadership who are considered cynical, it's the young leadership as well. This is clear in Israeli universities, where student government is a microcosm of national politics. Israel has a parliamentary system of government, meaning that numerous parties compete at election time. The left-of-center Labor party and the right-of-center Likud party are the largest, but neither ever receives enough seats in the 120-person Knesset to form a viable government. This means that whichever party receives the most votes in the nationwide election must form coalitions with the smaller parties in order to run the country. In universities, student unions work like the Knesset, with most parties having some political affiliation. At Tel Aviv University, for example, the New Generation party is aligned with Labor, and Labor gives them financial support to help draw in other students at election time. Students assured me, however, that once the university council is formed, their parties cannot use government money for their activities. And though a group like New Generation, which headed the Student Union in 2003, may run ideologically oriented activities, they must be nonpartisan when it comes to general student affairs.

Sound like a conflict of interest? Many students think so, even those in the unions. Efrat, the Student Union vice president at Hebrew University in Jerusalem, personally supports Labor, but she didn't run with the Labor-affiliated party. She won her position as a member of the Independent party—the only group at Hebrew University that does not affiliate politically and the one that wins year after year. According to Efrat, the success of the Independent party is obvious.

"People are sick and tired of politics," she told me. "They don't want politics in their lives. There's so much corruption."

Nir, another member of the Independent party, agreed. "Even though I love Israel, I have enormous problems with the government. I don't like the way it works." Nir said he voted Likud in the last national elections. "I like their basic way of thinking," he explained, "but I don't like the people there. The people make the system."

But if the student union is supposed to work solely for the general student body, I asked Nir and Efrat, then why do any students run for the union as part of nationally affiliated parties?

Efrat gave a snide grin and said, "Only one word: power. Most want to go straight from here to the Knesset."

"Do either of you have political aspirations after college?"

"I would never be a Knesset member," Nir said. "Politics means power. You have to have power to know how things work."

The way he said power, turning his mouth down in disgust, you'd think he was uttering a profanity.

In a country as small as Israel, the possibility of going straight from university politics to the Knesset isn't so far-fetched. Over the years, handfuls of politicians made names for themselves as Student Union leaders. Gila Gamliel is currently the most well known. She is a Jew of Yemeni descent and grew up in an impoverished development town, but she pulled herself out of her deprived circumstances through politics. She was Student Union president at Ben-Gurion University and, later, the first woman to be elected chairperson of the National Students' Association. When she was twenty-four, the Likud Central Committee (the body that chooses Likud's Knesset candidates) ranked Gamliel twenty-fourth. Likud won only nineteen seats that year, so Gamliel didn't make it into the government, but four years later, she got into the Knesset with room to spare. She was ranked eleventh, one seat ahead of defense minister and former chief of staff Shaul Mofaz. At twenty-eight years of age, she sits in an office larger than that of older Knesset members who have been in the government for years.

Gamliel has worked hard to achieve her position in Likud, but she's had a great deal of family support. Gamliel's family are longtime Likud activists. Her father built up the Likud party in her hometown and her brother is the local party chairman. Both her brothers are currently members of the Likud Central Committee. Gamliel is open about her political connections; it was family experience, she told me, that helped her navigate her way through national politics. But Gamliel has become infamous for allegedly bribing and blackmailing a fellow student at Ben-Gurion University into supporting her candidacy as Student Union president—a position that proved vital to her national success. Gamliel denies the accusations, but the teenagers and young adults with whom I spoke felt they could not trust her.

In fact, a culture of dishonesty seems to run through the Likud ranks; with only three thousand people choosing and ranking Likud candidates, corruption abounds. According to *The Forward,* the Likud primaries, or "crimaries" as they are known in Israel, resemble a *Soprano* episode. At the time of the last primaries, *Ha'aretz* reported that local bosses tried to bribe candidates into "delivering blocs of votes . . . in exchange for large sums of money and sexual and other favors."[*] When I asked former prime minister Benjamin Netanyahu about the Likud's primary system, he acknowledged that it did in fact breed corruption. "I changed the system to open primaries," he touted. (Labor has open primaries, which means their 100,000 party members rank the candidates.)

"You did?" I asked, wondering how I could have missed such a major political change.

[*] *Ha'aretz,* July 10, 2004.

"I did," Netanyahu repeated, "but the Central Committee revoked it."

"And there's nothing you can do about this now?" I pressed him.

"I changed it, the Central Committee revoked it." Netanyahu had clearly washed his hands of the issue.

Even if the majority of Knesset and party members are not corrupt, the culture of conduct in Israeli politics still repels young people. To student leaders like Nir at Hebrew University, it's people like Gamliel who turn power into a dirty word. Nir's aversion to national politics is a dangerous phenomenon. You need a certain amount of power—of clout within the system—to implement broad-scale change. Gila Gamliel understands this and might have bent the rules in order to reach a place where she could truly fight for young people and women. To her credit, she struggled to lower university tuition and helped new faces enter the government. But young Israelis like Nir and Efrat cannot reconcile the positive things Gamliel is doing in the government with the way she purportedly got there. Their disillusionment risks creating a political vacuum in which the potential leaders are not willing to utilize their potential. If they don't fight for power and a voice, their voice will be lost.

In Sari's eyes, government officials put trivial and selfish concerns ahead of their constituents. She saw one news report about the problem of cell phones in Knesset meetings; the members were constantly answering them under the table during important discussions. "That's what matters to them?" she asked, incredulous. "My teachers in school say it's not right to answer your phone in the middle of a class. And the people in the Knesset were saying 'I don't want to turn off my phone!' And these people are the leaders of my country?"

I asked Sari if she would ever consider a political profession. "No! Not at all" was her immediate response. "It's not that I want to live my small life. I do want to change something, but if I go there, they'll eat me."

"Eat you?"

"I'm not, like, I'm not poisoned. I will never go up there and fight and start screaming at people because of what I believe. I will never pay money to be advertised so that people will choose me."

I suggested to Sari that this atmosphere wasn't unique to Israeli politics, that we have similar problems with the American political system. But she was certain. "It's not like that in England," she said. "You don't see anyone answering phones in *their* meetings. But seriously. I'm not proud of my government. I'm really not."

I wondered what it would take for Sari and other young Israelis to feel proud of their leadership: Yoyo said he knew exactly what the country needed.

"A leader should be someone who has an inspiration," he explained. "But the people in the government and the parliament are not leading the country toward a vision. I haven't heard any politician say what Israel should be in thirty years."

Given his feeling about Israeli politics, it's not surprising that all Yoyo's role models are dead: Ford, Einstein, Nobel, and Herzl. And especially Ben-Gurion.

"He had the ability to have avant-garde thoughts. What people thought about but weren't strong enough to go outside and say." Yoyo told me about Ben-Gurion's decision to accept the 1948 UN Partition Plan even though the majority of the Jewish leadership opposed it, and his determination to disband the Jewish militants even at the cost of killing his own people.

"Having the power to say all this," he explained, "and to pass it on, and to make sure that people supported him, that's brilliant. For me, it's equivalent to E equals MC squared. We need a new Ben-Gurion now. "

Ben-Gurion is the kind of person, the kind of politician, Yoyo wants to be. He told me a Hebrew song that says, "You and I can change the world. It's been said before, but it doesn't matter." "Maybe I'm naive," Yoyo admitted, "but I'm concerned that this country is not what the people who founded it wanted. We should be as it's said in the Bible. We should set an example to other nations in the world: morally, and education-wise, and financially."

Shimon Peres is one of these historic founders. He immigrated to Palestine from Poland in 1934 and spent his teenage years living on a kibbutz, a Jewish farming collective. He got his political start as secretary of the Labor Youth Movement, and throughout his career he has served as minister of defense, minister of foreign affairs, and prime minister. Peres turned eighty the winter of 2003. He was then chairman of the Labor party and looked nowhere near retirement. He is, when judged by nearly any standard, a great man. Even Omri, who is fervently rightist, told me how much he admired Peres. "I don't like Peres's opinions, but I know that his mind is doing the best for Israel." Omri went on to call Peres one of the most honest men he'd ever seen.

Peres himself is a poet. According to my father, when Peres met the foreign minister of Iceland he said, "It's not every day that the leader of the Chosen People can shake hands with the leader of the Frozen people." Peres also waxes eloquent in his poetry. He speaks in metaphors: about the cosmos, and currents of electricity; about politics as a replacement for war; and about history, which he says is "generally not such a big occasion." His accent is thick—a Middle Eastern, Eastern European mix. His eyebrows are heavy, his forehead the "distinguished" kind. Over tea in his Tel Aviv office he told me candidly: "The former generation is a handicap, not a blessing. Because what they have to teach is obsolete and old-fashioned.

"You have to serve a cause," Peres continued. "I learned from Ben-Gurion that we say *we*. If you serve yourself, maybe you'll succeed, but I don't think you'll make a real change."

I asked Peres if channels existed in the Labor party for bright young leaders to rise. Peres said he was looking to the universities—to the Student Unions like the ones at Tel Aviv and Hebrew U. "I am going to the students and saying 'organize yourselves, and elect your own people to the parliament.' So instead of bringing politics to the students, I want to bring them to politics."

But Peres could give no straight answer as to how these university leaders could be elected to national government without the money and support of the old guard or without channels of mobility inside the party.

Peres isn't corrupt, but he is holding tightly to his position as Labor king. Barak said of him: "We used to joke that even in 2020, when I will be Peres's age, Peres will still be there and he will still be rejuvenating the party with our grandchildren."

Knesset member Avraham Burg did not share Barak's lightheartedness. According to him Labor was in the middle of a "serious leadership crisis." As one of the Labor party's younger members, he has quite a bit of experience behind him: fifteen years in the government and a position as former speaker of the Knesset. In 2003 he said there was only one person younger than him to have made it to the party's "premier league."

"Leadership should come and go," Burg warned. "Peres is always available. He does not like young people to take over. The Labor party can change the world if the old is the current and not the future. We are inaccurate, irrelevant, and shrinking."

Amram Mitzna agreed. He is the former mayor of Haifa who ran for prime minister against Sharon in 2002. After his defeat, Mitzna resigned as Labor chairman. The party wasn't behind him, he said, and it didn't give him enough authority to effect change. His replacement? Shimon

Peres. In Mitzna's Knesset office, I asked him what Labor needed to do to recapture the hearts and minds of Israel. He sighed like a person who has been too long on his feet. "We need reform inside the Labor party. It's the only thing that will save us, and a year after the elections we didn't try to change some of the laws, the procedures that will open the gates for new faces. . . ."

The party with the most success in opening the gates for younger leaders is Likud. They have instituted various affirmative action policies, such as reserving certain parliament seats for women and people under thirty. This makes it easier for new leaders to enter the party and for younger candidates to establish themselves. So Mitzna was taking the lead from Likud and making proposals. He wants one third of Labor's list to be new, at least forty percent of them women, and a regulation that after a Knesset member serves two or three terms, he or she must obtain a higher percentage of votes to be reelected.

I asked Mitzna how his plan was progressing. The party organs allow a person to change the laws, he said, "but you have to go through a lot of echelons. You see there are the members of the Labor party, which is about 100,000 people. Then there is the convention, which is about 5,000 people. Then you have the center, which is 3,000 people. And you have to go through all of them. And there are a lot of people who do not want to shake their situation."

I asked various young people what they thought about Mitzna's proposals and the challenges he faced within his own party. The comment that stuck out most came from the Student Union president at Tel Aviv University. Iftach, twenty-eight, was in the middle of his second term as head of the Labor-affiliated New Generation party. His shaved head and muscular arms made him look more like an army commando than a student politician.

"If you want to make change, you can make it." Iftach had little sympathy for Mitzna. "I got elected as the chairman of the Union and I'm not going to say to anyone that I don't have the power or the responsibility to make a change."

"So because you're able to make changes in the university, you don't excuse the national leadership for not being able to—"

Iftach cut me off. "Right now"—his eyes hardened—"I don't excuse anyone."

Despite his criticism of the national government, Iftach knows how difficult it is to build and maintain legitimacy, even on the student level.

"Students are very cynical of their union," he told me. "They think I'm only working for myself." But Iftach said that when you have to make difficult decisions, you can't always let the critics deter you. "You have to look for what you want to create in the long term," he said, and take the practical steps necessary to accomplish that goal. "It's the difference between talking about something and doing something."

In the winter of 2005, it seemed as though some members of the Labor party had finally taken action. At this time, Sharon faced opposition from the Israeli right for his decision to withdraw IDF forces from Gaza and dismantle settlements there. He needed to form a new coalition in order to prevent the collapse of his government. Tired of its inefficacy, Labor agreed to join with Sharon in a "national unity" government—a system in which the two central parties share the political mandate. Practically, this meant that Labor party members were elected to some of the cabinet posts and that the Labor party head became a vice–prime minister. When Labor held internal elections to determine who would be in the national cabinet, a handful of younger faces found themselves at the top of the list. This came as a surprise to some of the more seasoned Labor leaders who now found themselves sharing power with the young guard, and in some cases, replaced by them. Shimon Peres did not run in these elections; the national unity deal was predicated upon making him vice-premier.

Peres's eightieth birthday party was a massive event. There was an elaborate concert in Tel Aviv and a party packed with Israel's who's who, as well as world leaders from around the globe. All of them came to honor and pay tribute to Peres. But Peres wasn't the only star that evening. Bill Clinton, former president of the United States, attended the party and received no fewer than five standing ovations. After the concert, an Israeli government official pulled my father over and pleaded, "You're not using Clinton anymore. Couldn't you lend him to us—just for a little while?" This comment summed up what I'd been hearing from young Israelis. They were sorely in need of a Clinton-type leader, someone with energy and a vision. As Iftach said, the difference between talking and doing. It wasn't just the Israelis who were in need of this kind of leader. A Palestinian woman, applauding passionately for the former U.S. president, turned to me and said, "We really loved that guy."

What makes a leader legitimate in Israel? How do you capture the hearts and minds of the public as Labor has failed to do? To not be, as Burg said of his own party, "inaccurate and irrelevant"? The fact remains that Sharon was elected because he was the most relevant guy around. When he was first elected in 2001 and again in 2003, Israel was embroiled in an intifada. The country wanted a warrior to lead them, and they got exactly that. The slogan everyone associates with Sharon is "Let the army win."

"I don't blame Sharon," Uri told me. "He is doing what he was elected to do. There must be a reason why the people don't look for an alternative."

Some believed there were no alternatives. "It doesn't matter who you elect," Iftach told me. "The left, the right. It's always the same." At least there weren't any politicians giving the people a compelling reason why a warrior might not be in the national interest. After Camp David failed, Barak essentially convinced the country there was no Palestinian partner, so they certainly didn't want any peaceniks.

Israel's most hated, most popular peacenik is Yossi Beilin. Nobody seems to trust Beilin—his name is enough to evoke a scowl—yet about forty percent of the population supports his Geneva Initiative. Geneva is a comprehensive, highly detailed Israeli-Palestinian settlement that he drafted with Yasser Abed Rabbo, the former Palestinian minister of culture and information and Camp David negotiator. According to Beilin, Geneva is meant to show both societies that they do have a partner and to get them debating the critical issues inherent to settling their conflict. Geneva is not about imposing a settlement on the country, Beilin made clear, but about getting people to face the inevitable concessions upon which peace depends. Though Geneva is entirely a grassroots project, Beilin has longtime experience in the government. He was a Knesset member, deputy minister of foreign affairs, and from 1999 to 2001, Israeli minister of justice.

So why is the Israeli public so skeptical of Beilin? He's not even in the government. One Israeli suggested that people are afraid of him—of his experience, his daring vision for the country.

Yoyo thought otherwise. "You need people to be without a doubt about your concern for the security of the State of Israel. I think that's the problem with Beilin. People don't trust that he really understands the needs of Israel in terms of security."

I asked Sari if she thought the majority of Israelis would respect and support a peace activist like Beilin. "Yes!" she said. Then after a pause: "Well, hopefully." She paused again. "It's sad but maybe not. Because you have to be very pro-Israel. Only pro-Israel. At least now . . ."

"When you say being very pro-Israel, does that automatically mean being anti-Palestinian?"

"Now, ya. There's a demand for a person like that, but I don't think pro-Israel has to be anti-Palestinian. I'm sure it doesn't. And I don't think the person who leads Israel should be, 'Okay, I'll get peace if I give ninety percent of the land away.' I don't think that's the way. You have to believe in Israel for it to exist. On the other hand, you have to know what it takes to make peace."

Beilin says he understands the critics. "People don't want their lawyers to hug the lawyer of the other side," he told me. "And when they see them hugging, they say they are not really representing us."

Still, he is undeterred. He projects complete self-confidence—at least the *air* of legitimacy. "I will say that if you have forty percent support for Geneva, it's legitimate," he said. "You know, I'm not a beginner. I've done enough to believe that I can follow this path: to take an issue, to gather support for it, and to change the policy of the government. I've done it so many times. If it is sanctions against South Africa in the late eighties, or unilateral withdrawal from Lebanon" (which Israel invaded in 1982 and from which it unilaterally withdrew in 2000).

Beilin is trying to prepare the Israeli public for the kind of agreement he believes is inevitable. "The surprise of all the Israelis at the readiness of Barak to divide Jerusalem at Camp David was striking," Beilin said. "What we are doing is educating the people by saying, 'this is going to be the result.' "

Beilin says he isn't holding up Geneva as the Bible. It's a draft, he says, something he hopes will inspire discussion, support, and criticism. He says he's content to conduct this work outside formal governmental channels. "Thinking outside the box is a must for those who want to have an influence," he believes, "because the box is rusty. It doesn't mean that everything out of the box is wiser, but even when I was part of the center of the establishment, a member of the dominant party, I always worked outside the system."

Nowhere was this more true than in the Oslo talks, where Beilin began secret negotiation channels with Abu Mazen in 1992. Beilin was deputy foreign minister at the time, but he didn't tell his boss at the Ministry, nor did he tell his prime minister—Rabin. Only when he saw hints of success, he said, did he bring the secret channel to light. With Geneva, Beilin has taken the opposite approach: to put the negotiations on the table for everyone to see.

"We don't have too much time," he said gravely. "My deep feeling is that within six years, if this conflict is not finished, the whole story is over. The whole story of Israel as a Jewish and a democratic state is over. So we cannot now have a kind of educational cruise and forget about politics. We have to do whatever we can to get the government to change its policy."

The government is beginning to shift. Sharon has vowed to pull the army out of Gaza and to dismantle some West Bank settlements. He has even stood against his own party and risked governmental collapse. Still, the pervasive attitude in Israel is one of intense skepticism. People don't believe it's the Israeli government who's standing in the way of peace. They blame the Palestinians.

"In Israel there is a silent majority that is ready to make a Camp David deal," Barak told me. "The same majority that supports the wall or the fence." (Barak was referring to the security barrier, alternately an eight-meter concrete wall and a barbed-wire fence, that the Israeli government is constructing. Most Palestinians scorn the fence because in some places it reaches far into the West Bank to incorporate settlements, thereby isolating Palestinian enclaves. Most Israelis favor the barrier, because they believe it has significantly reduced terrorism inside Israel.)

"The moment there will be a Sadat-like leader," Barak continued, "this silent majority will stand on their feet and begin to walk toward peace. If Sharon, or whoever follows him, tries to block them, that person will be removed."

Barak says this silent majority are members of Meretz (a firmly left-of-center party), Shinui (which has a secular platform), Labor, and most of Likud. When it comes to the conflict, these people favor a negotiated settlement and a two-state solution, but they put security first. And when the vast majority of Jewish Israelis look at their Palestinian neighbors, they see a world of chaos, violence, and corruption that only a warrior can contain.

Hope for the Holy Land

⁂

The evening of Yitzhak Rabin's memorial rally, I began thinking about the people in this world who leave their mark. But I wasn't thinking about Rabin. Nor was I contemplating the Gandhis, Mandelas, Kings, or any of the other great men who struggle for decades to achieve equality and peace. That night as I left Tel Aviv, the men on my mind were Yigal Amir, Rabin's murderer; the 9/11 hijackers; and Khaled al-Islambouli, Anwar Sadat's assassin—men who changed history in an instant. As my car climbed the steep hill that winds toward Jerusalem, they seemed to rise up from the road, ghostly and elusive, each one a wizard wielding his fateful wand. It angered me to think that a straight shot from each of these wands—one bullet fired at Sadat, another at Rabin, and a rushing aircraft—could do such indelible damage.

Why, I wondered, was destruction efficient and straightforward while creation was complicated and time-consuming? There was no single action you could do to make peace but endless ways to provoke war. Even if positive acts—the civil rights movement, the end of South African apartheid, and Arafat and Rabin's legacy of mutual recognition between Israelis and Palestinians—did leave an imprint on history, it felt to me that the destructiveness in the world so easily consumed efforts to build and create.

My friend Jen, who was driving me home that night, had her own take on the matter. "Creation is not the opposite of destruction," she said. "The same lightning bolt act of pulling the trigger or flying a plane into a building could never produce good. Good acts are human work."

Initially, I didn't understand what Jen meant. Making peace was as much a human act as murder, but it seemed easier to kill people than to make them talk out their problems. Then, I began to see that Jen was asking me to view creation and destruction in a new context, not as opposites but as different processes altogether. Creation, I realized, is about building, and by its very nature connects and bonds human beings. This is what Jen meant when she said creation was human work. Though groups like al-Qaeda, the Ku Klux Klan, or the Nazis are closely united, their bonds are based upon the exclusion of other human beings. For these groups it's the ideology, be it cultural, religious, or political, that is of primary importance. If the ideology is more important than the human, you can simply get rid of any person who opposes you. Creation, on the other hand, is all about people, and that's what makes it so difficult to realize. Anyone who strives to create a solution for the Israeli-Palestinian conflict must consider the needs and requirements of two diverse and complicated societies. Such a process can be slow and frustrating, but if you want your indelible mark to be one of creation and not destruction, you have to take the time and invest in the long term.

Months after the Rabin rally, when I step back and look at young Israelis and Palestinians like Sari, Mohammad, Omri, Yara, and Reem, I see that each of them, in his or her own way, has accepted this difficult road of creating. They know that the conflict between their societies is a zero sum game; either they reconcile or they will inevitably destroy each another. While so many of their peers have been deterred by apathy and violence, my young friends are forging ahead. They are tireless, because they are determined to make their mark.

Senior Palestinian negotiator Sa'eb Erekat understands the source of their energy. "The world has changed," he told me. "When I was thirteen, my only option was throwing stones. I did not have an alternative. My daughter Dalal has an alternative. She has Seeds."

When Sa'eb Erekat says that his twenty-two-year-old daughter has Seeds of Peace as an alternative to throwing stones, he does not mean that Dalal's best friends are Israeli, or that she is highly involved in Seeds of Peace activities. The truth is, Dalal, along with many Seeds of Peace graduates, has focused mainly on her own community, schooling, and personal interests since she attended Seeds of Peace camp as a teenager.

It has been much the same with Omri since he went to camp in 2003. I arrived in Jerusalem in August 2003 feeling both hopeful and fearful for Omri and Mohammad's friendship. In the end, my fears won out. The two boys rarely saw each other, did not communicate much, and shirked my repeated attempts to organize a visit between them. For months I kept in touch with each boy separately, following his individual life, occasionally asking each one if he had heard from the other. I resigned myself to the fact that whatever superpower strength this dynamic duo held at camp, it did not bind them back home.

Mohammad was highly active in Seeds of Peace throughout my time in the region. He lives near the Jerusalem Center and went there most afternoons after school. Omri, however, was wrapped up in his own life. He had signed up to attend weekly discussion groups in Jerusalem (the Center staff even made special arrangements to put him and Mohammad in the same group), but he often skipped these activities for basketball practice or homework. It seemed to me that for this graduate, Seeds of Peace had slipped into the periphery.

Then one afternoon, Omri told me about the Seeds of Peace presentation he had recently given in school. I had visited Israeli high schools and had seen how intimidating it was for Israeli Seeds to stand in front of a large group and talk about their camp experiences. The audience was often less than receptive, reacting with whispering, eye-rolling, and open ridicule. Some of the students in Omri's class were the very kids who told him before he went to camp, "Promise us you won't come back a peace man!" And Omri had assured them, "You know I won't."

Nevertheless, Omri stood in front of thirty kids and pulled a Seeds of Peace T-shirt out of his bag. "Do you see this T-shirt?" he asked the group. "Do you know what this T-shirt means to me?" Omri told his classmates that if they saw such an ugly green shirt at the store they wouldn't pay twenty shekels—the equivalent of five dollars—for it. "But for me," Omri continued, "this shirt is worth more than one hundred dollars. This T-shirt represents a special period of time that I will never forget. This T-shirt will be with me as long as I live." Omri went on to ask the group who among them believed in peace. Only one or two hands out of thirty went up. "I used to think like you," he said. "I thought a good Arab is a dead Arab." But then he told them about Mohammad and his other Palestinian friends. He talked of their suffering and what it's like for them to see tanks parked outside their homes. About the fact that many Palestinians did want peace and were willing to fight for it. Omri spoke to the class and answered questions for nearly two hours. At the end he said to them, "Now how many of you believe in peace?" A handful of students were crying from all the emotion and about half the hands went up. Omri's mother told me the teacher had tears in her eyes.

Omri spoke about his class presentation with pride. He described the Seeds of Peace T-shirt with the same excitement and passion I'd felt from him when he told me about his father's army tags and his desire to be an IDF warrior. Listening to him, I began to understand the nature of Omri's relationship to Seeds. As he said, the T-shirt represented camp, a place where he could put his Palestinian friends and his desire for peace at the center of his life. When he returned to Israel, that period of time came to an end. Mohammad would not be an integral part of his life anymore, and Omri would always look skeptically at the Palestinian nation. At the same time, camp changed Omri. The tolerance he learned there would stay with him in the future. He would be thinking about that Seeds of Peace shirt for a long time, even if he wouldn't be wearing it.

Eight years after she first attended camp, Dalal Erekat also has that green T-shirt in mind. After she graduated from high school she won a scholarship to a university in London for a master's in international relations. When I last saw her, she was working on her thesis about Oslo and Camp David. Dalal is not simply following in her father's footsteps. If anything, watching her father struggle through so many negotiations has been a source of disillusionment for her.

"The Palestinians don't know how to negotiate," she told me one evening in Jericho. "When you walk into negotiations, you have to know every single detail about what you are discussing, and you have to be able to talk in a way so others will listen. Most of the people in the Authority don't know how to do this."

Dalal's proximity to the Palestinian Authority may have shown her ineffectual policies and closing doors, but her experiences with Seeds of Peace have opened tremendous opportunities. Dalal knows exactly what it takes to sit across the table from an opponent and hash out the core issues of the Israeli-Palestinian conflict. She attended the 1998 Seeds of Peace summit in Switzerland along with myself and Asel, Yoyo, Uri, and Ruba. We didn't solve all the issues, but even today, I remain impressed by the creative solutions we devised for issues like Jerusalem.

More important is the process that led us to these solutions. For ten days we debated, argued, cried, and forced ourselves to hear one anothers' needs and bottom lines, even though it meant putting down our defenses and laying out our vulnerabilities. As far as we were concerned, this wasn't a mock summit, but the real thing. We were proving to ourselves that we could put the skills we learned at Seeds of Peace and the trust we built there to practical use. At this summit, attended by 130 international high school–age Seeds of Peace graduates, and visited by heads of state and diplomats from Europe, the Middle East, and America, we were being shown an expansive view of the world, and in turn, we showed the world what we were capable of.

So when Sa'eb says his daughter has alternatives, he means an alternative worldview. Dalal and the other young people featured in this book have been given the opportunity to see how those outside of their own neighborhoods think, act, and look. In recognizing this diversity, it has become much more difficult for my Israeli and Palestinian friends to accept the hatreds their societies have prescribed for them. They have begun to recognize the creative solutions that exist, not only for the Israeli-Palestinian conflict, but for their own futures. They see options for self-expression beyond shouting Arab slurs or throwing stones: life over death, creation over destruction.

Because there are young people to whom death is tempting. I met the family of one young suicide bomber, eighteen-year-old Ayat al-Kharas, on a trip to the Dheisha refugee camp, located twenty minutes south of Jerusalem. Ayat blew herself up in the entrance of a Jerusalem super-market in March 2002, killing two Israelis (including a seventeen-year-old girl) and wounding thirty people. She was a high school senior, a straight-A student, and had recently become engaged. The al-Kharas family room had become a shrine to their daughter. Enlarged photographs of Ayat, her face as smooth and porcelainlike as the white *hijab* that covered her hair, hung on the walls. Her eyes were dark, her colored lips peaceful, with no more than a whisper of a smile. The central picture of the girl was embellished with brilliant Arabic calligraphy, a Koranic verse: "Fight them, God will let them suffer by you. Let them fall."

"We love all people. We are not terrorists," Ayat's mother said, drawing my attention away from the pictures. My friend Tamara sat next to us on the couch translating. "Ayat loved life," Mrs. al-Kharas said. "She loved to dance and sing. And she loved new clothes, especially." I smiled at this, but the mother's eyes returned a mean stare; her Arabic assaulted me like sharp slaps.

A child called out from the living room, alerting us to a television program—a documentary for al-Manara television (run out of Lebanon by the militant group Hizbollah) about the families of Palestinian martyrs.

Tamara and I removed our shoes and crossed the rug to sit on the thin mattresses that acted as couches. A large flashy television and its stand were the only pieces of furniture in the room. Two green curtains hung from the ceiling and were parted in front of the TV.

Mrs. al-Kharas appeared on the screen, imploring the audience. "I'd give both of my eyes to have her back," she sobbed. I looked over at the woman now, her once-mean eyes red and tearing, her stout body hunched over the mattress. Now the television showed a plain of waving grass and an open sky, suggestive of a condolence card or a pamphlet on spiritual healing. Two lines of Arabic appeared on the screen: "Twelve thousand volunteers are waiting their turn to be martyrs" the words said. The connotation behind this message was that these potential bombers could heal the wounds of Palestine. If I had been in charge of this documentary, however, I would have rewritten the message. In my eyes these twelve thousand were rending the wounds, not sewing them up.

Ayat carried out her mission with the help of the Al-Aqsa Martyrs' Brigades, the secular militant group associated with Arafat's Fatah party. According to Ayat's mother, the entire family was baffled by her action. "We didn't know any of those people," her mother said of the militants. "I had no idea this would happen; she told no one."

By all accounts, Ayat displayed no overt signs of anger or malice, though Tamara, who attended middle school with Ayat, remembers her being highly sensitive. All the family knew was that Ayat went to school every day, came home, and studied. In fact, she spent the night before the bombing studying for a science exam that she took the following morning. There must have been some reason, I pressed Ayat's mother, why she killed herself. Could she have experienced a loss, I asked, some unhappiness greater than that of her siblings and friends? Mrs. al-Kharas replied that while Ayat had known many people who died in the intifada, she wasn't particularly close with any of them. "Anyone who decides to be a martyr will do it," she said. "A child decides without the opinion of her parents. We can't control her."

"But don't you hold the men from the Al-Aqsa Brigades responsible for this?" I asked more forcefully than I intended. "Aren't you angry that they would allow a young girl to do such a thing?"

"They did not force her!" Ayat's mother snapped. "She wanted this. This is volunteer."

Yet I didn't believe that Mrs. al-Kharas had convinced herself of this. Midway through the documentary she focused her quivering eyes upon my own: "A mother is a mother," she was nearly begging. "I'm just like an American mom!"

For a while, we sat in silence. The documentary finished and someone switched the channel. Harrison Ford filled the screen, presidential and bloodied. Terrorists were hijacking Air Force One. I braced myself for a diatribe about the American media's demonization of Muslims and Arabs but quickly realized that the movie's hijackers were Russian. In the movie these men threaten to kill one prominent cabinet member on the plane every hour until their demands are met. For me, this has always been the movie's most heartwrenching point. "Twelve p.m.," the hijackers radio to the White House, "your national security adviser has just been assassinated. . . . One p.m., we've shot the secretary of state." And so on. This afternoon, as I watched *Air Force One* I realized it didn't matter whether the terrorists in the movie were Arabs, Russians, or even Japanese. I had been watching for less than a minute and already my heart was pounding. Harrison was throwing punches and dodging bullets. *He has to win,* I thought, realizing my fists were clenched. It was just a movie, I knew, and good action-suspense films will have this physical effect, but I was watching it in a refugee camp in the home of a suicide bomber.

It's not that I equated the terrorists on the screen with the al-Kharas family or even with Ayat. And I do not believe in an inherent cultural clash between East and West, but I was aware of a line drawn in the room. I sat on one side and everyone else sat on the other. Who were the al-Kharases rooting for, I wondered? In an ideal world, we'd be on the same team. We'd all see that Ford and his values of life and liberty were the universal "good" and that the hijackers, regardless of their nationalities, symbolized the universal perversion of all that, the embodiment of "bad." But you can't escape nationality—I seemed to be learning this lesson over and over. I wasn't sure that Ayat's mom would be able to look at the president's wife and daughter and empathize: "I'm just like an American mom." I wasn't sure I could look at this movie and not feel (as politically incorrect as it may be) the scenerio of "us against them."

I came out of these thoughts with the realization that I was the only person in the room paying any attention to the television. I had let my imagination get the better of me. I leaned over to Tamara. "Can it really be true that no one had *any* idea Ayat would kill herself?"

Tamara posed the question to Mrs. al-Kharas.

"Ayat's friends remember her telling them 'I will be leaving you,' "

Ayat's mother explained. "But she told them, 'you must continue your studies. To be educated is the hope of Palestine.' "

"They thought she was referring to her choice to get married," Ayat's older sister added in English. "You know, instead of attending university."

Hearing this was the greatest surprise of all. If Ayat truly believed that education was the key to saving Palestine, how could she possibly have killed herself? Her sister told me Ayat was sacrificing herself for her friends, that by giving up her own future, she was saving theirs. I considered this explanation and made little sense of it. As Ayat's sister was speaking of death and sacrifice, my attention was continually pulled back to Tamara, the twenty-year-old Seeds of Peace graduate who sat beside me. Here was a young Palestinian woman in her second year of university, studying to be a pharmacist. Her grandparents lived near the al-Kharas family in the Dheisha refugee camp and Tamara remembers watching Israeli soldiers kill her uncle when she was a little girl. Tamara is deeply religious, wearing both the *hijab* head covering as well as the traditional *jilbab* coat-dress. She has been active in Seeds of Peace since she was sixteen, worked for the local Bethlehem TV station this summer through a joint Seeds of Peace–Daniel Pearl Foundation initative, and, aside from pharmacy, is considering a career as a journalist. Tamara had also told me more than once that she could do much more for her country living than dead. In short, she saw one hope for healing the wounds of Palestine, and that was directing her efforts toward the future. Ayat, on the other hand, is frozen in the past. She will never leave the wall on which she is enshrined. This was the most depressing thought of all. I saw no reason why Ayat, a bright and well-loved student, could not have made the same accomplishments for her country that Tamara was determined to make. If Tamara, who came from such difficult circumstances, was a potential leader and healer of the wounds of Palestine, then why not Ayat? There's no telling what Ayat could have done with her life had she not cut it short. Ayat wanted Israel and the world to hear her plight, so she opened up her mouth and screamed. And in doing so, extinguished her voice.

In light of all the Palestinians who are expressing themselves through violent, destructive means, I don't find it surprising that Yasir Arafat appointed Sa'eb Erekat to be his head negotiator. Sa'eb is one of the only PA officials to have never been involved in violent resistance against the Israeli occupation. He was never a man of the streets, did not physically participate in the first intifada, and was never jailed for a long period of time.

Though alliances on the street are certainly important in gaining legitimacy in Palestinian society, being a fighter alone does not put you on the world stage, where Sa'eb has been since the early nineties. It does not help you garner respect in the international community, nor does it allow you to forge diplomatic relationships. Similarly, a leadership of fighters will never be able to build a developed and democratic Palestine. Qaddura Faris, who spent fourteen years in an Israeli prison but then made the transition to Palestinian politics, said it himself: "In the end, negotiation will end the Israeli-Palestinian conflict, not fighting."

Negotiating and fighting seem to be two ends of a spectrum, two contrasting political approaches. This does not mean a country must forgo its own security considerations in order to engage in dialogue. Yet I believe the path of negotiation is one driven by reason and long-term strategy as opposed to emotion and revenge. The sentiments of Ami Ayalon, former head of the Israeli Shin Bet, resonate with me here. When it comes to dealing with Palestinian violence, Ayalon said Israel's security community isn't thinking along logical lines. "In a state of war you need a warrior to lead you," he said, "no matter whether it makes sense."

Former Likud minister of justice Dan Meridor would agree. He told me that historically, human rights has been one of Likud's central platforms. I was surprised to hear this, because I had always associated the right-wing parties with tough policies toward the Palestinians, and therefore assumed they had always put Israel's security before human rights. According to Meridor, though, the Likud of today is not same party in which he grew up. He told me that Menachem Begin, Israel's first Likud prime minister, was the only prime minister to order the Shin Bet not to use violence in their interrogations. As minister of justice, Meridor put restrictions on the IDF and told Yitzhak Rabin, who was then defense minister, not to demolish Palestinian houses. Yet Meridor is no longer a proud Likudnik; he feels the party's morality has declined.

Yoyo feels this way about Israel in general. He learned through his own army service that instead of reining in the military for political and diplomatic considerations, the government acquiesces to these emotionally driven directives. As he believes, the Israeli government is failing its citizens by solely following the fighting path.

"This country is not what the people who founded it wanted," he told me. "We should be as it's said in the Bible. We should set a moral example for other nations in the world."

Yoyo is right that Israel's fighter-oriented attitude toward the Palestinians is lessening its status in the international community. Yet the problem stretches beyond the increasing skepticism of other nations and international bodies, such as the International Court of Justice. More insidious is the rise of anti-Semitism. I remember sitting in Shimon Peres's office before my interview, watching a news broadcast of a synagogue bombing in Turkey. A number of synagogues worldwide had been targeted in recent months and anti-Semitism was on the rise throughout Europe. I knew there would always be people who hated Jews, but I couldn't help wonder how much of this anti-Jewish activity was actually a reaction against Israel. It frustrates me that so many people equate Jews and the Jewish religion with the policies of the Israeli state. The fact is they do, and I believe this is something of which Israel should be conscious. If the founding of an Israeli state and the prowess of the Israeli army made the world a little safer for Diaspora Jews, today Israel's policies toward the Palestinians seem to be having the opposite effect.

Finally, Israel has a pressing domestic reason to adopt the negotiator's mind-set. It is connected to Yoyo's concern that his leadership lacks a national vision. According to him, with so much energy expended on fighting the Palestinians, the Israeli government has devoted little attention to the country's internal problems and divisions, especially the tension between religious and secular Jews. Yoyo fears that in the near future, the only way for the country to unite its Jewish citizens and to make them feel that they are contributing to the nation is by pitting them all against the external Palestinian threat (and I would add, by exacerbating the threat of Israel's internal Arab community). In this sense, Israel's emotionally propelled attitude toward the conflict is forcing Israel to lose sight of its very purpose: to be a Jewish and democratic nation, but a morally tolerant one, in which all its citizens—religious or secular, Arab or Jewish—can share the same freedoms and securities.

The young Israelis and Palestinians about whom I've written have seen how blinding the fighter's mind-set can be. They understand the importance of foresight and the necessity to question, to ask: Who do I want to be in ten years? What do I want my country to be in twenty? They are frustrated that many of the people currently in power are not asking these same questions. And even if the older generation is looking to the future, their vision will die with them unless they empower a younger generation to carry this vision forward. In this sense, to interest young Israelis and

Palestinians in political and social action—to teach them the way of the negotiator as opposed to that of the fighter—is the only way to invest in the future of these nations and ultimately solve the conflict between them.

Ruba speaks for many young Palestinians when she told me, "The young people of Palestine are really willing to do something. There's an energy in the people, but we are not getting advantage of this energy."

This is partly because Palestine is neither a real democracy nor a meritocracy, so it's very difficult for young Palestinians to utilize their talent and energy. They certainly don't have the option to write a book, attend graduate school, or travel the world, as my friends and I did after college. An organization like Seeds of Peace is adopting a handful of Palestinians each year and providing them with the support—the opportunities and alternatives—that their country does not. I strongly believe that all Israeli and Palestinian youth have the same leadership potential as every young person presented in this book. It does not matter whether they are refugees or settlers, religious or secular, affluent or underprivileged. I know Seeds of Peace youth from all of these backgrounds, and all of them shone once given the opportunity; show young people a way out of apathy and violence and they are all too willing to take it.

I saw this plainly one afternoon in Ramallah on a walk with my friend Badawi.

Badawi was one of the original 1993 Seeds. We had met at the Switzerland summit, where we were both assigned to negotiate the status of Jerusalem. He was nineteen then, with dark, skeleton-long limbs and wide sunken eyes like those of a starving child. His attitude toward Jerusalem was as austere as his face. For days, he approached the negotiations like battles, pouncing upon our compromises and tearing them apart. I didn't even try to see who Badawi was behind his politics, I was so offended by his implacable attitude, so turned off by his foreign features. It took me days to understand that Badawi wasn't a predator at all but a protector, defending Jerusalem the way any parent guards his child. In the end, however, it was Badawi whom we unanimously elected to be our committee's Arab spokesman. We had learned to respect his toughness, and he had lowered his defenses enough to enable our group to draft the first stages of an Israeli-Palestinian compromise over Jerusalem.

Somewhere between that summit and my arrival in Jerusalem in 2003, Badawi and I had formed a genuine friendship. I cannot describe how this was possible, as we had seen each other no more than three times in five years, but as with so many of my Seeds friends, our meetings carried the intensity of connections formed over months as opposed to minutes. I met him that day in Ramallah, shortly before he left Palestine to get his master's in engineering in France. Badawi had his future planned out: return to Palestine after his degree, build himself up through business, and invest his money and skills in revitalizing the country's physical infrastructure. Private business, he believed, was the only way to provide his people tangible support. The political system was so corrupt, it couldn't help anyone.

Badawi was explaining this to me as we entered one of the poorer areas of Ramallah. From the looks of the neighborhood, with its crumbling buildings, this was just the kind of place that could use Badawi's talents. It was a Friday morning, the Muslim day of worship, and schools were closed. The streets were empty except for small groups of boys chasing one another through the dusty, graffitied street or loitering outside the storefronts, most of them shut for the day.

We approached one group of boys outside a drugstore. Badawi called to them and they sauntered over, slapping each other on the back and hanging off one anothers' shoulders. I was struck by their unabashed affection, the kind of physical intimacy I rarely saw among teenage boys in the United States. The most striking thing about these boys, however, were their T-shirts. Out of the four, two wore shirts with American emblems: one was bright yellow with an American flag and "America" written in black above it; the other was black featuring the word "Coke." They were fourteen and fifteen. I had Badawi ask them what they wanted to do when they grew up. The one wearing the America shirt proudly announced that he wanted to be an engineer so he could build what he called "a bigger destruction force for self-defense." The boy in the Coke shirt said he wanted to go into business so that he could buy more guns for the Al-Aqsa Martyrs' Brigades.

The moment was uncanny. Badawi had just outlined the same career goals as these boys—business and engineering—but his purpose was to construct and create for his society, and not, as they desired, to feed it tools of destruction. When pressed, the boys told me that violence was their only means of expression. Without it, no one would listen to them.

I asked the boys about their T-shirts. They wanted military power, they said, to overthrow the Israelis. "We want to live like kids in the United States," they told me. "If we defeat the Israeli occupation we can do this."

I asked how they thought kids in the United States lived, and the boys concurred: There was no occupation, the streets were clean, and the government listened to the people.

"Abu Amr is a loser," one of the boys said. "He doesn't help us."

"But the U.S. government is a friend of Israel," the boy in the America shirt butted in. "They are blocking our way."

"The Europeans help us. Why not America?" another boy asked me then. His tone was imploring, as though he knew that for all the Europeans' assistance, only the United States had the power to sway Israeli policy. I realized that to this fifteen-year-old, it wouldn't matter whether someone like Badawi built one hundred gleaming roads as long as Israeli tanks continued to drive down them.

As I was about to leave, the boys became animated, rattling Arabic to Badawi. I had no idea what they were saying, but their faces were eager. I looked to Badawi for a clue.

"They want you to get them U.S. visas," Badawi said.

"Just for two months!" one of the boys broke in.

"You can hide us in your suitcase!" the boy in the Coke shirt exclaimed, as though the power of his voice could make such a thing possible.

I gave them an awkward smile. They were obviously joking, but there was something strained in their laughter. When Badawi and I left the group a few mintues later, I felt awful. I remembered driving away from the children playing soccer in the Sultan's Hill housing project in Gaza. As hopeless as I felt leaving those kids behind, they had run after the taxi with a kind of innocent hope. From these boys, however, I felt only anger, as though I should have been able to pull four visas out of my pocket and it was only selfishness that stopped me. I knew their situation wasn't my fault. I also knew that at heart these boys were angry at the policies of the U.S. government and not its citizens. They wore T-shirts proclaiming *America* and *Coca-Cola,* because the words symbolized a society of children who did not live as they did—children they longed to be.

I don't think it occurred to these boys that involving themselves in violent activities was counterproductive, that the brand of violent self-defense that Palestinian terror groups employed caused the IDF to further clamp down on the general Palestinian population, and this would put them no closer to their dream of living like American youth. Nor would they achieve this dream if their violent business got them hurt or killed. It was significant, however, that these boys did not speak to me about martyrdom. They wanted to be productive citizens—in fact, they were hungering for life. Which made their T-shirts all the more poignant; these boys dreamed of infinite possibility but knew how little Palestine had to offer them.

Perhaps a little bit of this possibility has come to Palestine. My last trip there was in the winter of 2005, a few months after Yasir Arafat's death and shortly after Abu Mazen's election. So another Abu had come to power—which disappointed Ruba, but did not automatically signal a perpetuation of cronyism and corruption. Unlike Arafat, Abu Mazen is no revolutionary. He is an academic who dresses in a suit and tie, a man with a thoughtful, grandfatherly expression. When you talk to him, you know he is listening.

"So what is going to change now that you are president?" I asked Abu Mazen in his refurbished presidential suite in the Muqata. "Tell me about the young people. What is your responsibility toward them?"

Abbas, who is sixty-nine, leaned forward in his chair and looked at me intently. "It is time to hand the younger generation the flag. We are sixty, sixty-five—seventy years old!" The way he said it, he sounded surprised that one as old as himself was actually sitting in the presidential chair. "We started in politics at your age." He winked at me. "It is now time to move on."

These are not empty words. Palestinians have held municipal elections throughout the territories, and elections for the Palestinian legislative council and for the Fatah General Assembly are scheduled for the summer of 2005. The Fatah elections are especially important, because the last elections within the party were in 1989. If Mohammad Dahlan's prediction is correct, most of the Fatah Central Committee members—the highest body within the party—will be voted out. This has already happened in the Palestinian cabinet. In February 2005, Prime Minister Ahmed Qurei (Abu Ala) proposed a cabinet full of former Arafat loyalists. The Legislative Council voiced intense opposition, castigating Qurei for his perpetuation of corruption within the Authority, and Abu Mazen stepped in to compile a new cabinet list. Of the twenty-four positions, seventeen appointees were new to the cabinet, and nearly all of them were experts in their fields of responsibility.

It may be a long time before these political changes translate into practical improvements on the ground—perhaps years before the boys I met on the street in Ramallah can confidently claim to have the opportunities like those available to most American children. Appointing new faces to the government isn't enough; these new leaders must work actively in their roles and take responsibility for their people as their predecessors did not. And of course, the challenges of occupation, terror, and the uncertainty of Israel's role complicate the future. That said, the changes that have transpired within Palestine between the end of 2004 and the beginning of 2005 are remarkable; there is a cautious optimism among Palestinians—not cause for celebration, but perhaps for hope.

When it comes to those Ramallah boys, you may think that I read too much into teenage apparel, but after so many years in Seeds of Peace, I am well-versed in T-shirt symbolism. When I encountered this group, I couldn't help but picture them, not in "America" or "Coke," but in Seeds of Peace green. They could be like any of those youngsters I'd met at camp earlier that summer or even those who attended Seeds its first year in 1993. Today when I look at the photo from the Oslo signing taken on the White House South Lawn, it could be their four young faces peeking out from behind Rabin, Peres, Arafat, and Clinton.

In the past, that wouldn't have meant much to me, because I cared much more about the world leaders in the picture than the young ones behind them. I felt so proud that the adults would honor Seeds of Peace by holding up our T-shirts. Years after Oslo failed and the priceless autographs have faded from my family's copy of the photo, it's no longer presidents and prime ministers who hold my attention; now, when I look at that photo, I am in awe of the thirteen-year-old faces. I identify three in the front row. "There's Tamer!" I tell my American friends. "And Ido and Ariel! I know those guys, but they don't look like *that* anymore."

When this picture was taken I knew neither the Seeds of Peace graduates nor the world leaders personally, and though it's impressive to say that I had tea with Shimon Peres and lunch with Yasir Arafat, it's not surprising given my father's relationship with both men. As I see it, the truly amazing thing is that this politically disinterested, sheltered American teenager would one day attend an international youth summit with Ido, get a tour of Israel Channel 10 from its youngest news producer Ariel, and celebrate Ramadan in a Cairo mosque with Tamer. Today, when I look at this photo, I see that *these* are the famous men, the ones who really matter. Unlike the boys in Ramallah, my friends from Seeds believe they matter to the world. They feel legitimate within their societies and, as important, feel legitimated by one another. They succeeded in the process of trust building where many of the Israelis and Palestinians involved in the Oslo process failed.

In fact, in July 2000, while the Camp David talks were failing, Camp Seeds of Peace was running as usual. I remember my father calling me at camp one night after lights-out and telling me about the lighter side of his negotiations. That evening, Yasir Arafat had sat next to him on the couch while he was watching the all-star game and asked for an explanation of baseball. My father had always believed that baseball was just like the peace process: both had fairly low expectations for success. In baseball, if you hit safely four out of ten times, you were a veritable hero. Both were full of strikeouts and errors. Despite these similarities, however, Arafat seemed none too impressed with the Orioles game on TV. Another evening, my dad said, was designated Camp David Movie Night, and the negotiators gathered to watch *Gladiator*. It wouldn't have been his pick for a peace summit, he acknowledged, but apparently no one could say no to Madeleine Albright. And finally, he said, the food at Camp David was much better than in most camp dining halls—Bill Clinton certainly seemed to like it.

As I listened to these stories and later when I saw the photos my father brought home, I couldn't help but think how similar Camp David was to Camp Seeds of Peace. Both are beautiful, secluded areas where representatives from conflict regions convene to talk out their problems. Both have activities to foster group bonding, such as movie night (though at Seeds the films are of the nonviolent variety), and both camps introduce their foreign guests to the great American game of baseball. Still, despite these similarities, there is a fundamental difference. When Camp David II concluded, the participants went home disillusioned and defeated. When Camp Seeds of Peace concluded, the participants returned to their countries emboldened and empowered.

I understand that Seeds graduates do not share the same national burdens and responsibilities as their political leadership. Though they do have their constituencies to think about—friends, parents, and teachers—they are not making the kind of sweeping decisions that might literally change the course of history. Seeds of Peace certainly never asked Omri to divide Jerusalem or Reem to give up the Right of Return. Just like Barak and Arafat, these two young leaders are also not perfect. A summer at Seeds of Peace did not completely eradicate their stereotypes and fears, nor did it blot out the pains of history. That these obstacles and perils are inherent in any journey is something I learned well enough throughout my own quest through the Holy Land. It is obvious to me that Israelis and Palestinians fell into despair after the collapse of Oslo and Camp David. If someone led me far away from home without the necessary provisions and without tools to navigate, I'd feel tricked, too.

I can understand this, because writing this book required me to make a huge physical and emotional separation from my own home and country. Still, I could not have asked for better guides than Omri, Reem, Mohammad, Sari, Yara, Hamdan, Yoyo, Uri, and Ruba. They might be a bit inexperienced—I certainly watched them let their guard down and stumble into quicksand—yet I also saw how determined they were to pull themselves out, and more than this, to avoid such dangers altogether. Despite their youth, they've become familiar with the tools of navigation. In the face of so many perils, I've watched them look within themselves, confront their insecurities, and tread forward with an equal balance of confidence and awareness.

Epilogue

Unlike the Ramallah boys, I know possibility. I am in awe of my country and the opportunities it provides. Among the greatest of these opportunities are the most simple: power and freedom. I live in a powerful and secure nation where I feel no existential threat to my country or my identity; and I live in a free society, where I can move, pursue my interests, and express myself as I wish.

My father often says the Palestinians wield the power of the weak, that they use the occupation to justify violent resistance and political unaccountability. On the flipside, Israel, with its military prowess, wields the more conventional power of the strong. I have come to see these powers as largely false; neither Palestinian resistance nor Israeli might has delivered these nations security and freedom. Indeed, I never appreciated these privileges until I lived among people who lacked them. I never appreciated how they established my sense of order in the world and my sense of self. Though I always visit the National Mall on Memorial Day—stand over the Reflecting Pool and search the memorial of names commemorating the Vietnam War—only after returning from the Middle East did I recognize the purpose of these monuments. When I look in the water or at the black, mirrored stone what I see more than anything else is my own face.

Over the six months I traveled between Gaza and Tel Aviv, a number of factors impressed upon me the necessity of personal and national self-reflection: It was listening to one of Israel's top security officials talk about the Israeli army being motivated by emotion rather than reason. It was seeing the injustice of the Israeli occupation in Gaza while at the same time hearing Palestinians spout frightening untruths about Israel and the

United States. It was the knowledge that two of the Israeli cafés I visited were eventually blown to bits. Most of all, it was learning that many people believed 9/11 "wasn't enough."

Reflecting on these experiences has affected me in two ways. First, it has shown me the fragility of my nation's power and freedom. I do not believe America is any more able to deal with terrorism than Israel, and though it is more difficult for terror to infiltrate the United States than Israel, Americans have already seen what angry human beings can do when they feel they have nothing to lose. As Americans we have *everything* to lose. If you've seen *The Siege,* a movie with Denzel Washington and Bruce Willis, you know what I'm talking about. In it, modern-day New York is put under martial law after a series of suicide bombings assault the city. Tanks roll through downtown Manhattan and the authorities quarantine the city's Muslim and Arab males in Shea Stadium. After 9/11, and certainly after living in societies battered by intifada, I don't find this film so far-fetched. As my father says, "One of these days someone is going to walk into a McDonald's with a backpack of explosives." When I told Tom Friedman about the movie *The Siege* he cynically suggested I title this chapter "Coming Soon to a Theater Near You." The fact is, in Israel, you get searched and scanned before walking into a movie theater and nearly every other public establishment. That's not the kind of life I want.

So the second product of my self-reflection as I wrote this book is my newfound patriotism. After living in the Middle East, I love and appreciate my country more than ever, and I feel an urgency to protect America and the opportunities she offers. To me, this means engaging with the world in a manner that empowers people and inspires their respect as opposed to one that creates resentment and hatred. I don't want my country's policies to allow anyone, however unjustified their claim may be, to tell me that 9/11 wasn't enough.

Here I take my lessons from the young adults I've followed in this book. These extraordinary leaders have convinced me beyond a doubt of the value of being a negotiator. They are not idealists—they know that force is sometimes necessary—and I share their pragmatism. Nothing angered me more than driving past Union Square in New York City one afternoon and seeing a red banner with a large, black "BUSH" in the middle, bordered by swastikas. To me, the sign presented as much of an extremist view as those who believe the United States ought to forcibly conquer the globe. So I am not what the Israeli army calls a universal pacifist, but I firmly believe that force without diplomacy breeds alienation and destruction. It's like Uncle Ben tells Peter Parker in *Spider-Man:* With great power comes great responsibility.

When it comes to the Israeli-Palestinian conflict, I believe America has a tremendous responsibility. My interest in seeing these societies reconcile is more than a humanistic desire to see the bloodshed stop. I believe that hostility toward the United States and excuses to exercise violence against us will continue until Israelis and Palestinians achieve a settlement. When I asked former secretary of state Colin Powell his opinion about this hypothesis, his response was clear.

"An unresolved Israeli-Palestinian conflict is a dark cloud over the United States," Powell told me. "As long as it continues it will be a source of instability in the Middle East and an excuse for hostility directed toward the United States."

Powell did not suggest that 9/11 happened because of the Israeli-Palestinian conflict, but he acknowledged the degree to which this conflict resonates throughout the Arab and Muslim world. These feelings seem to grow both from America's perceived bias toward Israel as well as our reluctance to seriously commit ourselves to a peace process. While Powell impressed upon me that the United States could not solve the conflict for Israelis and Palestinians, he firmly believed that an active U.S. role was crucial to helping these nations reconcile. No other country, he said, had enough influence with both parties to be an effective third-party broker. Moreover, Powell said it was irrelevant whether the American administration was headed by Democrats or Republicans. "The United States *must* get involved," he said.

I think the boys in Ramallah made this clear. As much as Palestinians and even Israelis may not like American foreign policy, they want us on their side—they need us. As I reflect on my journey among Israelis and Palestinians, I understand that as an American I need them, too.

Afterword

"I hope I don't cry," was the semi-facetious response I gave to people who asked if I was nervous about promoting my first book. This was September 2005, just days before *Inheriting the Holy Land* hit the stores, and I was excited to go on the road for my book tour. Since the age of ten, when I played Sebastian, the crab in a camp production of *The Little Mermaid* (I wore a pink lobster suit with enormous stuffed claws), I knew I'd end up onstage one way or another. Here was my chance; only this time the subject matter was serious. The Israeli-Palestinian conflict might often seem as absurd as a cartoon with talking sea life, but it is one of the world's most intractable, emotionally charged conflicts. I'd seen audiences heckle my father when he simply explained the U.S. government line. When he dared to express his personal opinion, people had tried to boo him off stage. This is what worried me; in *Inheriting the Holy Land,* my personal experience and opinion are central.

Over the months of book talks and presentations, I learned to stand up for myself. You can't please all the critics—what could I say to the Orthodox Jew who chastised me for eating Yasir Arafat's nonkosher meatball? And for an author who wrote a book at twenty-two, looks eighteen, and sounds ten on the radio, some criticism about my youthfulness was inevitable. Still, I found that my on-the-ground research provided plenty of substance with which to tackle the difficult questions. I may have been alone at the lectern, but a dozen Israeli and Palestinian young adults stood firmly behind me, lending their support.

Then, one evening in Cleveland, Ohio, I met my match. I was speaking at a synagogue—one of my final events—when a gentleman stood up and said, "You call your book a 'search for hope.' I've read your book, and I couldn't tell whether you found any. How about a coda?"

I was flummoxed. My first problem was that in all the presentations and interviews I'd given, no one had asked me this. People questioned whether *I* was hopeful about the future, and I had plenty to tell them about power of creation versus destruction, about my Palestinian friend Tamara who chose life over martyrdom, and about the boys in Ramallah who yearned for a better life despite their fixation with violence. But my examiner in Cleveland wasn't interested in Jen Miller's personal optimism; he wanted to know what the Israelis and Palestinians thought. Which lead me to a second problem: What did I mean by hope, in the first place? My online dictionary gave the following definitions:

Hope: 1. To wish for something with expectation of its fulfillment. 2. To have confidence; trust.

Did most Israelis and Palestinians expect to see an end to the violence, a political solution, or peace? These were not the same questions. More than that, I had never viewed hope as something easily assessed in a public opinion poll. You couldn't represent it in a pie chart or plot it along X and Y axes. To me, hope is an abstraction: an individual and often ephemeral state of mind that is difficult, if not impossible, to quantify.

My questioner forced me to consider a third problem. The subtitle of this book is *An American's Search for Hope in the Middle East,* but that quest was not the focus of my research in the region. I set out to find the humanity in this conflict; to understand how young Israelis and Palestinians responded to growing up in an intifada; and to present complex and diverse viewpoints in an accessible way. The more time I spent in the region, however, the more I discovered that humanity and hope are not always compatible. *Inheriting the Holy Land* humanizes the conflict by allowing individuals to express themselves without judgment, and that meant giving voice to the family of a young suicide bomber, to Omri and Mohammad's stolid responses to a bus bombing, and to the anger and hatred of Israelis and Palestinians. When I returned to Israel and the West Bank in December 2005 to research this afterword, much of what I found was also not hopeful. Many Israelis, including Omri, felt they were losing their faith in their country. Some even felt betrayed. Palestinians like Ruba and Hamdan expressed intense anxiety about the future and suggested that a productive life may not exist for them in Palestine: plenty of uncertainty here.

But is uncertainty cause for despair? If there's one thing adolescents and volatile political situations have in common, it's a propensity for drastic change within a short period of time. Observing both the political situation and my young friends in late 2005, I felt like a mother who suddenly realizes that her teenage children have lives of their own. It was a difficult realization but one that ultimately helped me put the conflict in perspective.

"You have a different look" was the first thing I said to Omri when we sat down for lunch at a trendy Tel Aviv café. I had selected this neighborhood, but our location seemed to reflect the transformation my friend had experienced since I last saw him in Israel. Usually, Omri and I met at the Central Bus Station, an immense building of unabashed seediness. The station was not actually central, but a concrete fortress amid the low-income neighborhoods, sex bars, and cheap shoe stores of southern Tel Aviv. The place itself teemed with crowds and reeked of cigarettes and urine—not an ideal place for quiet discussions or interviews, but convenient for Omri because of the station's proximity to Bat Yam, where he lived with his family. In December of 2005, Omri no longer lived in Bat Yam. He had moved to his father's house in Hertzaliya, one of the wealthiest cities in Israel.

I was used to seeing Omri in warm-up suits and sneakers, wearing a Star of David and army tags around his neck. On this day, however, he greeted me in a long-sleeved tee-shirt (white) worn beneath a short-sleeved Polo shirt (powder blue) and a white baseball hat with the Polo logo smack in the middle. I was shocked: Omri had gone prep. He told me up front that this physical change was due to his new home.

"I'm hanging around with different people with different lifestyles," he said with his usual frankness. "I still have the same values, but it's [just] the way I dress, I talk [that's changed]."

When Omri lived in Bat Yam, he was critical of Hertzaliya's rich Ashkenazi Jews and the sheltered world in which they lived.

"Hertzaliya is a big bubble," Omri admitted, but he called it a welcome change from Bat Yam's dirty, often unsafe neighborhoods. "I tried to hang out with my friends from Bat Yam," Omri said of the weeks after his move. But as he grew more integrated into his new surroundings, he not only lost touch with his old life but started looking down on it. "The people I used to date and hang out with, now they look to me like trash," he said. "Now the girls are more classy. I feel better with them."

I asked Omri if he wasn't being overly harsh toward his old community.

"It's not better but easier to live in a higher class," Omri explained, and made it clear that changing zip codes did not fundamentally change him. "I'm not in that high class," he assured me. "I go to their school and I live with them, but I'm not one of them."

Omri's father works as a gardener and electrician and lives in the Neve Amal, a large Hertzaliya neighborhood that has experienced its own transformation over the last decade. The community was once elderly and neglected, but an in-pouring of Jews from the former Soviet Union in the early nineties began to change the demographics and rejuvenate the neighborhood. The residents of Neve Amal are not wealthy, but Omri says his home is twice the size of his mother's Bat Yam apartment and includes a garden. "It's nothing like *their* houses," Omri said of the spacious modern structures in which his new friends live. Even so, he described Neve Amal with a passion that was quintessential Omri. "I love the way I live right now," he said.

Throughout our conversation, Omri emphasized the importance of adapting—how a change in environment required him to revise his appearance, behavior, and social expectations. Despite his criticisms of Bat Yam, he spoke of a sincerity between young people there that was absent between his new friends. "I can count on my friends in Bat Yam one hundred percent," he said. "But not in Hertzaliya."

Omri was quick to point out that he was making no judgments. According to him, all of this was simply "a matter of culture." A person in Hertzaliya couldn't expect to live like a person in Bat Yam. Accept this fact, he explained, and you could be happy.

For all of Omri's enthusiasm over his new home and what it provided (more privacy and living space, a safer environment, a better education), I detected his discomfort over the transition he'd made. Did he worry he'd sold out, I wondered?

"I told my mother a month ago that I changed," he admitted. "I became someone I used to look at as not so good. I don't really understand how it happened. I'm still trying to figure it out."

I soon realized, however, that Omri was grappling with a separation much greater than the one between Hertzaliya and Bat Yam. This division had little effect on his outward appearance, but it marked a significant change in his attitude and outlook: The central division in Omri's life now was the one between himself and his country. If anyone had sold out, he intimated, it wasn't him; it was Ariel Sharon.

When I first met Omri, he was fifteen—not old enough to vote, but itching to exercise his democratic rights. Now almost eighteen, he considered not voting at all.

"I can't identify with Sharon's party," Omri referred to the new Kadima or "Forward" party, which Sharon founded after breaking from Likud in the fall of 2005. "There are plenty of left wingers with Sharon's party," Omri continued. "That's not my way. I'm a right winger."

Sharon left Likud after his plan to withdraw settlers from Gaza alienated the far right members in the party. Now some Laborites, like Shimon Peres, were joining Kadima's ranks. Still, Omri was not the same ideologue I'd met at Seeds of Peace in 2003. He felt that Likud, now headed by former prime minister Bibi Netanyahu, was too right wing.

"We have to get out of Gaza somehow," Omri said, a startling contrast from the hard, angry boy who once spoke passionately about transfer. Then the familiar hardness returned.

"[But] the way we did it was awful," Omri shook his head. He explained that the government failed to provide adequate housing for the settlers after the withdrawal. He believed some were living in tents. He decried Sharon's unilateral action. "You have to have an agreement," he believed. "If you give, you have to get." He believed that Gaza after the evacuation was more dangerous to Israel than ever. In recent weeks, Palestinian militants had been launching Qassam rockets from the elevated areas once populated by Israeli settlers. With a longer reach, these rockets now threatened the Israeli city of Ashkelon. No longer a presence on the ground, the Israeli military had resorted to patrolling these vacated areas of Gaza by plane. Omri described the disgust he felt watching TV footage of Palestinians destroying Gaza's vacated synagogues. In the end, Omri called the Gaza disengagement "the biggest mistake," and felt Sharon was the one responsible.

"I could see people in favor of disengagement, the way they hate those settlers," Omri reflected on the weeks leading up to the withdrawal. "I didn't like my country in those days. I feel that I'm losing my love for my country."

It's true that Israeli society was fiercely divided over the disengagement from Gaza. Sari, who has close friends in the settlements despite her left-leaning political ideology, told me that friends who were once politically apathetic took up a cause.

"I'd get into a car with my friends, and you never knew what side they'd be on," she said. "You couldn't even make a joke about the pullout without turning heads."

When I asked Uri about this sudden passion for politics, he declared, "*That* was democracy!" He described the ribbons, bracelets, and bumper stickers that decorated everything from wrists to doorknobs: orange supporting the settlers and blue supporting withdrawal. But he agreed that the atmosphere was "heavy." Sharon's brand of unilateralism also made Uri uncomfortable so he put two stickers on his car: GET OUT OF GAZA NOW alongside YES FOR AN AGREEMENT. Again and again, the stickers were ripped off.

The explosion of ideology grew fierce. Thousands of settlers and their supporters flooded to Gaza to protest, though soldiers and police barred them from critical areas. There was even sporadic violence inside Israel proper, including people burning tires on major highways. Israelis speculated about the possibility of civil war. Sari said she automatically judged people wearing orange ribbons. To counter this negative reaction, she avoided wearing orange and blue and, instead, handed out white ribbons with a slogan about loving thy neighbor and purple ribbons that proclaimed the importance of compromise in the face of disagreement.

To everyone's surprise, the withdrawal precipitated little violence. The soldiers and police sent to evacuate the settlers were unarmed, and though the settlers expressed plenty of anguish and refusal, most evacuees went peaceably. Sharon emerged strengthened; his decision to split from the right-of-center Likud and chart a centrist path won widespread support. In the weeks leading up to his stroke in early 2006, polls reported that a third of the country was expected to vote for him and his new Kadima party that March. As mentioned, Kadima means "forward" and connotes a battle charge, a word that reflects upon Sharon's own reputation as a fearless military commander—a man willing to make the ultimate sacrifice for his country. This is exactly how he presented Gaza withdrawal to the public, and his political shrewdness paid off. Despite Sharon's incapacitation in March 2006, Kadima won the national election, installing Ehud Olmert, Sharon's number two, as prime minister.

Sharon's stroke did have repercussions. Voter turnout in Israel reached a historic low of 63.2 percent, and Kadima only won 28 seats in the Knesset, far less than expected. Israelis view Olmert as capable, but he lacks Sharon's gravitas. What many people forget, however, is that Olmert actually spearheaded the disengagement plan. I interviewed him in 2003, just after the plan was announced, and he was uncompromising. Disengagement, he explained, was necessary to ensure a Jewish-majority Israeli state.

"To be honest with you," Olmert said unapologetically, "if I need to live with a majority of non-Jews, I'd rather live with Americans or Canadians or Austrians, than with Islamic fundamentalists."

As he put it, "total unilateral separation from the Palestinians dictated by Israel" was the only current recourse. Then, as though he hadn't made himself clear enough, he added, "I'm talking about total separation, full stop. No gates, no movements of the population."

Such unilateralism wouldn't solve the conflict, Olmert admitted, but he did believe it would force the Palestinians to take responsibility for themselves without being able to blame the occupation for their troubles. It seemed to me that the security barrier was doing a great deal to curtail terrorism, but I worried that turning the West Bank into a Gaza-like prison would have long-term negative repercussions for both peoples. But Olmert was more concerned with the present.

"We're sick and tired of being engaged," he said and looked like he meant it. "Maybe you didn't get 100 percent of what you wanted," he said to the invisible Palestinians in the room, "but go to work and leave us alone."

Other constituencies in Israel felt as exasperated as Olmert and Sharon, but were not swayed by the benefits of disengagement. As Omri expressed, Sharon's action shattered the faith that many Israelis held in their leaders and in their country. In the Tekoa settlement, Shani and her family called the withdrawal an assault on democracy.

"Most of the people didn't want to leave the Gaza strip and we left anyway," Shani's daughter Yonit said, referring to the fact that Sharon refused to hold a public referendum on the disengagement. Though the Knesset approved the pullout, many settlers believed parliament members were pressured to vote for it. "People who went against the disengagement were fired." Yonit was certain.

What actually occurred was a reshuffling in the political system, whereby Sharon lost the support of his party and was forced to split from them. But the idea that Sharon deceived his constituency is something upon which Israelis of all political bents agree.

"People were being deprived of their lives, houses, dreams; and those dreams were made by the government," Uri said. "They were deceived for forty years."

"I don't think Sharon had this plan in mind for the last forty years," I disagreed. From everything I knew about Sharon, he held both the army and the settlements sacrosanct. That he had used one precious institution to tear down the other struck me as startling. It seemed difficult to believe that he'd had this plan in mind all along.

Maybe so, Uri conceded, but he believed West Bank settlers were being deceived this very moment. "They're prioritized as though they're the most important thing, but the priority is wrong," he said. "You can't say right now where the West Bank border will be drawn."

This is exactly what those in Tekoa fear. In 2004 when I first visited the community, Shani told me about a new road that was supposed to cut a forty-five-minute drive to Jerusalem down to twenty minutes. When I returned nearly two years later in late 2005, the road still wasn't finished, and Shani was sure why.

"The road is going to be for the Arabs," she said definitively, implying that it was part of a government plan to evacuate Tekoa. "For the first time in my life I can't say in my heart that the government is going to watch over me," Shani's voice sounded stretched out, thin. "I've seen my dream shattered in front of me. That's very sad."

Nahum Barnea, an Israeli journalist who writes for the daily paper, Yideot Ahranot, explained the root of the pain that Shani expressed in Tekoa: "For people in the settlers movement, the state of Israel is a religious miracle, a Messianic achievement." As Barnea saw it, the settlers were caught between two immutable symbols: Greater Israel and the sacred state.

"I wish we had a leader like Sharon," my Palestinian friend Ruba told me at her parents' home in Jericho during my December 2005 trip. I looked at her with surprise. Ruba hated Sharon. "He finds solutions for everything at the right time in the right way," she continued. "That's what he did in the disengagement."

Ruba was right. On the verge of political collapse and amidst a corruption scandal, Sharon not only rescued his career but solidified his position as the most popular politician in Israel.

"He thought, 'I'm going to pull out of Gaza and there will be more trouble,' and after six months he'll convince the people he has to go back." Ruba wasn't praising the Israeli prime minister but his perspicacity.

I was used to my friend's cynicism, but I found her comment about Sharon telling. In late 2005 and early 2006, the only people facing more uncertainty than Israelis were Palestinians. Lawlessness in Gaza was acute. Divisions within Fatah between the old and young guard had weakened Abu Mazen's Palestinian Authority to a state of inefficacy. To the shock of everyone—Palestinians included—Hamas won a majority in the 2006

Palestinian parliamentary elections. Many Fatah supporters switched to Hamas in protest over the Authority's corruption and more than this, dual Fatah candidates split the vote in many cities, practically ensuring Hamas's success.

The day I sat with Ruba, these events had not yet transpired, but there was plenty of anxiety. That very afternoon, militants stormed government offices in Gaza demanding transparent elections and jobs. Television footage showed the masked men walking up office stairs, firing into the air, and cradling their guns on balconies. There was something specious about the scenes, as though the gunmen were extras on a movie set waiting for their thirty seconds in the limelight. Hardly a threat to society. The fact that they were using a show of force to demand democratic process stuck me as ironic if not absurd. But some of these militants had physically threatened Fatah officials, and militias openly ruled the streets in Gaza.

I spoke with Hamdan, with whom I had visited in Gaza in 2004, about the situation. "You cannot control all the groups," he said. "Everyone has his own mafia. They're looking out for their own interests—for prey or bounty. The security forces are doing their best."

At first, this struck me as another irony. The armed men demanding jobs were looking for work inside the security services. I was reminded of Mohammad Dahlan who sat down to tea with Hamas members one day and was sent to arrest them the next. Hamdan didn't see the irony at all.

"The security officials are *engaged* with the disorder," he corrected me. "They have their own hidden interests. Most people do not feel safe. Most Palestinian youth want to leave their country."

This was not what a group of refugee children in Khan Yunis had told me in 2003, but Hamdan assured me: His friends were aching to get out. They had not had his luck in securing work. When I spoke with him in December 2005, Hamdan was about to graduate from Al-Ahzar University and was working as both a translator in the security services and an anchor for Palestinian Authority TV. His salary is about $325 a month, quite large by Gaza standards. He believes many of his educated friends will remain unemployed after graduation.

"So you'll stay in Gaza?" I asked him, relieved that at least one bright young Palestinian could stay to make a difference.

"No, no, no!" Hamdan quickly rejected this possibility. "Gaza's a big prison."

He said he might return in twenty years, but only after he'd given his life a chance. And in Gaza, Hamdan made it clear, that wasn't going to happen.

Ruba still envisions her life in Palestine, but she's anxious about the future. Over tea and cookies in her parents' living room, she shared her fears about Hamas and the growing threat of Islamic extremism. She wasn't certain that political participation and public accountability would force Hamas to moderate its violent behavior and rhetoric as some analysts believed. But Khalil Shikaki at the Palestinian Center for Survey Research was certain that the majority of Palestinians didn't want a return to violence. He believed this attitude would force Hamas to abandon its hardline views within a couple of years of joining the government. Still, without a unified Fatah, Shikaki warned, Hamas would take advantage of a fractured and decentralized Authority and more easily impose its conservative social and political agenda on the public. Thus far, Hamas was subscribing to the ceasefire Abu Mazen set as a prerequisite for the group's candidacy.

Ruba believed Hamas had the right to run. "If I want to live in a democracy, I should respect those people in the elections," she told me. But this didn't mean she wanted to see Hamas in the government. "I am terrified at the thought of having Hamas with a majority." She wrung her hands like a person awaiting bad news. "I'm terrified," she said again.

Rumors had begun to spread about Hamas: that their members would disrupt New Year's Eve parties where men and women socialized together.

"You mean they'd bomb Palestinians?" I asked, incredulous.

Ruba did not think Hamas would go that far, but she said they might throw stones and shoot into the air. "They don't think people should celebrate while Palestinians are being killed," she explained. "They don't want men and women together. They don't want alcohol."

These threats were beginning to bother Palestinians in less conservative cities like Jericho, Ramallah, and Bethlehem. Ruba was somewhat relieved that people were starting to take the threats seriously; it meant that some Palestinians who planned to support Hamas as a rejection of Fatah, might rethink their decision at the polls.

"In any society where there is a lot of poverty, people will go to God to feel secure," Ruba explained the phenomenon, which she detected not only in Palestine but throughout the Arab and Muslim world. "Palestinians don't think about Hamas's ideology when they vote," she said. "They just think: Hamas believes in God; they are great."

Shikaki explained that only 15 to 20 percent of Palestinians actively endorsed Hamas's conservative ideology. At the same time, he believed 60 to 70 percent of Palestinians were culturally traditional, and probably wouldn't find Hamas's social agenda threatening.

"If Hamas does win sixty to seventy percent of the vote," Shikaki said when I related Ruba's concerns, "your friend will certainly feel the heat."

But Ruba was feeling the heat already. Just a month before in November 2005, suicide bombers linked to Al-Qaeda attacked three hotels in Amman: the Radisson, Grand Hyatt, and Days Inn. I knew that Ruba's grandmother lived in the Jordanian capital and asked for her reaction. For a couple of moments she said nothing. Then she let out a deep, painful sigh.

"I was terrified," she said for the third time that afternoon. "Having an explosion in Amman is like having an explosion in Ramallah. Most of the people killed were Palestinians."

This was inevitable, given that a majority of Jordan's population is of Palestinian origin. But one of the bombings, perpetrated by a husband and wife pair (the wife's belt failed to explode and she was arrested), occurred in the middle of a Palestinian wedding. The groom's family was from Jenin, a city in the northern West Bank. His father and new father-in-law were both killed. Also among the dead were Bashir Nafe, a West Bank security chief whom I interviewed in 2004, and Abed Alloun, one of Nafe's top aides and my father's friend. I had spent many evenings with Abed and my dad, the three of us sitting in the Moroccan-style tent behind Jerusalem's Ambassador Hotel, smoking shisha and discussing recent tales of Palestinian political intrigue. Abed spent most of these evenings criticizing his boss's rivals in the government. The rivals changed frequently, because the bosses did: Bashir Nafe, Jabril Rajoub, Mohammad Dahlan—you could never be sure whom Abed was working for at any given moment. He was adept at riding the political wave. No matter if his superiors slipped and fell; Abed Alloun never wiped out.

He was an unctuous-looking man in his early forties with thinning hair, little kids at home, and three cell phones ringing at once. He provided me critical help in researching this book during the six months I spent in the region and afterwards. When my dad called with news of his death, I tried to picture Abed as he might have been found: lying dead on the ballroom floor of the Amman Radisson. I couldn't. It was impossible to think of Abed as no longer existing.

"Do most Palestinians you know believe al-Qaeda was responsible for the attacks?" I asked Ruba.

"Yes," she said. "But who is behind al-Qaeda? That is the question that is bothering every Palestinian and I think every Arab. Who would bomb themselves in the middle of Arab people just like them?"

"Do you think Israel is responsible?" I asked, hoping that Ruba had not latched on to the latest conspiracy theory reported in the media. "No, I'm not saying that," Ruba brushed off the possibility. "What's happening is not normal. These people," she said of al-Qaeda, "are fighting the United States and Israel for the sake of Palestinians. So why would they kill Palestinians?"

I told Ruba I didn't think al-Qaeda cared very much about the Palestinians, but rather about spreading Islam.

"He doesn't really want that," Ruba corrected me. "That's what I'm trying to tell you. Bin Laden wants control."

"But why bomb these hotels?" I questioned her.

Ruba said the bomber's martyrdom video lambasted the Radisson and other hotels for holding intelligence meetings between Palestinian, Jordanian, and Israeli officials, but this excuse did not satisfy her.

"If this is the reason then go and bomb an Israeli or American embassy." *But not Palestinian civilians.* The unspoken words lingered between us. Then after a pause she continued, comparing al-Qaeda leaders to the man she had always viewed as her worst enemy: "I never felt I would hate someone as much as I hate Sharon." Now two new people were at the top of her list: Zarqawi and bin Laden.

I suggested that tight security would prevent the success of an embassy attack and perhaps that's why the hotels were targeted.

"I know Jordan as good as Ramallah," Ruba snapped. "I can think of ten thousand ways of getting into a compound—if that is the reason."

"So in your mind the reason is—"

"Terror."

"But why?" I was beginning to feel as exasperated as she was.

"I can't rationalize it," Ruba said, with weakness in her usually sharp voice. "Unless it's a game between bin Laden and everyone in the world. And he wants everyone to feel what it means to kill civilians."

I was past the point of confusion, but I asked Ruba why bin Laden would kill Muslims.

There was no confusing her answer: "These people would want to kill me even before killing you," she looked me in the eye. "I'm Muslim but I'm not acting as a Muslim in their eyes. So I deserve to be killed."

I knew well enough that there was no easy way to define a Muslim or, for that matter, a member of any religion. When I called my friend Tamara in 2005, I was shocked to find that she'd gotten married since I last saw her the previous year. I congratulated her, masking my concern. Tamara was deeply religious, though a fiercely independent woman. She was studying to be a pharmacist at Al-Quds University and had sworn to me that she would not settle down until she had her degree and was in the work force. Now, I arrived in Bethlehem to find Tamara and her new husband settled into a one bedroom apartment a few blocks from her childhood home. When she opened the door, I hardly recognized her. Gone was the hijab which had covered her hair and the traditional jilbab coat dress that had sheathed her body. Instead, Tamara wore tight black pants and a fluorescent pink boatneck shirt. Long brown hair flowed down her back.

"You look different!" I raised my eyes at her, as I had at Omri.

"I can go like this in my own home," she explained. Now that there was no fear of her parents' male friends dropping by, Tamara could relax as she pleased. She invited me in to examine her new home. It was small and simple, but the couches—a wedding gift from her family—were made of hand-carved wood. Tamara took me from the sitting room to the kitchen to the bedroom, glowing with excitement.

Afterwards we sat down and she related the circumstances of her marriage. It turns out her husband Abdallah was a family friend, about ten years older than herself, who worked as an electrical engineer. He and Tamara always had a tempestuous friendship. They often fought and she never thought of marriage. Then one day, he asked for her hand. She was shocked and turned him down on the spot. Over the following weeks and months, he pursued her, coming by her university, even placing orders at the pharmacy where she interned. She began to soften.

"I prayed to God three times to ask him 'what do I do,' " she said. "And then I knew." She married Abdallah in August 2005.

I asked Tamara how her life had changed since the wedding. I'll admit, I was concerned for her. Palestinian society is traditional, and in many cases, women stop working or studying after marriage because of the pressure to have children. But Tamara's was a modern marriage, if I ever saw one. She was already better educated than her husband—he had only completed two years of college but he urged Tamara to pursue a PhD. Abdallah even hoped she would earn a scholarship to study abroad. As for household chores: Abdallah did the laundry. The two of them ate dinner at Tamara's parents' house so she didn't have to worry about cooking after a long day at school.

I spent an hour alone with Tamara before Abdallah returned from work. He had the same dark and serious look that he displayed in their wedding album photos, but I noticed a difference in his face. Instead of a smooth chin, Abdallah now wore a bristly beard, just beginning to fill in. Tamara addressed her husband's face without my having to ask. Her youngest sister, a baby of two months, had died recently. Out of respect for Tamara's family, the very secular Abdallah had grown the customary Muslim beard of mourning.

"It's okay if he fasts with me on Ramadan," Tamara said of Abdallah, who was clearly trying to respect her religiosity. "But I don't like this beard. He looks like Hamas." She looked at her husband with a joking smile. "Right bin Laden?"

It was heartening to see Tamara so happy but even more so to know that she had successfully balanced religious observance, social custom, and her desire to be independent. She would certainly face some resistance from the more conservative forces in her society, but she, more than any of my young friends, seemed hopeful about the future. Fortunately, she was not the only one.

Mohammad entrusted me with a letter for Omri and the look upon Omri's face as he read his friend's words was inspiring. The two had been out of touch for nearly a year, and to know that Mohammad was still thinking about him, gave Omri renewed hope. Despite Ruba's political concerns, she had not given up on her society. She'd been offered a scholarship for a master's program in conflict resolution, after which she planned to work for the PA's negotiating team.

But hope and despair aren't the whole story. As I talked with my friends in December 2005, I began to realize that these emotions were only two ends of a spectrum. In between were so many other states of mind: confusion, compassion, frustration, cynicism, humor, and love. Traveling through Israel, the West Bank, and Gaza, I not only witnessed this wide spectrum, but saw how easily these colors blended, faded and renewed themselves. Today, if I rest my hopes on anything regarding the Israeli-Palestinian conflict, it is this color, this volatility.

In most parts of the United States, a calm environment sets the standard for normalcy. The attacks of September eleventh came as such a shock to us, because we aren't used to violence on our doorstep. But Israelis and Palestinians are. For them, house demolitions and bus bombings aren't just constant: They're inevitable. The entrenched policies that fuel hatred and therefore violence are also responsible for this cynicism. When I began my research in 2003, Israelis and Palestinians never considered a change in Israeli settlement policy or the demise of Palestine's authoritarian national leader. At that time, there were two players in the game, each one perceived to be an intractable rock: Yasir Arafat and Ariel Sharon.

In light of this, the events that transpired between November 2004 and April 2006 are nothing short of extraordinary. Yasir Arafat passed away; Mahmoud Abbas was elected Palestinian president through the most free and fair elections the Arab world has ever seen; Ariel Sharon shattered the notion of Greater Israel by dismantling all of Israel's settlements in Gaza and four from the West Bank; Sharon broke from the right-leaning Likud party that he was instrumental in founding and formed a new centrist coalition; he then suffered a massive stroke which forced him from the political scene. To these events one might add the deposal of Shimon Peres as Labor party king and the assumption of Amir Peretz, the first non-Ashkenazi Jew to lead the party, as well as Hamas's decision (despite their previous boycotts of national-level elections) to run for the Palestinian Legislative Council and their eventual success therein.

These sweeping changes are the growing pains of societies in conflict, of peoples struggling to assert themselves in the face of insecurity. Is there hope to be found here? If not bright shining rays of hope, there is at least change: intense political volatility to counteract the dull and constant violence. In my mind, this kind of disruption and change flies in the face of all that is normal and inevitable in the region—in other words, all that is despairing.

April 2006

Index

ABOUT THE AUTHOR

JENNIFER MILLER grew up in Chevy Chase, Maryland. She first attended the Seeds of Peace International Camp for Conflict Resolution in 1996 as a camper and worked there as a creative arts counselor throughout college. She graduated from Brown University with a degree in literature and creative writing. She is currently writing a second book.